D0558582

RESEARCH CONFIDENTIAL

RESEARCH CONFIDENTIAL

Solutions to Problems
Most Social Scientists
Pretend They Never Have

ESZTER HARGITTAI, EDITOR

The University of Michigan Press • Ann Arbor

Copyright © by the University of Michigan 2009
All rights reserved
Published in the United States of America by
The University of Michigan Press
Manufactured in the United States of America
⊚ Printed on acid-free paper

2012   2011   2010   2009   4   3   2   1

No part of this publication may be reproduced, stored
in a retrieval system, or transmitted in any form
or by any means, electronic, mechanical, or otherwise,
without the written permission of the publisher.

A CIP catalog record for this book is available from the British Library.

Library of Congress Cataloging-in-Publication Data

Research confidential : solutions to problems most social scientists
    pretend they never have / Eszter Hargittai, editor.
       p.   cm.
    Includes index.
    ISBN 978-0-472-07026-8 (cloth : alk. paper) — ISBN 978-0-472-
05026-0 (pbk. : alk. paper)
       1. Social sciences—Research.   2. Social sciences—Fieldwork.
    3. Social scientists—Attitudes.   I. Hargittai, Eszter, 1973–
    H62.R4472   2009
    300.72—dc22   2009024926

To my mentors

PREFACE

The idea for a volume that explores the behind-the-scenes details of hands-on empirical social scientific research initially came to me during graduate school when I was grappling with numerous methodological issues and did not find sufficient sources to help me with them. I knew that many other scholars had done interesting and high-quality research relevant to what I was trying to accomplish, yet rarely were the gruesome details of data[1] collection available in the articles and monographs I consulted about these projects for assistance. While countless books exist about research methods, they either tend to be too general for the purposes of helping the researcher figure out the actual steps involved in doing a project, or they lack the first-person perspective—especially of junior researchers—that would make the advice relevant to somebody embarking on a project at an early stage in their career. It is these shortcomings of the literature that I hoped a volume like this would address. During my junior faculty years, I continued to start new projects with methodological details unfamiliar to me and continued to be frustrated by the lack of guidance available in write-ups of earlier projects by others. Finally, I decided that it was time to rectify the situation and decided to invite a group of talented young scholars to contribute to a volume that would stop the need for so many scholars to reinvent the wheel.

My keen interest in research methods owes much to the significant mentoring that I have been extremely fortunate to receive over the years from numerous exceptional scholars. Rather than give a long list of them all here, I am going to mention those who made a special mark regarding the ways in which I think about research design and methods in my work. During my graduate student days at Princeton, Paul DiMaggio, Frank Dobbin, Hank Farber, and Marta Tienda, and, during my junior faculty years at Northwestern, Greg Duncan helped in ways for which it is not possible to express gratitude in words. Their contributions to my everyday work have been tremendous and have stayed with me throughout the years. Both the patience and the insights I received were considerable, and I hope they realize that I continue to be grateful for their generosity. Additionally, while there were innumerable peers during graduate school and since then who have taught me important lessons and skills, the many interactions with the following people were particularly significant to the themes of this book, and I express my gratitude to them: Nina Bandelj, Brigid Barron, danah boyd, Jason Brownlee, Sarah Burgard, Marcy Carlson, Melissa Clark, Erica Field, Jeremy Freese, Kieran Healy, Amanda Lenhart, Ann Morning, Shawna Samuel, Christian Sandvig, Diane Whitmore Schanzenbach, and Steven Tepper. In day to day interactions with my colleagues at Northwestern, I'm indebted to Darren Gergle, Shane Greenstein, Peter Miller, Dan O'Keefe, and Jim Webster for helpful conversations about research methods. Interactions with students in my research group, the Web Use Project, and the Media, Technology, and Society PhD program at Northwestern University have been inspiring to the volume, so I thank them for that.

I am grateful to members of the 2007 Class at the Center for Advanced Study in the Behavioral Sciences for many helpful suggestions; in particular, I would like to thank Bruce Bimber, Gillian Hadfield, Ken Kollman, Kevin Quinn, Jonathan Rodden, and Mike Tomz. Dan O'Keefe and Jeremy Freese gave me helpful comments on the final write-up of the Introduction that was much appreciated. Readers of the Crooked Timber blog and Eszter's Blog offered wonderful ideas for the title. In the end, Jonathan Zittrain's "Research Confidential" suggestion won out, and I am delighted to have been able to benefit from his wit. Crooked Timber reader "Vivian" also deserves many thanks for inspiring the second part of the title.

I am very grateful to Alison MacKeen of Yale University Press, formerly at the University of Michigan Press, for taking an interest in this project from the start and for her enthusiasm and helpful input throughout the process. At the end stage, I very much appreciated Thomas Dwyer's, Alexa Ducsay's, and Christina Milton's support at the University of Michigan Press as well as the very helpful copy editing by Janice Brill.

I have been very fortunate to have time to work on this project due to the support of several people and institutions. First and foremost, I am very grateful to Dean Barbara O'Keefe of the School of Communication at Northwestern University for providing an incredibly supportive environment for pursuing one's projects. I am grateful to the Lenore Annenberg and Wallis Annenberg Fellowship in Communication through the Center for Advanced Study in the Behavioral Sciences at Stanford for a remarkable atmosphere and for the necessary time to realize such an undertaking. Harvard's Berkman Center for Internet & Society was my intellectual home when I put the finishing touches on the volume, and the opportunity to be part of that amazing community has been wonderful. The many stimulating conversations there have made me even more excited and inspired about thinking through the challenges of various research methods. Also, were it not for support from the John D. and Catherine T. MacArthur Foundation, especially Connie Yowell and Craig Wacker, I would not have had the need to revisit many methodological questions over the past years that underscored the importance of putting together such a volume.

This volume would not exist without the wonderful contributions of the authors who kindly responded to my request to join this somewhat unorthodox enterprise. I chose them because I admire their work. Many have been recipients of dissertation awards and prestigious fellowships and grants related to the work upon which they draw for their chapters. I am grateful that they were willing to open up about their experiences in ways that are not usual in academia and did so enthusiastically. My appreciation and admiration go out to each and every one of them.

Finally, I would like to thank my family and friends who are a constant source of support without which I would not be able to pursue projects like this one.

NOTE

1. I use the word *data* to refer to any type of empirical material collected about our social world. The word *data* is not used to indicate any one particular type of information. It is meant as an aggregate term to encompass both qualitative and quantitative material collected using numerous types of methodologies (in-person observations, historical archival research, survey instruments, etc.).

CONTENTS

INTRODUCTION

Doing Empirical Social Science Research

ESZTER HARGITTAI

Research Confidential is a comprehensive guide to doing empirical social science research. Bringing together vivid firsthand accounts of recently completed research projects, it introduces readers to a wide range of methods: from surveys about individual behavior to ethnographies of communities, from cross-national comparisons to archival research. At the same time, the book fills a notable gap in the existing literature. Although there is no shortage of books on research methods, few of them address the behind-the-scenes issues involved in collecting and analyzing empirical evidence. As a result, new researchers are rarely given a realistic idea of what to expect when they embark on a project. By focusing attention on the concrete details seldom discussed in final project write-ups or traditional research guides, *Research Confidential* aims to equip new researchers with essential information that is all too often left on the cutting room floor.

The dozen chapters in this collection were specially commissioned from young scholars who recently completed successful research projects in social scientific fields including communication studies, psychology, and sociology. Each of their chapters offers a thorough account of hands-on empirical research that was conducted in the context of a specific project, and each explicitly discusses hurdles that were encountered along the way and how they were negotiated. Some chapters focus on the behind-the-scenes challenges of familiar research methods (e.g., interviewing, ethnographic work, and secondary data analysis); others look at the challenges associated with cutting-edge genres of research associated with new media (e.g., collecting data from online populations, using text messaging to gather information about respondents). Whether covering traditional or new techniques, the chapters all make a unique contribution precisely by focusing on the nitty-gritty practical details and challenges that are usually omitted from final research reports. Together they provide a uniquely thorough, richly detailed, and accessible guide to the collection and analysis of empirical evidence such as large-scale data sets, interviews, observations, and experiments in a wide range of settings.

Research Confidential was inspired by the underappreciated insight that it is valuable to learn about the behind-the-scenes details of research *before* embarking on a project. As obvious as this point may be, it is seldom reflected in the existing literature: as noted earlier, project write-ups rarely include concrete details of how studies were conducted. This collection was designed to reverse this long-standing trend. Instead of relegating practical issues and concerns to a sidebar or an appendix—or ignoring them entirely—they are placed front and center, as the focus of each chapter. The motivation for this strategy is not to provide shortcuts or quick tips but rather to help prepare researchers who are committed to doing high quality work. *Research Confidential* aims to make the researcher's life easier by pinpointing pitfalls routinely experienced by others and alerting the researcher to these issues *before* projects get derailed and write-ups postponed (possibly resulting in delayed dissertations, missed employment opportunities, delayed promotions, etc.).

These chapters are all based on projects recently conducted by junior scholars either in the course of their dissertation research or during their junior faculty years. Our hope is that this focus will be especially valuable to younger scholars—graduate students working on independent studies and dissertations, junior faculty embarking on new studies, and advanced undergraduate students writing theses. The fact that each chapter draws on the work experience of younger researchers should reassure prospective or beginning scholars that engaging in successful empirical research does not require decades' worth of experience. The essays should also be of interest to more advanced researchers, especially those who are grappling with an unfamiliar method or are interested in familiarizing themselves with emerging methods.

Most books about research methods rely on hypothetical ideal-type scenarios. Readers are rarely informed about the myriad failed attempts, frustrations, lost data, and other issues that inevitably arise when doing empirical research. What this means is that each new cohort must begin afresh, duplicating previous efforts at data collection and analysis instead of being able to build upon and improve them. Conducting good research is sufficiently difficult in its own right; this difficulty should not be increased by withholding or burying precious lessons that could save young scholars from making mistakes that previous generations have already encountered and learned how to avoid. In fact, if the research enterprise is to improve in the aggregate over time, it is essential that new projects build on the knowledge amassed by previous studies and generations. This volume was designed to contribute to that collective enterprise.

Several overarching themes run through the collection as a whole. First: *Good research takes longer than you expect.* Ask almost any experienced researcher about what important lessons he or she has learned from doing empirical work and the first response is likely to be that people always underestimate how long data collection and analysis will take. If one is lucky, the work will only take twice as long as planned, but it can easily take five times longer—and, on occasion, even more than that. Almost everyone— including highly regarded scholars who have been in the field for years— has fallen into the trap of optimistically assuming that a project will be on track from the outset. But this never happens. *Ever.* It is important to be ambitious and to believe in making good progress, but it is equally important to be realistic. Walejko's chapter about her experiences surveying bloggers describes the many unanticipated issues that can arise during a research project and how they can impact research time lines. Albright's chapter discusses time considerations most explicitly by relaying how she and several colleagues decided, in the midst of an already packed calendar, to seize the unexpected research opportunity opened by the tragic events of September 11, 2001. Having a better understanding of the many vexing complications that can arise may help researchers set more realistic time lines for their projects.

A second recurring theme is the importance of ongoing detailed documentation of the research process: *Every step has to be recorded clearly.* Careful documentation is vital for several reasons. First, keeping track of processes and procedures makes it possible for them to be retraced if confusion or inconsistencies arise later when one looks back at the data and methods. Second, careful documentation is crucial for replicability. Both those on the research team and others need to be able to reproduce what has been done. If details are not recorded about the process then this becomes nearly impossible. Third, many research projects require coordination between several team members. As the chapter by Adam, Doane, and Mendelsohn demonstrates in detail, in order for everyone to be on the same page, information about progress needs to be documented and accessible to other research team members. Fourth, since distractions will almost inevitably steer researchers' attention to other projects, detailed documentation is essential to one's ability to pick up where one left off. Finally, the addition of new personnel to a project requires being able to share every detail of a study, a task that is nearly impossible if specifics were not documented clearly from the start.

A third general theme is the value of *obtaining feedback* from experts throughout the course of a project. Of course, obtaining such feedback may be easier said than done depending on one's position in the academic status hierarchy, and one purpose of this volume is to provide an alternative means of drawing on others' experiences. It is nevertheless generally the case that other researchers *are* available to give comments when asked to do so. And this kind of ongoing feedback from researchers who are separate from the project, whether they are students or senior scholars, can make an enormous difference to the quality of a completed study.

Even without actual researchers to consult, it can also be useful to imagine having to defend one's research choices in front of a crowd of experts. Would the decisions require many excuses? Are they based on convenience or scientific scrutiny? Any question that arises during the initial process is one that is likely to come up subsequently as well—in a job talk, conference presentation, or journal reviewers' comments. But because it is often too late at that point to correct the mistakes that were committed earlier in the project, it is essential to think about those methodological decisions critically from the beginning. The piece in this volume by Adam and colleagues describing the collection of biomarkers is especially informative in this respect insofar as it describes the numerous aspects of the research process that the researchers tested painstakingly at the outset in order to ensure that they were able to implement the correct tools in the final data collection process. As they note, once one starts gathering data, it is important to remain consistent across research subjects by using the same instruments and methods. To collect data from the second half of respondents in a *different* manner than the first set is clearly problematic. And yet if one makes the mistake of starting with a flawed method, then it jeopardizes the whole project to carry on in the same vein. Thus, while testing different procedures may require a significant amount of additional effort at the outset, failing to do so may ultimately lead to far worse setbacks, including rejections from journal editors, failed job talks, and so on.

A final recurring theme—and one that is a source of anxiety to almost any researcher studying human subjects—concerns the process by which one obtains permission from an institution to carry out such work. Although the specifics of how Institutional Review Boards (IRBs) deal with proposals differ greatly by organization, most projects nowadays require their approval, and thus the planning of any study must confront questions about procedures in a timely manner. Recognizing that this is now a nearly universal component of social scientific empirical research, several of the chapters describe IRB challenges. Williams and Xiong in particular go into considerable detail about how they handled questions from their review board while studying gamers online. Albright discusses how one can handle the approval-seeking process in the case of an unexpected research opportunity. Other chapters also make references to how it is best to address the logistics of IRB during various projects.

One caveat. Although this volume focuses on methods, it is important to remain aware throughout the research design and data collection process that without ideas none of this matters. That is, a good research project depends on good ideas that demonstrate a firm grasp of the field and the relevant literature in it. While this requirement is only occasionally addressed explicitly in this volume (the chapters by Bandelj and by Freese take on these matters most explicitly), it underpins all of them. In the same way that it is important to avoid working in a vacuum when it comes to methodological issues, it is also important to be aware of relevant theoretical discussions in one's field before embarking on a study.

While the different chapters of the book overlap at various points, they have been organized to help the reader consult the chapters that are most relevant to the type of inquiry he or she is interested in. This means that it is not necessary to know which method is most relevant *before* deciding which chapters of the book to consult. Anyone who has a general idea of their research interests should be able to find what they need easily and efficiently.

With that in mind, the chapters are organized into four categories: Beyond Self-Reports, Hard-to-Access Populations, Unexpected Opportunities, and Others' Data. The studies described in the first three chapters on Beyond Self-Reports give detailed accounts of methods that do not simply rely on respondents' reports of their own behavior. These methods make it possible for researchers to collect measurements that are more nuanced and more revealing than those produced by traditional methods. Adam, Doane, and Mendelsohn, for example, describe cutting-edge research on collecting biomarkers from respondents in order to measure physiological indexes of well-being. Pager discusses a successful method of field experiments—by now widely cited—that she has implemented in several studies as a vehicle to study employment discrimination. Clawson writes about the particular challenges of conducting an ethnographic study of a community of which the researcher herself is a member. As she shows, while this kind of participant status provides access to information that would otherwise be extremely hard to gather, it can also raise difficult ethical questions regarding disclosure and confidentiality.

The chapters on Hard-to-Access Populations address the challenges of locating and then gaining the confidence of people who are either hard to identify and track down or who belong to groups that cannot be easily accessed using traditional methods. Walling's description of conducting interviews with low-income people details some of the ways a researcher can gain the trust of those who may be especially skeptical of outside investigators. Walejko describes a study of academic bloggers and addresses the challenge of drawing a representative sample of people about whom no comprehensive directory listing exists. Williams and Xiong are also concerned with some of the new research parameters that have emerged due to recent advances in digital media. Their report on studies of online gamers, for example, touches on issues ranging from gaining legitimacy for new kinds of research topics to recruiting respondents to collaborating with corporate entities. Sandvig tackles the challenges of new media research from a different perspective; his chapter contemplates the difficulties involved in studying an area that requires considerable technical knowledge—knowledge that may not be trivial to acquire as a researcher from another field.

The chapters on Unexpected Opportunities consider examples of sudden research possibilities that arise either from abruptly occurring global events or from the unanticipated opportunities that can emerge in the course of a preexisting research project. Albright relates how she and several colleagues reacted to the events of September 11, 2001, as researchers, while simultaneously coping with everyday life as residents of New York City during a time of acute crisis and upheaval. Hargittai and Karr discuss an exciting possibility that came about when a project studying young adults' Internet uses, skills, and participation already under way offered a chance to piggyback on its large paper-and-pencil-based data collection effort in order to collect diary data about young adults using text messaging.

The last three chapters, on Others' Data, give pointers on how best to approach secondary data analysis. While not collecting one's own data may eliminate some of the challenges of empirical research, it raises other hurdles. Bandelj describes a cross-national project and the challenges entailed by trying to compile and compare data from innumerable different sources. Freese offers an illustration of how an intriguing theoretical question can be pursued by finding a relevant secondary data source to address it rigorously. Finally, Gallo gives a detailed account of the rich historical data sources that exist in archives and how best to locate and navigate them. Offering important insights into a wide range of relevant issues— from identifying and gaining access to the most relevant sources to reconstructing the thoughts, rationale, and logic of original investigators—these chapters offer an invaluable blueprint for approaching others' data sources.

While most of the projects discussed in this volume focus on investigating phenomena in the United States, and take the individual as their unit of analysis, many of the lessons learned from these studies can easily be applied to other types of investigations. For while conducting research in other countries will undoubtedly raise its own set of challenges, many of the relevant considerations will resemble those presented in the chapters here. Similarly, even studies of organizations, to name just one possible example, often require communicating with individuals in order to gain access to relevant data sources and respondents. Thus, readers should approach the chapters here with the understanding that much of the advice will apply to other settings as well.

Each of the chapters in this book allows readers to step inside the authors' research projects and to follow them in ways that are otherwise rarely possible. We hope that reading them will provide new researchers with the kind of knowledge and preparation that is usually possible only after years of hands-on experience, thereby sparing them substantial frustration and wasted effort and also improving the overall quality of their research.

SPIT, SWEAT, AND TEARS

Gathering Biological Data in Naturalistic Settings

**EMMA K. ADAM, LEAH D. DOANE,
AND KATHRYN MENDELSOHN**

Reality is the leading cause of stress amongst those in touch with it.
—Lily Tomlin

*One of the symptoms of an approaching nervous breakdown is the
belief that one's work is terribly important.*
—Bertrand Russell

Few social scientists concern themselves with the viscosity of saliva on a
daily basis. Our research team, however, has become expert on such matters. Even small samples of saliva offer social scientists insights into the
minds and bodies of individuals that surveys alone cannot provide. With
just a few drops, we can measure a variety of hormones and other biological markers that provide clues to the functioning of physiological systems,
including those serving functions related to the allocation of energy and attention, growth, sexual behavior, immune functioning, and responses to
stress. A new generation of social scientists (in part through pressure from
funding agencies) is realizing the importance of becoming truly multi-

method: in addition to combining qualitative and quantitative methods, they are now also incorporating biological measurement—often referred to as "biomarkers"—into their research.

Salivary biomarkers are just one of a wide range of biomarker measurement approaches, but the nonintrusive nature of salivary sampling makes it a particularly popular point of entry into this new genre of research. The apparent ease with which saliva can be collected has, however, also meant that many investigators adopt this approach without having a realistic sense of how complicated measuring and interpreting salivary biomarkers can be. This chapter describes some of the challenges and benefits of incorporating salivary sampling into social science research. Although it focuses on salivary cortisol in particular, it contains cautionary tales and lessons that can easily be generalized to other approaches to biological measurement.

Setting aside the not unimportant fact that many funding agencies are now encouraging social scientists to do so, why should social scientists want to incorporate biomarkers into their research? Perhaps because the constructs that social scientists already care about—social and policy contexts and the interpersonal interactions and experiences that take place within them—can have profound effects on biological processes. Alterations in biological processes, in turn, can have important influences on emotional and behavioral functioning as well as physical health (see fig. 1). Thus, physiological processes that used to be confined to the realm of biology and medicine are now understood to be embedded in social contexts, interacting with them dynamically, bidirectionally, and continually. A number of theoretical and empirical traditions incorporate this insight, including biopsychosocial (Engel 1980), biosocial (Booth, Carver, and Granger 2000), bioecological (Bronfenbrenner and Ceci 1994), life history (Worthman and Kuzara 2005; Ellis 2004) and early/fetal programming approaches (Barker 2004; Barker et al. 2002). Despite distinct theoretical and disciplinary orientations, the basic message is the same and is being heard now louder than ever: Biological and social/environmental processes are tightly and planfully intertwined—biological processes are in fact *designed* to change in response to changing experiences, with the aim of promoting flexibility, survival, and flourishing in the face of an ever-changing social-environmental landscape. As a result, examining the transactions between biology and social experience will enable us to better understand human behavior, development, and health.

In an effort to observe the ways in which experience and biology inter-

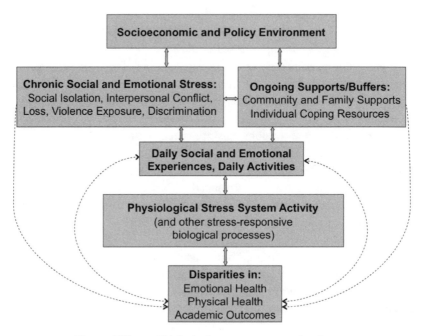

Fig. 1. Effects of biological processes on emotional state

act over moments, days, and years, our team now collects thousands of saliva samples per year from research participants, analyzing them in conjunction with questionnaires and diary reports of social experience gathered in naturalistic settings. This strategy allows us to identify how events and emotions occurring in the everyday lives of children, adolescents, and adults "get under the skin" to influence physiological processes. More specifically, we have spent countless hours preparing, collecting, and processing tiny vials of spit (see fig. 2) in order to identify how everyday life factors influence the stress hormone cortisol, and how differences in cortisol levels between individuals, and changes in cortisol levels within individuals over time, can in turn impact emotional and physical well-being. Although we have collected saliva from many different age groups, much of our recent research (and thus this chapter) focuses on youth aged 13 through 25 years of age—a population that has presented us with some unique challenges. By describing the trials and tribulations of implementing biological measures in our own research, we hope to provide tips and advice that will allow future researchers to avoid (or at least anticipate) the

Fig. 2. Social science data in liquid form

pitfalls of this type of research and to maximize its benefits. Before we can begin to convey these logistical and theoretical challenges, however, we need first to provide some background information about our hormone of interest, cortisol.

CORTISOL: BACKGROUND AND SIGNIFICANCE

Those readers with insomnia, or a bad case of television addiction, will be aware that late-night television ads refer to cortisol as "that nasty little hormone" and offer expensive (and non-FDA approved) "remedies" that promise to reduce your waistline and resolve multiple other "ills" by reducing your cortisol levels. It turns out, however, that the late-night television ads are largely misplaced in giving cortisol a bad rep. Cortisol is in fact essential for everyday survival, not only during times of stress, but also in low-stress situations. Cortisol is present in the bloodstream at all times and is referred to in this context as *basal cortisol*. Basal levels of cortisol play a central ongoing role in regulating metabolism and a variety of other physiological systems, including digestion, immune and inflammatory processes, and growth (Johnson et al. 1992). Basal cortisol levels change over the course of the day in what is called a *diurnal rhythm*—levels are typically highest in the morning upon awakening, increase approximately 50–60 percent in the first 30–40 minutes after waking (called the cortisol awakening response or CAR), then decline across the day to near-zero levels by bedtime (Kirschbaum and Hellhammer 1989, 1994; Pruessner et al. 1997). Cortisol levels also rise above these expected basal or baseline values when individuals encounter stressful events—a phenomenon called *cortisol reactivity*. This stress-related reactivity is what cortisol is best known for (and why it is often dubbed a "stress hormone," despite the fact that its basal regulatory role is equally essential). Stress-induced increases in cortisol have numerous effects on the body, including causing blood levels of glucose to increase in order to provide the individual with the energy needed to face the stressor at hand (Johnson et al. 1992). Thus, for the most part, cortisol is a necessary, functional hormone—our friend rather than our foe. It is only when cortisol is chronically or frequently elevated, or when it fails to elevate in situations when it is needed, that it is thought to be problematic and to contribute to disease states (McEwen 1998). Enter the social scientist, bent on discovering what types of situations or experiences cause this hormone to elevate and hoping to observe when, for whom, and under what circumstances abnormal or problematic functioning might emerge.

The first of these tasks—looking at what elevates cortisol—was originally (and is still frequently) undertaken in the lab context, often according to the following instructions: Round up some unsuspecting undergraduates looking for course credit, expose them to all sorts of stressful tasks, then make them spit a couple of times before and after the stressor. Next, find out what conditions are most effective at causing cortisol levels to spike, and which types of individuals are most likely to show these increases, et voilà: stressors and stress-reactive individuals will have been found.

While important, these lab-based studies nevertheless have several limitations. First of all, undergraduates are not necessarily like everyone else—they may, for example, be more competitive than average; also, racial and economic diversity is limited on some college campuses. Some researchers have attempted to address this limitation by bringing in individuals from the broader community to participate in these lab-based paradigms. But a second problem also emerged—many researchers attempting lab-based paradigms were baffled by the fact that participants' cortisol levels at the start of the task often tended to be high, with cortisol levels declining over the course of a session, rather than increasing as one would expect them to do in response to the stressors. A comparison of levels at the same time of day at home revealed the answer to the mystery—participants were showing "anticipatory" cortisol reactions. That is, they tended to be more frightened by the prospect of many lab tasks than by the tasks themselves. Put another way, their bodies were preparing them for a potential stressor in advance rather than waiting for them to encounter the actual challenge—and this of course made it hard to look at how cortisol levels responded to experiencing the lab tasks.

To solve this problem, researchers have identified certain standardized, highly stressful lab-based tasks that consistently manage to elevate stress hormone levels (see Dickerson and Kemeny 2004 for a review). In addition, modern-day laboratory-based cortisol researchers have outsmarted the problem through a variety of strategies, including: implementing long baseline periods (multiple samples before the stressor), allowing time for anticipatory stress to wane, and making sure that home comparison samples are collected at the same time of the day so as to make it easier to quantify the degree of anticipatory stress reactivity present at the start of the session. Nonetheless, there are some things that lab-based paradigms cannot accomplish. First, they cannot identify the stressors that actually occur in people's everyday lives that manage to activate cortisol levels in naturalistic environments. Second, they cannot examine people's basal cortisol levels over the course of an entire day (unless you plan to lock participants up in a hotel or hospital room for a 24-hour period, which gets costly and may serve as a stressor in and of itself, thereby making it difficult to observe basal cortisol).

The lab-based tasks that are known to be effective in activating cortisol (making a speech and then performing backward arithmetic in front of a very stern-looking panel of judges) are not necessarily representative of situations that people encounter every day. Certainly, these tasks are designed to capture aspects of experience (e.g., fear of negative social evaluation) that do occur in our daily lives. But why approximate real-life experience when you can get out there in the world and measure it directly? One reason is that measuring cortisol in everyday environments is exceptionally complicated: it not only involves amazing feats of creative problem solving but also an array of gadgets and hours of painstaking work in order to be done right. Examining cortisol in relation to everyday life events in naturalistic settings can also lead to many unexpected (and sometimes amusing) turns of events, no matter how careful the planning. These efforts and amusing stories are rarely apparent in the final written research article, which is why we choose to share them here. Gathering spit, while at first distasteful to the squeamish social scientist, opens many new scientific doors, and the resulting information is worth all the investigator sweat and tears involved in implementing this novel "beyond self-report" method. Our discussion addresses a number of questions relating to the why, who, how, when, and what of salivary cortisol. That is, we examine *why* one would measure salivary cortisol, *who* should measure it and *how*, *when* it should be measured, and *what* to do with the data when they are obtained, in terms of analysis and interpretation.

THE WHY'S, WHO'S, HOW'S, WHEN'S, AND WHAT'S OF SALIVARY CORTISOL

Why Measure Salivary Cortisol?

Reading about the challenges of adding a biological measure such as cortisol to a social science study may prompt readers to wonder, *why bother?* We have already noted that federal funding agencies have recently begun strongly encouraging researchers to incorporate "biomarkers" into social science research. Pressure from funders is of course by no means sufficient reason to do so and should be resisted unless there is a compelling research question that adding biomarker(s) is likely to answer. Gathering biomarkers in the hopes of coming up with such a question *eventually* is not a compelling rationale for imposing an additional burden on research participants, or spending money on biomarker analysis. Furthermore, a post hoc (after-the-fact) analysis is rarely sensible, particularly in the case of cortisol, as the specific research question needs to guide the specific data collection strategy.

Our own research was guided by our interest in whether individual differences in basal profiles of cortisol are altered over time by the experience of life events or by the accumulation of life events over the years, with individuals who experienced a larger number of such events, or more severe events, over the years showing more dramatic changes in cortisol profiles. We were also interested in whether acute increases in negative mood or perceived stress predict acute increases in cortisol levels in naturalistic settings. Finally, we wanted to understand whether individual differences in basal profiles, or differences in how cortisol-reactive individuals are to everyday stressors, help to predict the likelihood of depression in subsequent months or years. In one study, we examine these questions longitudinally, over an eight-year period, in a diverse sample of approximately 200 youth transitioning from late adolescence (high school) to young adulthood.

The first of these questions—whether changes in basal cortisol correspond to changing life events—required us to choose a measurement protocol that would accurately define the diurnal cortisol rhythm. The second required us to measure multiple cortisol samples over the course of an entire day, along with simultaneously recorded diary reports of events and emotions, in the hope of capturing momentary cortisol increases associated with stressful situations in everyday life.

In general, research has moved beyond the stage where cortisol is considered simply a handy "indicator" of subjective levels of stress. The studies that are most compelling and most likely to receive funding are those that consider the way in which its interaction with social and contextual stressors may influence later developmental or health outcomes. Above all, the reason for adding a biomarker should be clearly known in advance, to help ensure that the data gathered are appropriate to answer the specific question at hand. This may seem an obvious point but it bears repeating since we know of a number of studies in which the investigators decided to simply "gather stress hormone (cortisol) data," only to be later disappointed when they learned that the measure of cortisol they obtained was not sufficient for the question they eventually decided to ask of it. Having a sensible question in advance obviously requires considerable familiarity with the theoretical literature about the ways in which environments and biological processes interact as well as with past research and theory on the particular biomarker of interest (in our case cortisol). Such familiarity requires either extensive reading or collaboration with someone who already has theoretical expertise and research experience in the relevant areas.

Whose Cortisol Should We Measure, and Who Should Do the Measuring?

Because salivary sampling procedures are noninvasive, they can be used to measure cortisol levels in infants, children, adolescents, and adults. Procedures are typically so straightforward that they can be implemented by individuals on their own after receiving a brief in-person demonstration, guided phone conversation, or even a clear set of written and pictorial directions. Obviously, infants and young children need to be assisted and supervised by an adult to complete the sampling appropriately, and the sampling protocol changes slightly depending on the age of the subject. Salivary cortisol procedures have been successfully implemented across a wide range of socioeconomic, racial-ethnic, and cultural groups (Adam et al. 2006; Cohen et al. 2006).

Also in the "who" category is the question of who will introduce the protocol to participants and answer people's questions. This may seem like a trivial detail, but our experience is that the idea of salivary sampling can either elicit a strong "yuck" response, or a strong "Cool, that's interesting" response, depending on how the idea is presented, and that this response has important implications for participation rates and degree of compliance with sampling protocols. Whether participants lean toward one response or the other depends greatly on the comfort level and enthusiasm of the person explaining it to them. That enthusiasm depends in turn on the type and quality of training that is received. Interviewers that understand, if only at a layperson's level, the novelty and importance of the measure ("from your saliva we will be able to tell how the stresses in your life are affecting your body") are much better at conveying the importance of the measure to participants.

Finally, the importance of having participants who do conduct salivary sampling in their home settings maintain frequent contact with the research team cannot be emphasized too much. Researchers should use regular phone conversations to (1) instruct participants on the procedures; (2) remind them when they are starting the study; (3) check in with them regarding how the sampling is going; and (4) remind them to return their materials (via prepaid mailers or courier boxes that we send out to them). Our typical phone-call pattern involves one call to consent and schedule participants for the study; one call the night before to ensure they have the materials, remember that they are supposed to start the next day, and know what to do; one call the evening they are supposed to have completed the study in order to make sure they did so (and to reschedule them to complete part or all of the study if they did not); and an average of two phone calls asking them to put the materials in the mail to us (sometimes many more). In some cases, for participants living nearby, we arrange to drop by their house to pick up the materials if necessary.

This intensive phone contact schedule requires a large team of callers—we typically have five or six undergraduate research assistants working as callers at any point in time. Each is assigned one or two evenings per week when they are on call duty. In order to make this less onerous, and because participants are often best reached in the evening hours, we allow callers to work from their own home/dorm rooms. We even purchased a family cell phone plan for the purposes of this calling, assigning each undergraduate volunteer his or her own study phone.[1] In order to ensure that their calling is coordinated (and we do not, for example, call the same person twice about the same thing), each caller records their progress on a secure online spreadsheet to which the entire team has access. It also takes another several undergraduate volunteers consistently working to complete data entry of the diaries, questionnaires, and cortisol samples as they come in, and a central lab manager to coordinate all this activity. So, one important point regarding the "who" question as it applies to this type of research is that it takes a lot of "whos" to get the job done. Larger social science projects can choose to contract out to professional data collection organizations in order to accomplish this work. Unless that organization has prior biomarker experience, however, a relatively high degree of investigator involvement in training, supervision, and data quality control is important.

How Is Salivary Sampling Accomplished? What Tools, Equipment, and Protocols Are Utilized?

One rarely discussed aspect of all research is the painstaking effort required to choose exactly the right research tools, whether that be the best-validated questionnaire, the best-worded interview question, or in the case of salivary cortisol measurement, exactly the right width of straw through which to have participants spit. In our research, many straws were tried and failed before the best one was found—not too thick, not too thin, just the right length when cut in 3 sections. (Of course, within a year of locating the perfect straw, the store we frequented stopped carrying that brand, and we had to start all over again.) We cannot emphasize enough how important the "little things" are in biological measurement—such as implementing the correct collection and storage protocol. In some cases, there is debate even among experts as to the best protocol, thus making it hard for beginning researchers to know which approach is best and whose recommendations to follow. The obvious advice is to use previously developed protocols that have recently been published in top journals so that they can be referenced to justify the chosen equipment and procedures. It is, however, important that those articles be recent, as knowledge changes quickly and the most up-to-date advice is best obtained by consulting experts in the field by phone, e-mail, or in person, or by attending a training workshop on the "hows" of biomarker data collection.

Sweat the Little Things. In the case of salivary sampling, some of the "little things" we worry about are whether it is okay to stimulate saliva flow using something sweet and/or tart like Kool-Aid crystals (it is generally preferable not to do this [Schwartz et al. 1998]) and whether levels of various salivary analytes are affected by using cotton swabs to absorb saliva (Shirtcliff et al. 2001) or by the type of material used to make the vials in which samples are collected and stored (Ellison 1988; Hofman 2001). Another key issue is how long samples can remain at room temperature (rather than being frozen, which increases stability) without values being substantially affected. It turns out this varies by salivary analyte (the fancy word for the various things you can measure in saliva). For cortisol, several days or even a week at room temperature is not problematic, which is handy as it allows us to send samples to and from our lab by courier or even regular mail (Clements and Parker 1998).

When in Doubt, Use the Most Conservative Protocol Possible. In general, it is best to err on the cautious side in collection protocols, if possible, in order to avoid any unfortunate run-ins with overly persnickety reviewers later on. As a result, for adults, adolescents, and older children, we choose to collect our samples by "passive drool"—using no stimulants or absorptive material, but rather simply having participants spit into a vial directly or through a small straw. For infants and younger children, some deviation from this preferred protocol is often necessary, as they are unlikely to be willing or able to spit neatly into a vial. Absorption of saliva using a small spongelike pad on the end of a stick, careful use of a few (less than 1/16th teaspoon) sweetened Kool-Aid crystals, and absorption of saliva using cotton are methods often used with younger populations, with the rationale that getting a sample with a small degree of bias is better than getting no sample at all, given that the amount of bias tends to be consistent across samples (Gordon et al. 2005). Regardless of stability at room temperature, we typically have participants refrigerate samples as soon as possible and freeze them as soon as they are returned to the lab. Samples are preferably stored in a low-temperature (–80 degrees Celsius) freezer, but a regular household freezer is fine so long as it is *without* an autodefrost cycle that would subject samples to repeated freeze-thaw cycles. Although we know cortisol levels are not significantly affected by being shipped at room temperature (Clements and Parker 1998), we choose to ship them on dry ice whenever possible. Using the most conservative protocol—that is, the one that works well for the widest range of salivary analytes—is also helpful in the event that you have or later get permission from participants to analyze their samples for additional analytes.

Try to Be Consistent. It is important to use the same materials for all participants in a study. If you think materials are going to cease to be available or change their formulation over the period of your study, it is wise to buy all the necessary materials at the beginning of the study (provided you have enough room to store them and they do not have an expiration date). We ran into an unfortunate circumstance many years back, when we used to use sugarless gum as a stimulant for saliva flow. We had always used this protocol in the past, but when we went to implement it in a new study, we were horrified to discover that our chosen brand of gum advertised in bold letters "New Flavor." This meant that any prior validation work (in which the use of gum was compared to no use of stimulants) would need to be repeated, as we didn't know whether the changes to the gum would somehow influence values. It was this event that convinced us to become "stimulant free" in our future studies of adolescents and adults.

When Do I Obtain My Saliva Samples?

The "when" question is by far the largest and thorniest, particularly in the case of cortisol. We spend much of our day obsessed with timing-related issues: choosing when to gather samples, ensuring samples are taken at the times requested and that those times are accurately recorded, ensuring that we know exactly when samples were taken in relation to participants' wakeup times that day and that samples and equipment are sent back to us in a timely manner. All of these timing issues, as you will see, have posed *major* challenges.

One factor that bears directly on the "when" decision is whether the investigator is interested in basal cortisol rhythms, or reactivity. The notion of basal cortisol *level* doesn't hold much meaning, as the interpretation of cortisol levels varies dramatically according to time of day. Most researchers are therefore interested in examining one or several cortisol *parameters*. In order to best capture each parameter, a differing set of precisely timed samples is required. As mentioned earlier, cortisol levels are high in the morning upon awakening, increase 50–60 percent in the first 30–40 minutes postawakening, decline rapidly at first, and then decline more slowly to near-zero levels at bedtime. Various aspects of this basal rhythm are of interest, including the average elevation of the curve, the size of the increase in cortisol postawakening, and the steepness or rate of decline in levels across the day. It took several years of playing with fancy statistics to figure out the best way to model this diurnal rhythm (see Adam 2006b; Adam et al. 2006) and to understand that increases in cortisol above this typical rhythm may in part reflect cortisol reactivity to events occurring throughout the day.

One cortisol parameter that is particularly interesting is the difference between the waking stress hormone value and a sample taken 30 minutes later.[2] The size of this cortisol awakening response has been found to be correlated with chronic stress, among other things (Schulz et al. 1998). This response involves a rapid and acute increase in hormone, followed by a rapid decline, which means that if participants do not time these samples accurately, and take them either late or early, the researcher has missed the boat on capturing this response. But when participants are going about their own business, taking samples on their own, at home, how do you ensure they take that second sample exactly 30 minutes after the first? And how do you know that they took the first sample when they woke up? What does "waking up" mean, anyway? As soon as you open your eyes for the first time that day? As soon as you shake off the layer of fog from your brain and remember that you have a study to do? Right after your morning triple latte with extra foam? We typically ask participants to gather wakeup samples "as soon as they open their eyes for the first time, before they hit the snooze button," which helps but does not guarantee a prompt wakeup sample. The timing of samples later in the day is also of concern, although subtle deviations in timing later in the day have less of an effect on estimates than deviations in timing occurring during the morning hours, when cortisol levels are changing more rapidly.

Having decided that following participants around at all times (particularly overnight) was not a viable solution, both our lab and others have improvised various solutions for objectively determining levels of participant compliance. The solutions come in the form of gadgets ranging in cost from $2 to $800 apiece. The cheapest gadget on our technology continuum is the simple kitchen timer, available at dollar stores everywhere. Troubled by how to get our groggy participants to take their wakeup plus 30 minute sample exactly 30 minutes after the first sample, it occurred to us that a simple kitchen timer, set to 30 minutes after the first sample, might just do the trick.

Armed with a PhD, 2 MA degrees, and several hundred thousand dollars of foundation and federal funding, the intrepid Principal Investigator (PI) of our team (EA) set off on a quest to find the perfect kitchen timer. We needed a timer that would be small enough to fit in a small-sized courier box, but large enough to be seen without glasses/contacts, and that was mechanical rather than digital (for ease of setting it). The timer had to have a very visible 30-minute mark and needed to look at least somewhat professional, ruling out the various ones shaped like eggs, chickens, cows, pigs, teakettles, and so forth, no matter how tempting it was to buy these comical devices with federal research funds. Buying a boring-looking timer, we reasoned, would also reduce the number of such timers participants would "forget" to return to us with their kits. After visiting at least 10 dollar stores in the Chicago area, the ideal timer was located, at a cost of $2.99 apiece, and the store relieved of its entire stock.[3] Despite our best efforts, the ugly kitchen timers are our least-returned item of research equipment, perhaps appreciated for their ability to prevent the overcooking of ramen noodles and frozen pizzas, or even, one could only hope, causing our participants to aim for even greater heights of culinary achievement. So one moral of this story is to *budget for equipment replacement costs*—a consideration that is of course even more important when such losses extend to include more costly pieces of equipment.

The gadget most commonly used to examine participant compliance with sampling protocols in salivary cortisol research is the TrackCap (AARDEX Ltd., Switzerland), a small bottle with an electronic monitor in the cap (costing approximately $100) that records a time stamp every time the bottle is opened. Typically, some element of the saliva sampling supplies is placed in the bottle so that participants need to open the bottle to do their sampling. This provides an objective recording of their sampling times that we can compare to their self-reported sampling times. This works well, except when participants decide to outsmart us by dumping all the supplies out of the bottle the first time they open it (telling participants they must use the TrackCap to get paid is a partial solution to this problem). It turns out that just knowing they are being monitored increases accuracy considerably among participants (Kudielka, Broderick, and Kirschbaum 2003), so monitoring participants serves to determine how accurate their timing is while at the same time increasing that accuracy.[4] Occasionally, the TrackCaps have provided us with more information than we have asked for—on one occasion, a participant used it to store a uniquely scented plant product in the bottle for a week after his or her study data collection was complete, thus providing us with an objective (but unfortunately unpublishable since we lacked the consent necessary to use this particular data) record of his or her substance use over that period.

The most expensive gadget for helping to monitor compliance is the actigraph or accelerometer, a wristwatch-looking device that keeps an ongoing record of participants' motion. Although this device is not yet prominent in the published literature, several labs, including our own, have begun to use it. The actigraph costs from $400 to $800 per unit, depending on the brand and model you purchase. Ours are at the high end of the range, and include many bells and whistles (almost literally), such as the ability to beep at particular times of day to remind people to do their diary entries and cortisol sampling. Of course, cheaper signaling devices are available, but they do not do what the actigraph can do—give you an objective measure of when participants got up that day, when they go to bed, the quality of their sleep, and the level of physical activity throughout the day. The data provided by the actigraphs on sleep timing and efficiency open up all sorts of new and important scientific questions regarding the interface between sleep, stress, cortisol, and psychopathology. This information also has the added feature of giving us an objective measure of when participants got up that day, which can be compared with self-reported waketimes.[5] Although some degree of judgment is necessary in interpreting actigraph data, they nonetheless provide a convergent source of information on participant sleep-wake schedules and the ability to examine the impact of physical activity levels on stress hormone levels.

One message the next generation of researchers should take from this is that there are many technologies not originally intended for social science research that can be adapted to serve our purposes, and brand new technologies that may enrich our understanding or increase our methodological rigor are becoming available all the time. There is some push, often reinforced by research methods training, to do things in exactly the same way that they have been done in the past. Many great advances (as well as careers) are made, however, when individuals are willing to be creative, take risks, and add something new to the methodological tool kit of their profession.

How Many Cortisol Samples Do I Need?

Closely related to the issue of when to measure cortisol is the question of how many samples are needed. This is a source of considerable angst for individuals considering adding salivary sampling to their studies: they want to measure cortisol, and measure it well, but they also want to use the fewest number of samples possible in order to minimize participant burden, maximize compliance, and minimize costs. Rather than simply guessing, we recently decided to approach this question scientifically, starting with a very sampling-intensive data-collection protocol and examining how much reliability decreased with each additional sample that was dropped. It turns out that samples added during the middle of the day on the same day do not add much to the estimation of the basic diurnal rhythm, whereas samples added on a different, second day improved reliability more considerably (Adam 2009). In order to assess momentary reactivity to events and emotions occurring throughout the day, however, multiple points across the full day are required (Adam 2006).

Additional research is needed to find the optimal numbers of samples for maximizing information for minimal costs. Until then, the best advice is to collect as many samples as you can afford, preferably across several days and/or situations, and to use existing protocols that have appeared frequently in the literature. A low-cost protocol for assessing basal cortisol involves one sample taken at wakeup, one at 30 minutes after wakeup, and one at bedtime (Adam et al. 2006). This protocol allows a (rough) estimate of average cortisol levels across the day, the steepness of the diurnal cortisol rhythm, and the size of the cortisol awakening response. A more intensive protocol allowing examination of these same parameters as well as momentary cortisol reactions to events occurring across the day involves sampling repeatedly across the full day, including points at wakeup, bedtime, and wakeup plus 30 minutes, as well as 3 to 7 points in between (Adam 2006; van Eck et al. 1996). In either case, repeating the protocol across multiple days improves estimation considerably.

WHAT TO DO WITH THE DATA? HOW TO ANALYZE AND INTERPRET THE DATA?

Statistical Modeling of Cortisol Data

The best sampling plan in the world is useless without appropriate methods for modeling the cortisol data statistically so as to isolate the parameters of interest. For the first author's initial naturalistic cortisol study, approximately 25 percent effort went into reading background literature and planning the study, 10 percent went into grant writing, 25 percent went into data collection, and 40 percent went to figuring out optimal methods of data analysis that would glean the best information from the material at hand.

It took several years of playing with the data to figure out the best way to model the diurnal rhythm of cortisol (Adam 2006; Adam and Gunnar 2001; Adam et al. 2006) and to discover that you can model cortisol reactivity to events occurring in naturalistic settings by identifying the deviations above each individual's latent, fitted, or average diurnal rhythm using multilevel modeling techniques (Adam 2006). Using multilevel growth curve modeling, it is possible to derive a latent estimate of each individual's basal pattern of cortisol production across the day (presumably reflecting trait cortisol variation) and then predict individual differences in basal cortisol patterns from trait variables of interest (Adam and Gunnar 2001; Adam 2006; Hruschka, Kohrt, and Worthman 2005; van Eck et al. 1996). Other researchers have used latent-state-trait modeling to isolate and predict variance in cortisol that is stable within individuals across time, and is thus presumed to represent "trait" rather than state or error variance in cortisol (Kirschbaum et al. 1990; Shirtcliff et al. 2005). Use of multilevel or latent variable approaches is not a necessity in cortisol research—many studies are published predicting individual cortisol samples or using simple aggregation approaches to combine values across samples. It is the experience of our lab and others, however, that use of latent variable approaches tends to yield stronger and more consistent effects.

Whatever approach is used, it is essential to remember that there are many different indicators or parameters of naturalistic cortisol activity, each of which is interpreted differently, and many of which have separate literatures dedicated to them. As described earlier, commonly measured cortisol parameters include average cortisol level as measured by taking the area under the cortisol curve across the full day, size of the cortisol awakening response, slope of the diurnal cortisol curve,[6] and the degree of reactivity to and speed of recovery from acute stressors. Each of these different measures of cortisol activity has different predictors and is predictive of different outcomes (Adam, Klimes-Dougan, and Gunnar 2007).

Incorporating Health and Demographic Control Variables

As important as proper modeling of the cortisol levels themselves is the proper measurement and inclusion of statistical controls/covariates. Cortisol activity is influenced by a wide range of factors over and above the psychosocial variables of interest to social scientists. Thus, in addition to providing saliva samples, participants should also provide information, typically by way of a questionnaire report completed within the same week as the saliva sampling, about health and lifestyle confounds that can influence cortisol levels and patterns. Such a questionnaire should definitely include age, gender, a list of current medications taken, presence of any chronic or acute health problems, weight and height for calculation of body mass, time of waking on the day of testing, and for postpubertal (and premenopausal) women, whether or not she is currently pregnant, and number of days since her last menstrual period. It should also address lifestyle factors that may influence cortisol such as levels of use of nicotine, alcohol, caffeine, and physical exercise (of these, nicotine use has perhaps been the most strongly related to cortisol in past research), typical hours of sleep and sleep quality, as well as hours of sleep and sleep quality the night before cortisol testing. It can also, where possible, be helpful to ask participants to keep diary records of their activities in the hour prior to taking each sample, such as napping, smoking, caffeine or alcohol consumption, vigorous physical activity, drinking, eating, or medication use. It is typical to ask participants to restrain from eating, drinking, smoking, napping, or exercise in the hour prior to taking any particular cortisol sample, but when this is not possible, knowing about these events allows you to identify and statistically control for confounding influences on particular cortisol samples. It is also helpful to ask whether anything unusually stressful or out of the ordinary happened that day.

Some variables influence cortisol levels and patterns so greatly that they serve as grounds for exclusion from the sample altogether. Common exclusion criteria include the presence of an endocrine disorder such as Cushing's or Addison's disease, acute physical illness (e.g., flu) on the days of testing, use of steroid-based medications for allergy or asthma, and being in the third trimester of pregnancy. Other variables are often included as statistical covariates, such as gender, oral contraceptive use, nicotine use, body mass, and time of waking on the day of cortisol testing. There is some sign that socioeconomic as well as racial/ethnic characteristics are associated with cortisol levels (Cohen et al. 2006; DeSantis et al. 2007). In some cases, these are the variables of interest, with investigations aimed at understanding the mechanisms by which these demographic differences come to be related to individual differences in cortisol. When they are not the variable of concern, it is advisable to add them as covariates. Another variable that can be added as a statistical covariate is the degree of compliance with the timing of cortisol sampling, as determined by use of the electronic monitoring devices—where low compliance has a systematic effect on cortisol measures, adding this covariate can be helpful (Adam et al. 2006). Obviously, large enough sample sizes are required to employ multiple controls for confounding variables, and this should be taken into account in power analyses. Although novice cortisol researchers are often concerned that employing multiple covariates will reduce effect sizes for the psychosocial variables of interest, it is the experience of our research team that proper employment of covariates has the opposite effect—results are strengthened when other factors influencing cortisol are taken into account in statistical models.

Data Cleaning and Transformation

Before proceeding with fancy statistical analyses, a great deal of grunt work must be accomplished, including cleaning and preparing the cortisol data. When data are received from the laboratory that performed your assays,[7] the researcher will receive two values for each sample (provided the samples were assayed in duplicate, i.e., each sample twice, which is preferred as it increases reliability of measurement). The average of these two values is typically used. Different laboratories use different units to report cortisol values. In North America, the units most frequently used are μg/dL, while in Europe, nmol/L is often used (to convert from the first to the second, multiply by 27.59).

A visual inspection of the raw data will quickly reveal some extreme outlying values. The data associated with such samples should be inspected to see if (1) time of day was recorded incorrectly by the participant or data entry person, for example, reversing AM or PM, such that what appears to be a very high PM value is actually a normally high morning value; (2) the sample looked odd in any way or appeared contaminated; (3) the person was napping, eating a large meal, or engaged in vigorous physical activity just prior to taking the sample; or (4) whether he or she meets any of the exclusion criteria described previously, such as being ill on the day of testing. In cases in which the reason for the outlier renders the sample invalid, such as being physically ill, the sample should be excluded. In most other cases, when the origin of the high value is unknown, or there is no clear justification for exclusion, the impact of particular outliers may be reduced by windsorizing—that is, reassigning extreme values a value that is 3 standard deviations above the mean or a value equal to the upper limit of detection of the assay. A natural or base 10 logarithmic transformation is also typically applied to cortisol values in order to reduce a commonly found strong positive skew in the data (a natural log transform is slightly preferable, as the resulting data are easier to interpret). Frequently, transformed values will be used in actual statistical analyses, while cortisol values in original units are presented in tables for greater ease of interpretation.

Another question of concern regarding outliers is whether one should report extremely high (or low) cortisol values to participants. This is a decision that should be made in advance and in conjunction with one's Institutional Review Board. In our experience, because our knowledge of the precise medical meaning of cortisol differences is still relatively limited, it is most common not to report unusual cortisol values to participants. If one were to report such values, follow up by the participant with a physician experienced in the medical interpretation of cortisol differences would of course be essential.

SPIT HAPPENS

This phrase, featured on a babies' bib that was prominently displayed in the lab space of the first author's dissertation adviser,[8] suggests two possible interpretations: (1) There is a lot of spit in the world, just waiting to be collected and examined by the savvy and pioneering biopsychosocial scientist, and (2) You cannot entirely control everything in the research process—unexpected events will happen. In short: things are going to get messy (something that is true both literally and figuratively when you are working with saliva). In addition to the various mishaps described above, this section describes a few of the unexpected events that have occurred and resulting lessons learned during our research experiences thus far. Appearing in no particular order, they serve as a montage of anecdotes illustrating research "messiness."

Saliva Quality Issues. Despite clear instructions not to eat and drink in the hour before sampling, approximately 15 percent of our saliva samples come back with an array of colorful chunks and swirls (resembling miniature lava lamps). Were every single sample with a contaminant to be excluded, there would be considerable data loss. Instead, when samples are returned, any issues regarding quality and quantity of the sample are noted in a spreadsheet. That is, each sample should be logged in immediately upon its arrival at the lab, with notes regarding date and time of sample, quantity, and anything unusual that can be observed regarding sample quantity or quality. Signs of blood should especially be noted, as this has known influences on cortisol and may be sufficient reason for exclusion of a particular sample. In studies in which blood contamination is a frequent concern, the presence of blood in samples can and should be tested (Kivlighan et al. 2004).

Saliva Samples Mistaken for Trash. Small vials of spit in plastic bags clearly marked "completed samples" are apparently somewhat vulnerable in the household refrigerator: several of our adolescent participants' hard work fell victim to the overzealous cleaning and decluttering efforts of their family members. Thankfully, in most of these cases, the adolescent was kind enough to do the data collection a second time, being sure to first instruct all family members to keep their hands off their spit. More tragically, close to 5,000 samples (our entire first wave of data collection) fell victim to the overzealous cleaning efforts of a laboratory doing our assays, after the analysis of cortisol levels in the saliva was complete. Cortisol was in fact the primary biomarker of interest in this study, but we had intended to seek funding to assay the leftover saliva for other hormones that we had obtained consent to examine. Thankfully, multiple additional waves of data are being collected, such that we can examine the additional analytes in later waves and even predict prospectively from them. Note that this type of mishap is the exception rather than the rule in terms of laboratory experiences: for the most part, the existing laboratories conducting salivary assays provide excellent, rapid, helpful, and reliable service. Obviously, however, it is crucial to provide the laboratory with crystal-clear instructions about what to do with samples after an assay is conducted.

Actigraph Disasters. Although actigraphy seemed like the ideal solution to tracking our participants' sleep-wake schedules, there were several bumps along the road in implementing this method in relation to salivary cortisol sampling. First of all, we needed an actigraph watch that would beep to signal participants to do the cortisol sampling—a requirement that added several hundred dollars to the price of each watch. In prior studies, we had used a less expensive (approximately $40) programmable digital watch to signal the sampling times. To save on costs, we considered the possibility of having participants wear two watches—the actigraph to measure activity, and the digital watch to signal sampling times. However, given that we were already asking adolescents to (1) wear an ugly watch that would interrupt them several times a day and (2) spit for us repeatedly, we figured that asking them to wear *two* watches at once could be the straw that broke the camel's back in terms of whether or not they would be willing to participate in our research.

So, we bit the bullet and spent the extra few hundred dollars per watch in order to purchase the actigraphs that beeped. In our first few pilot tests, however, beeps that our research team had no trouble hearing were missed repeatedly by participants. After some discussion, we realized that this was probably due to the fact that our research participants were members of the iPod generation and likely had another device making noise in their ears at the same time our watch was trying to capture their attention. We also discovered that, although the actigraph devices were themselves fairly waterproof (could be worn in the shower), the small opening from which the sound was supposed to issue had a tendency to fill with water, muffling the sound. After conversations with the company about obtaining watches with a louder and longer beep (they had a louder version in the development phase), our temporary solution was to program the actigraph watches to beep *twice in a row* so that the beeps went on for longer and were thus harder to miss or ignore.

We also struggled with how to minimize the possibility of actiwatch losses. Should we tell participants the value of the watches, or would that prompt some to "keep" the instrument? Deciding that honesty was the best policy, we eventually let adolescent participants know that our study would go out of business if we lost too many of these expensive instruments. In order to discourage them from removing them during the day, we also came up with the idea of having adolescents use nonremovable wristbands, similar to the kind issued in hospitals (or rock concerts). We even managed to get the wristbands personalized, with the name of the study and our phone number, stating "Property of the Sleep and Stress Study."

Despite telling the adolescents these devices were extremely expensive, and fixing them to adolescents' wrists with bands that needed to be cut to be removed, a painfully large number of our fleet of 27 actigraphs went astray over the course of several years, with the following compelling reasons being among the list of excuses.

1. I emptied the FedEx packet out into pile of laundry in my friends' dorm room, and could not locate watch amid the chaos.
2. I went to the emergency room—the actigraph was cut off and never seen again.
3. I left it in the library and went back and couldn't find it.
4. My backpack was stolen with the actigraph in it.
5. It fell under my bed and I couldn't find it.

Issues with Time. Although it may seem that we are obsessed with time, the strong impact that the time of day has on cortisol levels (approximately 70 percent of the variance in cortisol levels is determined by time of day) makes it essential we know when samples are taken (hence all our timing devices described earlier). Despite our frequent reminders to record the time of each sample, however, samples still come back to us without times recorded. Each of our labels is preprinted to indicate which sample of the day it is, so on the relatively rare occasions when time is not recorded, we can use the label to identify approximate time of day (i.e., when the sample was supposed to be taken), and use either the intended time of sampling or the TrackCap recorded time as the time of the sample. This is typically preferable to discarding the sample altogether. When samples come back to us without a label at all, however, they are destined for the trash.

Another time-related issue we encountered when using multiple devices with internal clocks was that the devices must all be calibrated not only to the same minute but also to the correct time zone. The latter problem arises when research participants in our longitudinal study inconveniently decide to plan their own lives, moving to locations that are optimal for their own development, as opposed to staying nearby, in order to make life easier for our research team. A surprising number of participants appear to believe that their life priorities should come first. All jesting aside, given the many larger priorities in people's lives, we never cease to be amazed at and grateful for how far our participants will extend themselves to contribute to our research. For example, on occasions when completed materials were lost in the mail, or watches failed to beep when they should have, participants have kindly agreed to repeat the procedures for us right away. In another example, we have had participants complete their study procedures even when their own lives are not going so smoothly—we have had participants provide diary reports and samples during exam week, right after breakups with their boyfriends/girlfriends, and even from a police station.

Holiday Card Hand Cramps. One year, to express our appreciation for our participants, we decided[9] it would be a good idea to personally and individually handwrite long notes of thanks to approximately 200 participants on (religiously neutral) winter holiday cards.[10] A team of seven people was charged with this task. Four days, a dozen sparkly colored pens, and seven serious hand cramps later, our masterpieces were done, and hopefully appreciated by at least a few participants. One moral of this story is that it is often hard to anticipate how long any particular research task will take. As Eszter Hargittai cautions in the Introduction to this collection, when in doubt, and even when *not* in doubt, assume that each task will take at least two to three times longer than you initially estimate.

Incentives Shrink with Age. As the multiple longitudinal waves of our study have proceeded, we have discovered an amazing fact—the same amount of money appears to shrink with the passage of time, repetition of study tasks, and the aging of our participants. That is, what appeared to be a passable incentive to a 16-year-old ($10) does not hold much appeal to a 19-year-old, and what used to be a reasonable incentive in the freshman year of college ($40) does not appear to be enough when they are juniors and seniors. Thankfully, several of our participants were kind enough to inform us directly that our incentive payment was no longer sufficiently motivating, and we have been able to adjust our incentive plan accordingly before too many participants were lost. One message in this is that it is worth considering your research participants to be your allies: asking them directly if there are ways that their experience of the research process could be improved often yields valuable information that can be used to correct the course of current research or to improve plans for future projects.

Dear Diary. One thing we have learned from the diary component of our study is that a pen can sometimes be a dangerous weapon in the hands of a late adolescent late at night (particularly on occasions when they are under the influence of more than their hormones). Several late-night diary entries were characterized by messy handwriting and passionate declarations of either love or hate for our research project and all involved with it. The diary reports typically return to normal the next day. A more disturbing turn of events in the diaries is the serious declarations of distress they sometimes contain. The undergraduate volunteers who are doing data entry for our project are trained to immediately call the laboratory manager and/or study PI if they see anything in the diaries indicating extreme distress or, even more seriously, suicidal ideation or intent. Interestingly, some of the more revealing entries emerge in the most open-ended section of our diaries, in which we invite participants to share random thoughts and doodles. In several cases, signs of distress have been conveyed in no uncertain terms in either verbal or pictorial form, prompting us to intervene to help connect the adolescent with appropriate services.

Stressful Life Events. Given the title of this section, you may think we are going to tell you how we measure exposure to stressful life events for participants in our study. We do of course look at this, using a well-validated interview measure. A more relevant topic, however, for revealing the dirty underbelly of the research process is the way in which "spit happens" in our own lives as well as the life of the research project and its participants. Dealing with your research team's life events should perhaps fall outside the bounds of what is expected from either academic advising or study management, but in reality, bad stuff happens to good people, even the good people who are supposed to be running your study like a smoothly oiled machine. One can ask lab members to leave their personal lives at home, but in reality, one needs to be prepared to deal with both the affective consequences as well as the practical implications of study team members being temporarily distracted or even incapacitated by stressful life events. In jest, we have suggested sending lab members home with spit kits to examine the impact of these events on their stress hormone profiles, in the interests of quantifying the physiological impact of their misfortune, but thus far, alas, this strategy has not been implemented. Although others will have differing opinions on this point, in our experience a relatively "open" climate in which lab members feel they can share, at least with the lab manager, the fact that significant events are going on in their lives has been important for keeping our research team running smoothly and has helped our lab members and the study as a whole to navigate the bumps along the road. To provide some perspective on why this might be relevant, a partial list of the known life events that occurred to members of our lab or to a member of their immediate family over a recent two-year period is listed below. There has been some rather nonscientific talk among lab members that there may be a curse on our lab, but we prefer to chalk it up to bad luck.

3 car accidents
3 car break-ins
3 cancer diagnoses
1 laptop stolen
1 hard drive crash
1 open heart surgery
2 cases of meningitis
1 homeless man sleeping in child's bed with gun
1 muskrat drowning in household toilet[11]

Lest the reader become too depressed, we do have positive events happen on occasion as well—such as a marriage or two, the birth of one 8-pound and two 10-pound baby boys (thankfully to different mothers), an academic promotion, a number of graduations, and even a wide range of successful presentations and publications from the project.

CONCLUSION

Having reached the end of our story, one moral to take away is that adding biological measures to social science research can be extraordinarily complex, introducing a wide range of issues that are not normally faced in typical survey, interview, or even observational research. It is also worth noting that cortisol is considered by those who study the biology-environment interface to be among the most complicated of biological measures to implement and interpret. Because it is also one of the best known, it is often one of the first biological measures that investigators new to this type of measurement seek to incorporate. On the one hand, it is deceptively simple—"a hormone that shows how stressed you are, I want to measure that!"—on the other hand, remarkably complicated. Having been informed of some of the complications in this chapter, some investigators may choose not to go down this methodological pathway. Others, we hope, will go on to tread it carefully, aware of the complexities involved and with the knowledge that they will need to do considerable background reading and/or collaborate or consult with individuals who have experience with these measures. Another message we want to impart, however, is that you do not have to have it *all* figured out in advance: research consists in large part of learning by doing (often by trying and failing the first time) and creative problem solving. Finally: no matter how prepared you are, you need to expect the unexpected because, no matter how hard you try to control your research process, spit happens.

NOTES

The research described in this chapter was supported by a number of different sources, including a William T. Grant Foundation Scholars award to the first author, the Spencer Foundation, the Alfred P. Sloan Foundation, NIMH R01 MH65652 and NIMH R03 MH63269, and the Institute for Policy Research at Northwestern University. We would also like to heartily thank all our research participants for their generous contributions of time and effort (and body fluids!) to this research endeavor.

　　1. Our purchase of the family cell phone plan was motivated by several factors, including (1) It was not fair to have our volunteers using their own cell phone minutes; and (2) We wanted to preserve the privacy of our callers. We later realized it

had the added bonus of allowing us to track the number of calls each caller was making each night and how long the phone calls were taking.

2. Studies focusing on this parameter specifically have participants take samples every 15 minutes over the first hour after waking; those that want to measure the CAR as well as activity across the full day often employ a more efficient (but less precise) protocol involving just two samples—at wakeup and 30 minutes after waking, which is thought to be the typical peak of the CAR response.

3. Surprisingly, the storekeeper did not seem interested in engaging in a scholarly debate regarding the morality of a dollar store selling items that not only cost more than $1 but are not even sold in multiples of $1.

4. An important corollary of this is that you could actually improve compliance simply by telling participants they are being monitored, whether or not this is actually the case. In several large studies, to reduce expense, we had the idea of using a mixture of real and cheaper nonfunctioning TrackCaps, such that only a subset of participants are actually being monitored. The nonfunctioning caps were made by special order, overcoming the companies' initial resistance to selling us products that didn't actually work, with the promise to buy a considerable number that did.

5. Truth be told, it was in fact the actigraph's potential as a compliance monitoring tool that originally caught our attention, followed later by a realization of the full potential of this instrument and the incorporation of sleep processes as a central measure in the study.

6. This is often measured by finding the slope of a regression line fit through all cortisol points across the day. The slope is determined by regressing time of day (preferably time since waking) on all the cortisol values, excluding the CAR sample, which is thought to be determined by different mechanisms (Clow et al. 2004).

7. When choosing a laboratory, it is important to obtain information regarding the quality of its assay, including at a minimum the degree of intra- and interassay variation in cortisol levels (less than 10 percent on each is good) and the upper and lower limits of detection of the assay (the highest and lowest values the assay can reliably detect). This information will also be required when writing up the manuscript.

8. Megan Gunnar, to whom this chapter is hereby dedicated, as her training contributed to many of the insights presented herein. Any errors in the chapter are fully the responsibility of the editor . . . er, rather, the authors.

9. Editorial comment from second and third authors to the first author/study PI: "Actually, I believe YOU decided it would be a good idea and coerced us into doing it." The first author's memory of this particular decision is vague. She does, however, recall that her research team told her (and kept up the practical joke for at least five hours) that they had sent out a rather unflattering photograph of her inside every single holiday card.

10. Again, at least two hours of scouring discount stores was required to locate cards that were (1) attractive, (2) religiously and culturally and gender neutral, and (3) relatively inexpensive.

11. Thankfully, no one was seriously hurt in the final two scenarios, except for the luckless muskrat, who apparently fell through the ceiling tiles in exactly the right place, at exactly the right angle to land wedged face down in the toilet bowl.

REFERENCES

Adam, E. K. 2006. Transactions among Adolescent Trait and State Emotion and Diurnal and Momentary Cortisol Activity in Naturalistic Settings. *Psychoneuroendocrinology* 31(5): 664–79.

Adam, E. K. 2009. Strategies for Modeling Diurnal Cortisol Slopes in Population-based Research: Implications of Number and Timing of Salivary Cortisol Samples for Slope Estimates.

Adam, E. K., and M. R. Gunnar. 2001. Relationship Functioning and Home and Work Demands Predict Individual Differences in Diurnal Cortisol Patterns in Women. *Psychoneuroendocrinology* 26:189–208.

Adam, E. K., L. C. Hawkley, B. M. Kudielka, and J. T. Cacioppo. 2006. Day-to-Day Dynamics of Experience-Cortisol Associations in a Population-based Sample of Older Adults. *Proceedings of the National Academy of Sciences* 103:17058–63.

Adam, E. K., B. Klimes-Dougan, and M. R. Gunnar. 2007. Social Regulation of the Adrenocortical Response to Stress in Infants, Children, and Adolescents: Implications for Psychopathology and Education. In *Human Behavior, Learning, and the Developing Brain: Atypical Development*, ed. D. Coch, G. Dawson, and K. Fischer, 264–304. New York: Guilford Press.

Barker, D. J. P. 2004. The Developmental Origins of Adult Disease. *Journal of the American College of Nutrition* 23 (90006): 588–95.

Barker, D. J. P., J. G. Eriksson, T. Forsén, and C. Osmond. 2002. Fetal Origins of Adult Disease: Strength of Effects and Biological Basis. *International Journal of Epidemiology* 31:1235–39.

Booth, A., K. Carver, and D. A. Granger. 2000. Biosocial Perspectives on the Family. *Journal of Marriage and the Family* 62:1018–34.

Bronfenbrenner, U., and S. J. Ceci. 1994. Nature-Nurture Reconceptualized in Developmental Perspective: A Bioecological Model. *Psychological Review* 101 (4): 568–86.

Clements, A. D., and C. R. Parker. 1998. The Relationship between Salivary Cortisol Concentrations in Frozen versus Mailed Samples. *Psychoneuroendocrinology* 23 (6): 613–16.

Clow, A., L. Thorn, P. Evans, and F. Hucklebridge. 2004. The Awakening Cortisol Response: Methodological Issues and Significance. *Stress: The International Journal on the Biology of Stress* 7 (1): 29–37.

Cohen, S., J. E. Schwartz, E. Epel, C. Kirschbaum, S. Sidney, and T. Seeman. 2006. Socioeconomic Status, Race, and Diurnal Cortisol Decline in the Coronary Artery Risk Development in Young Adults (CARDIA) Study. *Psychosomatic Medicine* 68:41–50.

DeSantis, A., E. K. Adam, L. D. Doane, S. Mineka, R. Zinbarg, and M. Craske. 2007. Racial/Ethnic Differences in Cortisol Diurnal Rhythms in a Community Sample of Adolescents. *Journal of Adolescent Health* 41:3–13.

Dickerson, S. S., and M. E. Kemeny. 2004. Acute Stressors and Cortisol Responses: A Theoretical Integration and Synthesis of Laboratory Research. *Psychological Bulletin* 130:355–91.

Ellis, B. J. 2004. Timing of Pubertal Maturation in Girls: An Integrated Life History Approach. *Psychological Bulletin* 130 (6): 920–58.

Ellison, P. T. 1988. Human Salivary Steroids: Methodological Considerations and Applications in Physical Anthropology. *Yearbook of Physical Anthropology* 31:115–42.

Engel, G. L. 1980. The Clinical Application of the Biopsychosocial Model. *American Journal Psychiatry* 137 (5): 535–44.

Gordon, M. K., E. Peloso, A. Auker, and M. Dozier. 2005. Effect of Flavored Beverage Crystals on Salivary Cortisol Enzyme-Immunoreactive Assay Measurements. *Developmental Psychobiology* 47 (2): 189–95.

Hofman, L. F. 2001. Human Saliva as a Diagnostic Specimen. *Journal of Nutrition* 131 (5): 1621S–25S.

Hruschka, D. J., B. A. Kohrt, and C. M. Worthman. 2005. Estimating Between- and Within-Individual Variation in Cortisol Levels Using Multilevel Models. *Psychoneuroendocrinology* 30:698–714.

Johnson, E. O., T. C. Kamilaris, G. P. Chrousos, and P. W. Gold. 1992. Mechanisms of Stress: A Dynamic Overview of Hormonal and Behavioral Homeostatis. *Neuroscience and Biobehavioral Reviews* 16:115–30.

Kirschbaum, C., and D. H. Hellhammer. 1989. Salivary Cortisol in Psycho-biological Research: An Overview. *Neuropsychobiology* 22:150–69.

Kirschbaum, C., and D. H. Hellhammer. 1994. Salivary Cortisol in Psychoneuroendocrine Research: Recent Developments and Applications. *Psychoneuroendocrinology* 19 (4): 313–33.

Kirschbaum, C., R. Steyer, M. Eid, U. Patalla, P. Schwenkmezger, and D. H. Hellhammer. 1990. Cortisol and Behavior: 2. Application of a Latent State-Trait Model to Salivary Cortisol. *Psychoneuroendocrinology* 15 (4): 297–307.

Kivlighan, K. T., D. A. Granger, E. B. Schwartz, V. Nelson, M. Curran, and E. A. Shirtcliff. 2004. Quantifying Blood Leakage into the Oral Mucosa and Its Effects on the Measurement of Cortisol, Dehydroepiandrosterone, and Testosterone in Saliva. *Hormones and Behavior* 46:39–46.

Kudielka, B. M., J. E. Broderick, and C. Kirschbaum. 2003. Compliance with Saliva Sampling Protocols: Electronic Monitoring Reveals Invalid Cortisol Daytime Profiles in Noncompliant Subjects. *Psychosomatic Medicine* 65 (2): 313–19.

McEwen, B. S. 1998. Stress, Adaptation, and Disease: Allostasis and Allostatic Load. *Annals of the New York Academy of Sciences* 840:33–44.

Pruessner, J. C., O. T. Wolf, D. H. Hellhammer, A. Buske-Kirschbaum, K. von Auer, S. Jobst, I. Kaspers, and C. Kirschbaum, 1997. Free Cortisol Levels after Awakening: A Reliable Biological Marker for the Assessment of Adrenocortical Activity. *Life Sciences* 61:2539–49.

Schulz, P., C. Kirschbaum, J. Pruessner, and D. Hellhammer. 1998. Increased Free Cortisol Secretion after Awakening in Chronically Stressed Individuals Due to Work Overload. *Stress Medicine* 14:91–97.

Schwartz, E. B., D. A. Granger, E. J. Susman, M. R. Gunnar, and B. Laird. 1998. Assessing Salivary Cortisol in Studies of Child Development. *Child Development* 69 (6): 1503–13.

Shirtcliff, E. A., D. Granger, A. Booth, and D. Johnson. 2005. Low Salivary Cortisol Levels and Externalizing Behavior Problems in Youth. *Development and Psychopathology* 17:167–84.

Shirtcliff, E. A., D. A. Granger, E. Schwartz, and M. J. Curran. 2001. Use of Salivary Biomarkers in Biobehavioral Research: Cotton-based Sample Collection Methods Can Interfere with Salivary Immunoassay Results. *Psychoneuroendocrinology* 26 (2): 165–73.

van Eck, M., H. Berkhof, N. Nicolson, and J. Sulon. 1996. The Effects of Perceived Stress, Traits, Mood States, and Stressful Daily Events on Salivary Cortisol. *Psychosomatic Medicine* 58:447–58.

Worthman, C. M., and J. Kuzara. 2005. Wiley-Liss Plenary Symposium: Life History and the Early Origins of Health Differentials. *American Journal of Human Biology* 17:95–112.

FIELD EXPERIMENTS FOR
STUDIES OF DISCRIMINATION

Experimental methods provide a powerful means of isolating causal mechanisms. Traditional experiments typically begin with clearly defined "treatment" and "control" conditions, to which subjects are randomly assigned.[1] All other environmental influences are carefully controlled. A specific outcome variable is then recorded to test for differences between groups. Frequently, in an effort to ensure a naive or "natural" reaction to the experimental condition, subjects are not told the purpose of the experiment. Experiments are often considered to be the "gold standard" for studies of causal effects precisely because of their ability to carefully isolate the effect of one variable on another. Because so much social science research is dedicated to developing causal arguments, experimental techniques clearly offer a valuable approach.

At the same time, experimental methods have been criticized for failing to provide realistic conditions in which to study important social relationships. Many experiments are conducted in laboratory settings, far removed from the regular interactions and environments of everyday life. Experiments also typically rely on undergraduate psychology students as their subject pool, thus further limiting the generalizability of the findings to a broader population. To the extent that experiments compromise external validity (generalizability to the wider world) for enhanced internal validity (precise estimation of causal effects), the trade-offs entailed by using experimental methods must be carefully considered.

This chapter on field experiments offers one solution to the problems of generalizability in experimental methods. Field experiments blend experimental methods with field-based research, relaxing certain controls over environmental influences in order to better simulate real-world interactions. While retaining the key experimental features of matching and random assignment that are important for inferences of causality, this approach relies on real contexts (actual employment searches, real estate markets, consumer transactions, etc.) for its staged measurement techniques. For example, rather than asking undergraduate subjects to rate hypothetical job applicants in a lab experiment, a field experiment would present two equally qualified job applicants to real employers in the context of real job searches.

In what follows, I consider the use of field experiments in one specific domain: the study of labor market discrimination. This case makes it possible to highlight the unique features of field experiments while also considering the potential complexities and pitfalls of this particular methodological approach. Field experiments offer unique advantages in isolating the causal effect of discrimination within the context of real-life settings. At the same time, the logistical requirements of field experiments—particularly in studies of hiring behavior—are often quite taxing, and, for that reason, it remains an uncommon method of social science research. In the following discussion, I describe the methodology of field experiments, discuss their strengths and limitations, and relate several firsthand experiences that illustrate the complexities and frustrations involved in original data collection of this kind.

THE USE OF FIELD EXPERIMENTS FOR STUDIES OF DISCRIMINATION

Discrimination has long been a fascinating and frustrating subject for social scientists. It is fascinating because it is thought to be a powerful mechanism that underlies many historical and contemporary patterns of inequality; it is frustrating because it is elusive and difficult to measure. Over a century of social science interest in the question of discrimination has resulted in numerous techniques intended to isolate and identify its presence, and to document its effects. Field experiments offer a unique approach to the study of discrimination because they provide carefully controlled comparisons of treatment on the basis of selected characteristics (e.g., race, gender, age) within the context of real-life decision making.

Field experiments designed specifically for the measurement of discrimination are typically referred to as *audit studies*. The audit methodology was first pioneered in the 1970s with a series of audits conducted by the Department of Housing and Urban Development to test for racial discrimination in real estate markets (Yinger 1995; Wienk et al. 1979; Hakken 1979). The approach has since been applied to numerous settings, including mortgage applications, negotiations at a car dealership, and hailing a taxi (Turner and Skidmore 1999; Ayres and Siegelman 1995; Ridley, Bayton, and Outtz 1989; Yinger 1995; Massey and Lundy 2001; Cross et al. 1990; Turner, Fix, and Struyk 1991; Bendick, Jackson, and Reinoso 1994; Neumark 1996).[2] In the case of employment discrimination, two main types of audit studies offer useful approaches: correspondence tests and in-person audits.

CORRESPONDENCE TESTS

The correspondence test approach, so named for its simulation of the communication (correspondence) between job applicants and employers, relies on fictitious matched résumés submitted to employers by mail or fax. In these studies, two or more résumés are prepared, each reflecting equal levels of education and experience. The race (or other group characteristic) of the fictitious applicant is then signaled through one or more cues, with race randomly assigned to résumé type across employers (i.e., minority status is assigned to one résumé for half the employers, to the other résumé for the other half) in order to ensure that any differences between résumés will not be correlated with the measured effects of race.[3] Reactions from employers are then typically measured by written responses (to staged mailing addresses) or callbacks (to voice mail boxes) for each applicant. An exemplary study of this kind was recently conducted by Marianne Bertrand and Sendhil Mullainathan (2004).[4] In it, the researchers prepared two sets of matched résumés reflecting applicant pools of two skill levels. Using racially distinctive names to signal the race of applicants, the researchers mailed out résumés to more than 1,300 employers in Chicago and Boston, targeting ads for sales, administrative support, and clerical and customer service positions. The results of their study indicate that white-sounding names were 50 percent more likely to elicit positive responses from employers than equally qualified applicants with "black" names.[5] Moreover, applicants with white names received a significant payoff to additional qualifications, such as increased work experience or academic honors, while those with black names did not. The racial gap among job applicants was thus higher among the more highly skilled applicant pairs than among those with fewer qualifications.

The advantage of the correspondence test approach is that it requires no actual job applicants (only fictitious paper applicants). This is desirable for both methodological and practical reasons. Methodologically, the use of fictitious paper applicants allows researchers to create carefully matched applicant pairs without needing to accommodate the complexities of real people. The researcher thus has far more control over the precise content of "treatment" and "control" conditions. Reliance on paper applicants is also practically desirable because of the logistical ease with which the application process can be carried out. Rather than coordinating job visits by real people, in which case testers may affect outcomes in ways unanticipated by the audit protocol and interactions with employers are subject to differing circumstances (such as when the employer is out to lunch, busy with a customer, etc.), and so on, the correspondence test approach simply requires that résumés be sent out at specified intervals. In addition, the small cost of postage or fax charges is trivial relative to the cost involved in hiring individuals to pose as job applicants.

But while correspondence tests do have many attractive features, there are also certain limitations of this design that have led many researchers to prefer the in-person audit approach.

Problems Signaling Key Applicant Characteristics

Because correspondence tests rely on paper applications only, all relevant target information must be conveyed without the visual cues of in-person contact. In the case of gender or ethnicity, identifiable names can easily convey the necessary information by using gender-specific or ethnically identifiable names (see Riach and Rich 1991–92; Lahey 2005). In the case of age discrimination, several studies have relied on high school graduation dates to convey the applicants' age difference (Bendick, Brown, and Wall 1999; Lahey 2005). Researchers who wish to study black-white differences, on the other hand, face a somewhat more challenging task. The Bertrand and Mullainathan (2004) study discussed earlier, for example, used racially distinctive names to signal the race of applicants. Names like "Jamal" and "Lakisha" signaled African Americans, while "Brad" and "Emily" were associated with whites. While these names are reliably associated with their intended race groups, some critics have argued that the more distinctive African American names are also associated with lower socioeconomic status, thus confounding the effects of race and class. Indeed, mother's education is a significant (negative) predictor of a child having a distinctively African American name.[6] The use of names to test for black-white differences, then, is complicated by the social context in which racially distinctive names are situated.

Other correspondence test studies have used the "extracurricular activities" or "voluntary memberships" section of the résumé to signal the applicant's race.[7] Membership in the student league of the NAACP, for example, would strongly signal an African American applicant. The matched "white" applicant would then be given a race-neutral activity (e.g., Student Democratic Alliance) that, in the absence of any racial identifiers, is typically (by default) associated with whites.[8] Whatever strategy is used, it is important that résumés are pretested carefully before using them in the field. Names, extracurricular activities, neighborhoods, and high schools may each have connotations that are not readily apparent to the researcher. Directly assessing these connotations/associations is an important first step in developing the materials necessary for a strong test of discrimination.

Limited Sample of Jobs

One other important limitation of the correspondence test method relates to the types of jobs available for testing. The application procedure used in correspondence tests—sending résumés by mail—is typically reserved for studies of administrative, clerical, and other white-collar occupations. The vast majority of entry-level jobs, by contrast, more often require in-person application procedures. In the case of jobs such as busboy, messenger, laborer, or cashier, for example, a mailed-in résumé would seem highly out of place. To study the low-wage labor market thus requires in-person application procedures. While in-person audit studies also face a restricted range of job openings, in-person application procedures allow for a substantially wider pool than can be achieved through paper applications alone.

IN-PERSON AUDITS

The use of in-person audits, as opposed to mail-in résumés, represents a more elaborate simulation of the hiring process.[9] In-person employment audits involve the use of matched pairs of individuals (called testers) who pose as job applicants in real job searches. Applicants are carefully matched on the basis of age, race, physical attractiveness, interpersonal style, and any other employment-relevant characteristics to which employers may respond in making hiring decisions. As with correspondence tests, all applicants' résumés are constructed to reflect equal levels of schooling and work experience. In addition, the in-person presentation of confederate job seekers must be carefully controlled. Testers must participate in extensive training to familiarize themselves with the details of their profile and to learn to present themselves to employers according to a highly structured protocol. Daily debriefings are necessary to ensure that the implementation of each test proceeds according to plan.[10] Though in-person audits are time consuming and require intensive supervision, the approach offers several advantages over correspondence studies. In-person audits provide a clear method for signaling race (through the physical presentation of job applicants); they allow for a wide sample of entry-level job types (that often require in-person applications); and they provide the opportunity to gather both quantitative and qualitative data, with information on whether or not the applicant receives the job as well as how she or he is treated during the interview process. In the following discussion, I consider some of the specific dilemmas and possibilities of the in-person audit approach.

Matching

The selection of testers who will play the role of job applicants is one of the most critical components in the design of an employment audit and arguably one of the most time intensive. Testers must be chosen on the basis of personal attributes that make them individually well qualified to perform what can be a highly demanding job that requires a substantial degree of autonomy. But they must also be chosen on the basis of personal attributes that make them a good match for another well-qualified individual (their test partner). To take into account the wide range of characteristics to which employers may pay attention in evaluating applicants, testers should be matched on concrete factors, such as age, height, weight, and level of education, as well as more subjective criteria such as articulateness, ease of personal interaction, physical attractiveness, and nonverbal communication style. Though the relevance of these characteristics may vary by job type or employer, they are all potentially influential in hiring decisions and thus must be considered in deciding on potential matches. Taking all these considerations into account meant that I wound up interviewing between 50 and 80 candidates for each tester I hired.[11]

The matching process is an art as much as it is a science (a fact that has provoked criticism by some) (Heckman and Siegelman 1993). While there are a number of psychometric scales for measuring personality attributes, verbal ability, and so on, there are certain intangible qualities that are arguably more important in making a first impression. Including a wide range of external evaluators (individuals not directly involved in the research project) can provide important feedback about the holistic impressions formed by each potential tester, and the degree of similarity between proposed pairs.

It is worth noting that audits of contexts other than employment require less attention to physical appearance and personality characteristics. Housing audits and audits of consumer markets, for example, are typically based on a far narrower (and more easy to control) set of tester characteristics. Likewise, requirements are less stringent when treatment conditions can be randomly assigned. In testing the effects of a criminal record, for example, testers can alternate which individual presents himself as the ex-offender over the course of the study, thus evening out any unobserved differences within the tester pair. Again, by way of example: if one tester is slightly more attractive, he will be a slightly more attractive offender in some cases and a slightly more attractive nonoffender in others. Any individual differences will even out if each tester serves in the treatment and control condition in an equal number of cases.[12] But in testing the effects of race, by contrast, the treatment condition cannot be randomly assigned. The quality of the matches thus becomes extremely consequential, as race can be fully confounded with any other individual characteristic. To the extent that differences will persist, researchers should err in the direction of choosing black testers with slightly more desirable attributes. Results will then represent a conservative test of discrimination, essentially providing a lower-bound estimate.

Constructing Résumés

Once tester pairs have been matched, they are assigned résumés reflecting equal levels of education and experience. Substantial thought must go into choosing high schools and neighborhoods that have similar reputations and student/resident compositions; likewise, work histories must be developed to reflect not only equal amounts of prior work experience but also similar types of work experience.[13] In addition to pretesting résumés to assess their comparability, résumé types will ideally be assigned independent of treatment condition (e.g., any given résumé will be used by both black and white testers, to control for any unmeasured differences). In some cases, the résumé will be the only point of contact between the tester and the employer (e.g., in cases where the person in charge of hiring is not present at the time of the test, and the tester leaves a résumé); it is thus important that all relevant information can be effectively conveyed on this single-page document.

Training

No matter how carefully matched two testers may be, they can only act as successful audit partners if they learn to interact with employers in similar ways. A wide range of questions can arise in the course of a conversation or interview with an employer, and testers must be prepared to share similar information and communicate similar types of profiles in their descriptions of past (fictitious) experiences. Before starting actual fieldwork for an audit study, testers typically participate in an extensive training period during which they rehearse the content of their profile, practice the appropriate way to phrase answers to interview questions, and work on aligning their responses with those of their test partner's. Training can consist of videotaped mock interviews, practice interviews with employer confederates, and practice audits with real employers. In addition to the initial training period, daily debriefings with testers can help to identify problems that may arise, or additional content that needs rehearsing.

Problems of Implementation

With any field experiment, the unpredictability of the real world often interferes with carefully planned research designs. Traffic can back up (or public transportation can break down), making it impossible for one tester to make it to an employer at the specified time. A job can get filled in between the time the two testers come to apply. A tester may run into someone she or he knows during an audit; an employer may know the manager of a fictitious job listed on the tester's résumé. The key to maintaining the integrity of the experimental design lies in the ability to respond quickly to unexpected happenings, and to tweak existing protocols constantly in order to take account of new situations. In cases where the protocol appears not to have been fully (or effectively) implemented, the test should be canceled. While it is impossible to catalog the countless number of potential disruptions that may arise, researchers must be vigilant throughout the course of the study. Effective and continual supervision of the testing process is one of the most important elements of a successful audit study.

Supervision

The quality of the data from an audit study depends on the degree to which testers effectively follow the established protocol. And yet evaluating testers' performance is difficult, since the majority of the testers' work is completed with no direct supervision. In order to monitor the quality of the testing process, a number of formal procedures can be put into place. First, immediately following each visit to an employer, testers are typically required to fill out an extensive summary form, including a large number of closed-ended questions (job title, race/gender/age of employer, whether screening tests were required, whether testers were asked about criminal background, etc.). In addition, testers usually write a lengthy open-ended narrative, describing their contact with the employer and the content of interactions they had during the test. These summary forms allow researchers to monitor the relative experiences of tester pairs and to identify any anomalies in the testing experiences that may confound measurement of the treatment variable. Second, the researcher (or project manager) should be available for daily debriefings with each of the testers, following the completion of each day's work. On occasions where something unexpected occurs, the project manager should be contacted immediately. Third, weekly meetings can be useful for allowing testers the opportunity to brainstorm together about how to make the logistics of testing as efficient and controlled as possible. Finally, spot checks of tester performance can provide helpful tools for surveillance and continued training. On a number of occasions, we arranged for our testers to unknowingly apply for jobs with employers we knew (and had contacted in advance), to allow for an external assessment of their performance. In a few cases, we arranged for hidden cameras to record these spot checks. This was an especially effective tool for additional supervision. We used the tapes as an additional training tool at our team meetings, to facilitate discussion about the details of the protocol and to identify any remaining differences in presentation style between tester pairs. It also helped in keeping the testers on their toes—they never knew when we might be watching them!

In general, effective and continuous supervision is critical to the success of a field experiment. The vast majority of problems that arise in the course of fieldwork for an audit study are relatively minor and can be resolved quickly, provided effective monitoring. It is only when problems continue unchecked that they can pose a significant threat to the validity of the research.

Managing the Emotional Side of Testing

I knew that managing an audit study would require intensive supervision of every aspect of the fieldwork, as described previously. But one thing I could not have anticipated was the psychological toll this process can take on the testers involved. The ethics review of studies of this kind (managed through the university Institutional Review Board) focuses on the risks and benefits posed to research subjects, in this case the employers. Certainly their well-being is important and deserves careful review. But the IRB does not encourage consideration of the testers' well-being, as they are merely paid employees for the project. Nevertheless, considering this aspect of an audit study represents an important concern for researchers.

In the first audit study I conducted, in Milwaukee, I became aware of the strain some testers were experiencing early on. One tester reported feeling discouraged and frustrated that he had had very few responses from employers. For a successful, bright college student, the change in status to a young black criminal was extreme, and the difference in treatment he received seemed to take a toll. The emotional reactions of testers to the experience of discrimination have multiple important consequences: for the well-being of the testers themselves; for the validity of the tests (which may be affected by the testers' emotional state of mind); and for the perseverance of testers on the project (turnover among testers can cause major disruption, as finding high-quality matches takes time).

Fortunately, after gaining more experience with the project, this tester (and others) seemed to feel more comfortable in their interactions and better able to perform in their assigned roles. But these initial reactions made clear the degree to which such interactions can deal a serious blow to one's self-confidence and motivation. In all of my planning for this project, I had not appreciated how taxing these daily exposures would be for the testers.

In the Milwaukee audit study, I attempted to mitigate the reactions of testers by conducting daily debriefings with testers individually. I wanted to avoid invidious comparisons among testers that might lead to further feelings of discouragement. I met with each tester one on one following each day of testing to discuss their experiences and, if necessary, to provide an outlet for them to process or vent their feelings.

As it turns out, however, I am not sure that keeping the testers separated was such a good idea. In the second study I conducted—in New York—we had a much larger group of testers who came together each morning and each evening in our project office. They had their own dedicated space, and they grew close to one another over the course of months of daily fieldwork. The camaraderie they developed as a group actually seemed to do more to keep their spirits high and to insulate them from the damaging effects of exposure to discrimination than anything I could have provided. I would not have expected this to be the case. But in the future, I think I would rely more on the group support of peers experiencing similar feelings than on one-on-one processing between tester and project manager.

Tester Compensation

The issue of how to compensate testers for their time and effort can also wind up being more complicated than it may seem initially. Some have suggested paying testers per job application completed. This is undesirable, as one doesn't want the testers to feel any incentive to rush from one employer to the next. Testers should spend as much time at each employer as necessary to maximize their chances of getting the job—and they should be compensated for doing so. Others have suggested paying testers a bonus for each callback they receive, as a means of providing additional incentives for testers to work hard at following the protocol and making a good impression. This strategy is also undesirable if one believes there is discrimination in the labor market. If whites are systematically advantaged in their search for work, white testers will receive greater compensation than black testers for no greater effort. Building a discriminatory system of payment into one's research design only contributes to the very inequalities audit researchers seek to measure.

In the audit studies I have been involved in, testers were always paid at an hourly rate. Though this system of compensation provides no special incentives for performance, it is the only system that both is fair and provides appropriate compensation for thorough completion of the protocol.

As a final note on matters of compensation, university researchers should be warned about the bureaucracies one must deal with in hiring and paying testers for their work. Nonuniversity employees must go through a special application process before they are approved to work on university or grant-funded research. Often this approval process takes weeks to complete, and testers can often work more than a month before seeing their first paycheck. For young men and women working for an hourly wage, this can pose difficulties. In my first study, it took more than six weeks before the testers were approved for payment. For two of my testers this was a huge problem, as they had rent to pay and other bills piling up. I ended up writing them personal checks, with a (written) agreement that they would pay me back once they received their first paycheck. This was a risk on my part, but I did not want them to suffer just because the university bureaucracy moved so slowly. Meanwhile, I had to pester the various payroll administrators on a weekly basis to make sure we experienced no additional delays. The transition from researcher to employer involves many unexpected obligations.

Quantitative and Qualitative Outcomes

One of the attractive features of the in-person audit design is its ability to measure a wide range of outcome variables, reflecting a range of applicant experiences. The primary outcome variable is typically a quantitative indicator of positive response by the employer: a callback or job offer. In addition, however, the audit process can detect a number of more subtle indicators of differential treatment. In some cases, for example, testers are channeled into jobs other than the ones originally advertised (e.g., the job ad was for a retail sales clerk, but the employer offers the tester a job stocking shelves). In other cases, employers may express revealing comments in the course of a conversation or interview. Tracking the level of attention, encouragement, or hostility testers elicit can provide important information about the experiential aspects of the job-seeking process. Indeed, by observing the kinds of treatment testers receive in their ongoing job searches, one can identify the experiences that may lead certain workers to become discouraged from seeking work altogether.

Testing for Litigation versus Research

One of the common questions about the audit methodology concerns how it can be used to reduce the problems of discrimination. The audit method was initially designed for the enforcement of antidiscrimination law. Testers were used to detect racially discriminatory practices among real estate agents, landlords, and lenders, providing the evidence necessary to pursue litigation.[14] Audit studies for research purposes, by contrast, are oriented not toward a specific intervention but rather to obtain accurate measures of the prevalence of discrimination across a broad sector or metropolitan area. The difference between these two types of studies is further reflected in the design of the study. Testing for litigation requires multiple audits of the same employer (real estate agent, etc.) to detect consistent patterns of discrimination by that particular individual and/or company. Testing for research, by contrast, typically includes no more than a single audit per employer, with discrimination detected through systematic patterns across employers, rather than repeated acts of discrimination by a single employer. The distinction here is important in what we can tell from audit studies intended for research purposes. In these studies, *it is not possible to draw conclusions about the discriminatory tendencies of any given employer.* Indeed, even in the complete absence of discrimination, an employer confronted with two equivalent candidates will choose the white applicant in 50 percent of cases. Using a single test of each employer, therefore, does not allow for individual-level assessments of discrimination; only by looking at systematic patterns across a large number of employers can we determine whether hiring appears to be influenced by race or other stigmatizing characteristics.[15] The point of research-based audit studies, therefore, is to assess the prevalence of discrimination across the labor market rather than to intervene in particular sites of discrimination. At the same time, and notwithstanding their different objectives, research audit studies provide important information about discriminatory practices that can support calls for strengthening antidiscrimination policy or other policy initiatives designed to protect vulnerable workers.

Ethics of Audit Research

Discussions of audit studies inevitably lead to ethical questions. Audit studies require that employers are unwittingly recruited for participation and then led to believe that the testers are viable job candidates. Contrary to the ethical standards for research established by the federal government, this design does not allow for the use of informed consent by research subjects for participation, and it often avoids debriefing subjects after the study's completion. How then are audit studies permitted to take place? As it turns out, there are specific criteria that regulate the use of research of this kind, and a well-designed audit study can arguably meet each of them. Later I provide a discussion of the relevant concerns and potential solutions to the ethical problems posed by research of this kind.

The use of deception in social science has long been met with suspicion. While individual researchers may feel they can clearly distinguish between appropriate and improper research practices, examples from the past indicate that researchers' individual judgments may not always conform to the standards of the discipline (e.g., Milgram 1974). Because of past transgressions, legislation concerning the use of human subjects now governs all social science research and includes, as one of its fundamental criteria, the use of informed consent from all research participants.[16] In the case of audit studies, however, the nature of the research requires that subjects remain unaware of their participation, and the condition of informed consent therefore cannot be met.

While current federal policy governing the protection of human subjects strongly supports the use of informed consent, it is recognized that certain types of research that fail to obtain formal consent can be deemed permissible. According to the regulations, a Human Subjects Institutional Review Board (IRB) "may . . . waive . . . informed consent provided (1) the research involves no more than minimal risk to human subjects; (2) the waiver or alteration will not adversely affect the rights and welfare of the subjects; (3) the research could not practicably be carried out without the waiver or alteration; and (4) whenever appropriate, the subjects will be provided with additional information after participation."[17] Each of these conditions can arguably be satisfied in the context of audit studies of discrimination. While there are potential risks to subjects, reasonable efforts can be made to reduce the costs to subjects and thereby impose only minimal risk.

Most audit research poses two primary potential risks to subjects: (1) loss of time and (2) legal liability. In the first case, subjects are asked to evaluate a pair of applications submitted by phony applicants. Time spent reviewing applications and/or interviewing applicants will therefore impose a cost on the subject. Most employment audit studies limit their samples to employers for entry-level positions—those requiring the least intensive review—in part to minimize the time employers spend evaluating phony applicants. Entry-level positions are typically filled on the basis of cursory overviews of applications and limited personal contact (Fix and Struyk 1993). Contact with subjects is thus minimal, consisting of requesting an application and/or answering a few brief questions. Audits of higher skill jobs, by contrast, impose a greater burden on employers, as the hiring process for such positions typically requires a greater investment of time and effort.[18]

A second potential risk posed by audit research is the potential for employers and/or firms to be held liable for discrimination if the evidence documented in the audit were to be released publicly. In fact, as mentioned earlier, the evidence provided by audit studies intended for research cannot be used to support claims of discrimination against any individual employer. Nevertheless, great care must be taken to protect employer identities so that even association with a study on discrimination cannot be made. To this end, any identifying information should be kept in a secure location, and any publicly released publications or presentations should omit all identifying characteristics of individuals and firms.

The issue of debriefing subjects following the completion of the audit study is also complicated. Though IRB protocol typically supports the debriefing of subjects whenever possible, in certain cases acknowledging the occurrence or nature of a research study is deemed undesirable. It could be argued, for example, that subjects could be placed at a greater risk should their behavior, as a result of the audit study, fall under greater scrutiny by superiors. In the case of human resource personnel or managers who are thought to be discriminatory, the consequences may be more serious than if no attention were brought to the audit whatsoever. While the chances that negative consequences would result from this research are in any case very small, some IRB committees take the view that eliminating the debriefing stage is the most prudent strategy. The purpose of audit research is *not* to harm individual employers. Rather, the research seeks to improve our understanding of the barriers to employment facing stigmatized groups in their search for employment.

As a final matter, it should be emphasized that the ethics of audit research is not only of concern in the university context. The legal standing of testers has also been closely scrutinized by the courts. In fact, the issue of testing has reached the highest judicial body, with the U.S. Supreme Court upholding the standing of testers in a 1982 decision.[19] A more recent ruling by the Seventh Circuit Court again upheld the standing of testers in cases of employment discrimination while also broadening their endorsement of this methodology. In each of these rulings, the courts have been primarily concerned with the use of testing for pursuing litigation against employers (rather than for pure research, as is the case here). Implicit in these holdings, however, is the belief that the misrepresentation involved in testing is worth the unique benefit this practice can provide in uncovering discrimination and enforcing civil rights laws. According to former EEOC chairman Gilbert Castellas, "Using employment testers in a carefully controlled manner is an important tool for measuring the presence or absence of discrimination. If we can shed light on barriers to fair hiring in entry-level jobs, which are the gateway to self-sufficiency and economic independence, we will have made an important step in assuring equal opportunity for everyone."[20] Indeed, despite certain burdens imposed by audit studies, the ultimate benefit from research of this kind extends far beyond the contribution of a single study. Rigorous and realistic measurement of discrimination is fundamental to understanding and addressing persistent barriers to employment facing members of stigmatized groups.

Critiques of the Audit Method

While most researchers view the audit methodology as one of the most effective means of measuring discrimination, the approach is not without critics. Before assuming that a field experimental design automatically confers high levels of both internal and external validity, the possible vulnerabilities of the audit methodology thus deserve careful consideration. Economist James Heckman is among the most vocal critics of the audit methodology, particularly when used to study the effects of race. Heckman's primary criticism focuses on the problems of effective matching.[21] The validity of an audit study depends on its success in presenting two otherwise equally qualified job applicants who differ only by race. Given the vast number of characteristics that can influence an employer's evaluation, however, it is difficult to ensure that all such dimensions have been effectively controlled. Note that in testing for the effect of a nonembodied characteristic—a characteristic that can be randomly assigned to test partners—these concerns are less relevant. Because testers are able to alternate their roles (e.g., performing as someone with and without a criminal record), any remaining differences within the tester pairs effectively cancel out over the duration of the study.

By contrast race is not something that can be experimentally assigned. We must believe, then, that audit researchers have been successful in identifying and matching on all relevant characteristics—something that, according to Heckman, leaves substantial room for bias. Heckman's primary critique focuses on the problem of unobservables—those characteristics "unobservable to the audit study [researchers], but . . . at least somewhat visible to the prospective employer and acted on in hiring . . . decisions." According to Heckman, blacks and whites (at the population level) may differ in the average and/or distribution of important characteristics. As an example, consider a hypothetical case in which whites on average have a faster response time in interview interactions than blacks. That is to say, the delay in seconds between a question posed by an interviewer and the initiation of response is shorter on average for whites than for blacks. (To be sure, response times are just one potential example, and I emphasize that it is a case that to my knowledge has no empirical basis. Heckman himself does not suggest any concrete examples of potentially relevant unobservables that could affect hiring outcomes, but it is instructive to consider a concrete hypothetical case for the purpose of clarity.) Because any difference in response time would be extremely subtle, it may not be immediately recognizable to researchers and may even register for employers only at a subliminal level. Nevertheless, if this trait produces an incremental advantage for the individual with a faster response time—because he is perceived as sharper or more engaged—we may mistake the employer's response for discrimination when in fact nonracial evaluations are driving the differential response.

A related problem emerges if blacks and whites differ in key characteristics, not on the average, but in the level of dispersion. To continue with the same example, imagine a case in which blacks and whites each have a mean response time of .5 seconds, but blacks demonstrate greater heterogeneity along this dimension than whites. Differential results may then be observed depending on the overall qualifications of the testers relative to the requirements of the job. If testers are highly qualified relative to the positions for which they apply (which tends to be the case in audit studies), differential dispersion on any key variable will favor the group with lower dispersion (because a smaller proportion of applicants in this group will be at the low end of the tail relative to a high-dispersion group).

Heckman's critique raises some important considerations and surely encourages a more rigorous scrutiny of the audit methodology. In each case, it is worth considering when and how these concerns can be effectively addressed. Heckman's concern is that if, on average, blacks and whites differ in the mean or variance on any unobserved productivity-related variable, estimates from matched-pair studies will be biased by design. If auditors were randomly drawn from the population and matched on a rote basis according to readily measurable characteristics, this critique would surely be valid. It is a mistake, however, to assume that the researcher is at a necessary disadvantage relative to the employer in identifying productivity-related characteristics. In fact, the researcher is him- or herself an employer in the planning and implementation of an audit study. The job of a tester is not an easy one, and finding a suitable team to complete this type of project requires extensive screening and careful selection. The job requires solid writing skills (for the written narratives that follow each audit), good communication skills (to communicate the necessary information in an interview and make a good impression on the employer); high levels of motivation (to keep up day after day), reliability (to accurately conduct and report each test), navigation skills (to find locations throughout the city), and an endless number of other qualifications. Thus, apart from the more explicit traits of height, weight, race, and age, researchers must search for testers who can perform well in an intensely demanding position.[22] As an employer him- or herself, the researcher must identify subtle cues about applicants that indicate their ability to perform. Whether or not these cues are explicit, conscious, or measurable, they are present in a researcher's evaluation of tester candidates as they are for employers' evaluations of entry-level job applicants. Like employers, researchers are affected by both objective and subjective/subconscious indicators of applicant quality in their selection and matching of testers, in ways that should ultimately improve the nuanced calibration of test partners.

A related concern of Heckman has to do with the possibility that matching (even when done successfully) may itself produce distortions in the hiring process. Because audit partners are matched on all characteristics that are most directly relevant to the hiring process (education, work experience, physical appearance, interpersonal skills, etc.), employers may be forced to privilege relatively minor characteristics simply because they need to devise a means of breaking the tie. "By taking out the common components that are most easily measured, differences in hiring rates as monitored by audits arise from the idiosyncratic factors, and not the main factors, that drive actual labor markets" (Heckman 1998, 111). If employers care only marginally about race but are confronted with two applicants equal on all other dimensions, race may take on greater significance in that particular hiring decision than is true under more normal circumstances, when evaluating real applicants who differ according multiple dimensions.

Again, this critique is an important one, though in this case one that can be addressed more easily. If the only outcome of interest in an audit study is whether or not an applicant gets the job, Heckman's concern is certainly relevant. If forced to choose a single hire, employers will use whatever basis for differentiation exists, whether that particular attribute is valued highly or not. Audit studies that measure callbacks as an outcome variable, by contrast, avoid situations in which employers can choose only one applicant. In fact, employers typically interview an average of eight applicants for each entry-level job they fill.[23] If race is only a minor concern for employers, we would expect both members of an audit pair to make it through the first cut. To the extent that race figures prominently even in these early rounds of review, we can infer that race is invoked as more than a mere tiebreaker. In these cases, the evidence of race-based decision making is quite strong.[24]

A third important critique of the audit methodology raises the problem of experimenter effects, or the possibility that the expectations or behaviors of testers can influence the audit results in nonrandom ways. For example, if a tester expects to be treated poorly by employers, he may appear more withdrawn, nervous, or defensive in interactions. The nature of the interaction may then create a self-fulfilling prophecy in which the tester experiences poor outcomes, but for reasons unrelated to the experimental condition (e.g., his race). Indeed, the possibility of experimenter effects represents one of the most serious threats to the validity of the audit experiment. Although there is no way to rule out this possibility conclusively, there are several precautions that can be taken to minimize the problem. First, effective training and supervision are critical to the successful implementation of an audit study. Testers must be excessively familiar with their assumed profiles and the audit protocol, such that appropriate responses to employer queries become almost automatic. Extensive role plays, videotaped interviews, and practice audits help testers to become comfortable with their role and to gain important feedback on their performance. Likewise, during the course of the fieldwork, daily debriefings and regular troubleshooting sessions are critical to identify any potential problems or to refine the protocol in ways that best suit the specifics of the study. Finally, after the fieldwork is completed, it is possible to conduct an indirect check on the problem of experimenter effects. Typically a significant proportion of tests are conducted with little or no in-person contact, either because the employer is not present or does not have time to meet with the applicant. By comparing audit outcomes for testers who did and did not interact with employers, we can assess the degree to which in-person interaction leads to a different distribution of results. If testers are acting in ways that fulfill their expectations of discrimination, we would expect outcomes for those tests conducted with interaction to show greater evidence of differential treatment than those without. If the results show no difference, or show weaker evidence of differential treatment, we can be more confident that experimenter effects are not driving the results.[25] As a final note, it is worth reiterating that a key advantage of correspondence tests (relative to in-person audits) is the ability to present matched pairs of résumés to employers without the use of real testers. That these studies typically also demonstrate consistent evidence of discrimination provides one further reassurance that the outcomes from in-person audit studies are not merely the product of mismatched testers or participants' enacted expectations (Bertrand and Mullainathan 2004).

CONCLUSION

Despite its various complexities, the audit method remains the most effective means of measuring discrimination in real-world settings. By participating in actual job searches, and by simulating the process of actual job applicants, we can get as close as possible to the interactions that produce discrimination in contemporary labor markets. While the audit design cannot address all relevant aspects of labor market disadvantage, it does identify discrimination at the point of hire as one powerful mechanism regulating the employment opportunities available to job seekers in low-wage labor markets.

NOTES

Parts of this chapter appeared in chapter 3 of Pager 2007. The author gratefully acknowledges support from NSF (SES-0547810), NIH (K01 HD053694), and a William T. Grant Scholars Award.

1. Random assignment helps to remove the influence of any respondent characteristics that may affect outcomes by breaking the link between respondent characteristics and selection into treatment conditions.

2. For a review of experimental field experiments in international contexts, see Riach and Rich 2002.

3. The present discussion focuses on the case of racial discrimination, but these methods can be readily applied to studies of discrimination on the basis of gender, age, neighborhood, and numerous other social categories.

4. In fact, very few correspondence studies have been conducted in the United

States. This approach has been more widely used in European and Australian contexts. See Riach and Rich 2002 for a review.

5. White male names triggered a callback rate of 9.19 percent, compared to 6.16 percent among black male names.

6. Fryer and Levitt (2004) report that "Blacker names are associated with lower income zip codes, lower levels of parental education, not having private insurance, and having a mother who herself has a Blacker name" (786).

7. See Bendick, Jackson, and Reinoso 1994. It would be undesirable, however, to use only extracurricular activities to signal race. This subtle cue would likely be missed by many employers in the course of their cursory review.

8. To the extent that applicants presenting "race-neutral" extracurricular activities are not assumed to be white in 100 percent of cases, more conservative results will be obtained. For an example of this approach, see Dovidio and Gaertner 2000.

9. For an in-between approach using telephone contact (with voice and style of speech signaling race, class, and gender), see Massey and Lundy 2001.

10. See Pager 2003, app. A.

11. Advertising for testers is another complicated matter. One must make hiring selections based on very specific criteria—including profiles for age, gender, and race—but it is not typically appropriate to list these criteria in a job ad. My flyers and announcements indicated that I was searching for African American and white men between the ages of 20 and 23 to serve as research assistants for a study of employment discrimination. Needless to say, I received some angry complaints for my use of age, race, and gender preferences in the ad.

12. Note that even in cases where the experimental condition can be randomly assigned, it is nevertheless desirable to match testers as closely as possible, so as to minimize extraneous noise in the comparisons of tester outcomes.

13. Typically résumés are constructed to reflect a range of entry-level work experience, including, for example, jobs in sales, restaurants, and manual labor.

14. In these discrimination cases, testers serve as the plaintiffs. Despite the fact that the testers themselves were not in fact seeking housing (or employment) at the time their application was submitted, their treatment nevertheless represents an actionable claim. This issue has received close scrutiny by the courts, including rulings by the highest federal courts. The U.S. Supreme Court upheld the standing of testers in their 1982 decision (*Havens Realty Corp. v. Coleman*, 455 U.S. 363, 373 [1982]). A more recent ruling by the Seventh Circuit Court again upheld the standing of testers in cases of employment discrimination, broadening their endorsement of this methodology.

15. This feature has certain desirable properties from the perspective of gaining approval from an Institutional Review Board (i.e., university ethics committees). Concerns about confidentiality and risks to employers are reduced when no single participant can be identified as a discriminator.

16. DHHS CFR45.46.116.

17. 56 Federal Register 117, p. 28017, June 18, 1991.

18. In the present research, I further limit imposition on employers by restricting audits to the first stage of the employment process. In most cases, then, I

look only at whether or not an employer invites the tester for an interview, rather than including the interview and job offer stages as well. Limiting the research design to the initial process can thus further reduce the burden to subjects.

19. *Havens Realty Corp. v. Coleman*, 455 U.S. 363, 373 (1982).

20. This statement was drawn from a press release issued on December 5, 1997, and can be found at http://www.eeoc.gov/press/12-5-97.html. Accessed April 27, 2009.

21. Heckman 1998, 107–11. Elsewhere, Heckman and Siegelman (1993) identify five potential threats to the validity of results from audit studies: (1) problems in effective matching; (2) the use of "overqualified" testers; (3) limited sampling frame for the selection of firms and jobs to be audited; (4) experimenter effects; and (5) the ethics of audit research. Each of these issues is addressed in detail in Pager 2007, app. 4A. See also the series of essays published in Fix and Struyk 1993. In addition to the criticisms expressed by Heckman, audit studies are often costly and difficult to implement and can only be used for selective decision-points (e.g., hiring decisions but not promotions).

22. Given these extensive demands, it is common for researchers to screen between 50 and 100 applicants (already selected on age, race, and gender) before finding a single matched pair.

23. See Pager 2007.

24. Indeed, we see evidence of more discrimination in audit studies testing actual job offers. This could be due to the kinds of tiebreaker effects discussed by Heckman, though it may also result from the fact that job offers are more consequential, and thus employers may exert their preferences more forcefully at this final stage.

25. See Pager 2003, app. A, for an example of such a test.

REFERENCES

Ayres, Ian, and Peter Siegelman. 1995. Race and Gender Discrimination in Bargaining for a New Car. *American Economic Review* 85:304–21.

Bendick, Marc, Jr., Lauren Brown, and Kennington Wall. 1999. No Foot in the Door: An Experimental Study of Employment Discrimination. *Journal of Aging and Social Policy* 10:5–23.

Bendick, Marc, Jr., Charles Jackson, and Victor Reinoso. 1994. Measuring Employment Discrimination through Controlled Experiments. *Review of Black Political Economy* 23:25–48.

Bertrand, Marianne, and Sendhil Mullainathan. 2004. Are Emily and Greg More Employable than Lakisha and Jamal? A Field Experiment on Labor Market Discrimination. *American Economic Review* 94:991–1013.

Cross, Harry, Genevieve Kenney, Jane Mell, and Wendy Zimmerman. 1990. *Employer Hiring Practices: Differential Treatment of Hispanic and Anglo Job Seekers*. Washington, DC: Urban Institute Press.

Dovidio, John F., and Samuel L. Gaertner. 2000. Aversive Racism and Selection Decisions. *Psychological Science* 11:315–19.

Fix, Michael, and Raymond J. Struyk, eds. 1993. *Clear and Convincing Evidence: Measurement of Discrimination in America.* Washington, DC: Urban Institute Press.

Fryer, Ronald G., Jr., and Steven D. Levitt. 2004. The Causes and Consequences of Distinctively Black Names. *Quarterly Journal of Economics* 119:767–805.

Hakken, Jon. 1979. *Discrimination against Chicanos in the Dallas Rental Housing Market: An Experimental Extension of the Housing Market Practices Survey.* Washington, DC: U.S. Department of Housing and Urban Development.

Heckman, James J. 1998. Detecting Discrimination. *Journal of Economic Perspectives* 12:101–16.

Heckman, James, and Peter Siegelman. 1993. The Urban Institute Audit Studies: Their Methods and Findings. In *Clear and Convincing Evidence: Measurement of Discrimination in America*, ed. Michael Fix and Raymond J. Struyk, 187–258. Washington, DC: Urban Institute Press.

Lahey, Joanna. 2005. Age, Women, and Hiring: An Experimental Study. NBER Working Paper 11435.

Massey, Douglas, and Garvey Lundy. 2001. Use of Black English and Racial Discrimination in Urban Housing Markets: New Methods and Findings. *Urban Affairs Review* 36:452–69.

Milgram, Stanley. 1974. *Obedience to Authority: An Experimental View.* New York: Harper and Row.

Neumark, David. 1996. Sex Discrimination in Restaurant Hiring: An Audit Study. *Quarterly Journal of Economics* 111:915–41.

Pager, Devah. 2003. The Mark of a Criminal Record. *American Journal of Sociology* 108:937–75.

Pager, Devah. 2007. *Marked: Race, Crime, and Finding Work in an Era of Mass Incarceration.* Chicago: University of Chicago Press.

Riach, Peter B., and Judith Rich. 1991–92. Measuring Discrimination by Direct Experimentation Methods: Seeking Gunsmoke. *Journal of Post-Keynesian Economics* 14:143–50.

Riach, P. A., and J. Rich. 2002. Field Experiments of Discrimination in the Market Place. *Economic Journal* 112:480–518.

Ridley, Stanley, James A. Bayton, and Janice Hamilton Outtz. 1989. *Taxi Service in the District of Columbia: Is It Influenced by Patrons' Race and Destination?* Washington, DC: Washington Lawyers' Committee for Civil Rights under the Law.

Turner, Margery, Michael Fix, and Raymond Struyk. 1991. *Opportunities Denied, Opportunities Diminished: Racial Discrimination in Hiring.* Washington, DC: Urban Institute Press.

Turner, Margery, and Felicity Skidmore, eds. 1999. *Mortgage Lending Discrimination: A Review of Existing Evidence.* Washington, DC: Urban Institute Press.

Wienk, Ronald E., Clifford E. Reid, John C. Simonson, and Frederick J. Eggers. 1979. *Measuring Discrimination in American Housing Markets: The Housing Market Practices Survey.* Washington, DC: U.S. Department of Housing and Urban Development.

Yinger, John. 1995. *Closed Doors, Opportunities Lost.* New York: Russell Sage Foundation.

PART OF THE COMMUNITY

LAURA CLAWSON

July 2004. Having spent the summers of 2001 and 2002 doing fieldwork among Sacred Harp singers on Sand Mountain (in northeast Alabama), in 2004 I used my local contacts to help Dana, an anthropology graduate student, find housing for the summer. During a short trip, I was in Dana's living room with Allison, a singer in her twenties whose father is a respected singing-school teacher and whose family has been singing Sacred Harp for generations. Looking at a stack of videos, CDs, and instructional booklets produced for small-scale sale that various singers had given Dana to help her with her research, I wondered aloud why nobody ever gave me *their sale products given that I, too, was studying Sacred Harp.*

"They just think of you as part of the community," Allison replied.

One of the great temptations of ethnography is to consider oneself a complete insider, someone around whom no editing takes place. The record is littered with people who have in one way or another made too grand a claim in this regard and been shot down. But the temptation persists, and ethnographers of groups that can be glamorized or sentimentalized are often especially eager to see themselves through that lens, to be not just a staid academic but someone grittier and more "real."

Studying a community in which your subjects are in close relationships with each other increases the temptation, offering not only acceptance by individuals but a sense of membership. But how do you and your subjects decide when you are an insider and when you are a researcher? How do you manage your commitments as a community member while maintaining enough independence to produce sound analysis? This issue must be navigated during both the fieldwork and writing processes, with each stage involving distinct challenges. At the same time, there are significant benefits to deep engagement in a community of research subjects. Indeed, the fieldworker who does not become sufficiently engaged to feel the temptations of belonging is likely to produce work lacking in understanding or empathy. Every ethnographer grapples with these questions, and many methodological pieces have dealt with variations on them. In this chapter, I consider my own experiences through the lens of such earlier work. Though researching a community, and one you are a part of, introduces both complication and richness, I would argue that doing so does not pose unique challenges but rather extends those faced by all ethnographers.

The Temptation. In a review essay on Loic Wacquant's *Body and Soul*, Paul Stoller draws on his own experience as an ethnographer.

> Several years ago, I phoned Issifi Mayaki, one of my Nigerien friends who lived in New York City. Issifi, whom I had known for more than 10 years, was one of the principal characters in *Money Has No Smell*, my ethnography of West African immigrants in New York City . . . When I met new immigrants from Niger who had come to visit their compatriot at his market stall in Harlem, Issifi would introduce me as his "brother."
>
> "Paul is one of us," he liked to say. "He speaks our language and understands our ways."
>
> After several rings, Issifi's brother picked up the phone.
>
> "This is Paul," I said introducing myself.
>
> "Who is it?" I heard Issifi asking in the background.
>
> "Paul."
>
> "Oh that's the white man," Issifi said to his brother, not knowing he had been overheard. "I'll take it." Moments later he picked up the receiver. "Paul! How are you, my brother?" (Stoller 2005, 197)

This anecdote immediately—and even viscerally—captures the potential embarrassments and disappointments that can be incurred by believing that your relationships with your subjects are uncomplicated. But aside from the momentary dismay such an experience engenders, it also suggests a serious intellectual danger: If you believe too strongly in your own insider status, believe that your subjects really do see you as a "brother" like anyone else they call by that title, your analysis and conclusions are likely to be predicated on that erroneous belief. And however close to the subject you are, however genuine the feeling between you, there will be moments when that belief is wrong—either about their feelings toward you or yours toward them.

THE RESEARCH PROJECT

Sacred Harp

For my dissertation I conducted participant observation in four communities of Sacred Harp singers. Sacred Harp singing is an a cappella singing tradition practiced continuously in the Southern United States since the publication of the 1844 tunebook from which it takes its name. At the time *The Sacred Harp* was originally published (it has been revised several times since), it was one of a number of nineteenth-century tunebooks set in shape notes, a late eighteenth- or early nineteenth-century system to teach sight-reading. Today, though a few other shape-note books survive, *The Sacred Harp* is the one in most widespread and active use.

The invention of shape notes occurred during one of several waves of music education initiatives in the early United States, though shape notes later fell out of style during a subsequent push for better music education. Shape notes are in almost every respect identical to standard Western musical notation but, instead of the standard uniform circle, the noteheads take four different shapes, with each shape corresponding to a syllable in a solfège system much like the more famous "do re mi." Sacred Harp singing uses four shapes, a triangle called "fa," circle called "sol," rectangle called "la," and diamond called "mi." With only four shapes, some notes repeat in each scale—the major scale runs "fa sol la fa sol la mi fa" and the minor scale is "la mi fa sol la fa sol la."

At a Sacred Harp singing, the names of the notes are sung before the words, both because the notes continue to be a useful tool for singing new or difficult songs and because doing so is a tradition that has endured for many generations. Another key musical difference between Sacred Harp and most Western music is that, in Sacred Harp, both tenor and treble are sung by men and women an octave apart; the melody is carried by the tenor, and the harmony parts are unusually complex.

Shape notes were invented in the Northeast and were common there for some time, with a number of Northern shape-note books published before the epicenter of their use shifted southward. *The Sacred Harp* was published in Georgia and used most heavily there and in Alabama, though its use did spread to other states through the South, including Florida and Texas. The book has been revised several times—most recently in 1991—with songs by living composers being added each time. The older songs in the book, and many of the more recent ones, employ the eighteenth- and early nineteenth-century religious poetry of Isaac Watts, Charles Wesley, and Philip Doddridge, focusing less on the individual than on the grandeur of God, often as expressed in His creation of nature.

Sacred Harp singing is not intended for performance, but to be sung by everyone in attendance, ideally in large groups (as many as several hundred people). Participants sit in a hollow square, with tenors facing altos and trebles (sopranos) facing basses, and a space in the middle where the song leader stands. These leaders change every song, with anyone who attends a singing allowed to choose a song and lead it by standing in the middle facing the tenors and marking time as the class of singers follows the leader's choice of tempo and verses. Though a few people may come to listen, typically sitting at the periphery of the square, there is no space formally set aside for an audience.

Although many communities have weekly or monthly local singings lasting two or three hours in the afternoon or evening, the all-day singing or multiday convention is the central event of Sacred Harp, and most established singing communities host at least one, beginning between 9:00 and 10:00 in the morning and running until 2:00 or 3:00 in the afternoon, with hourly breaks and a potluck lunch, or "dinner on the grounds," provided by local singers at noon. The day begins and ends with prayer, which is understood as a major part of the day's purpose by some people and as a formality by others.

Southern Singing

Since its original publication, *The Sacred Harp*'s use has been concentrated in the South. Small churches in rural areas there often held formal services only once or twice a month, and many churches would host a singing on a weekend without services. Sacred Harp was therefore firmly connected to the church without being part of services in most churches. Since these small country churches were frequently associated with particular extended families, Sacred Harp singing, too, was often a family event of sorts.

Even as the development of improved transportation during the twentieth century made it easier for singers to travel to each other's events rather than staying within a small area, other developments weakened attendance. Large families became less common, young adults were more likely to move away, and some churches replaced congregational singing with instrumental music or choirs. Still, substantial numbers of singings continued to be held, often connected with families in which the tradition remains strong.

In Alabama and Georgia, Sacred Harp singing is very much a religious tradition. The prayer offered at the beginning and ending of a singing and before lunch is considered indispensable and is often given by a minister in attendance.[1] Some leaders draw attention to the religious message of the lyrics of their chosen song. Most of all, though, church standards of decorum apply at singings—Southern singers typically wear good clothes as they would to church, do not clap between songs, and generally stay quiet and respectful of their environs between songs.

Northern Singing

During the folk revivals and early music movement of the 1960s, Sacred Harp was one of the many forms of roots music recorded and released by collectors like Alan Lomax. As a participatory form that is not well suited to being performed for audiences, it never achieved the popularity of—and was never popularized like—ballad singing or fiddle tunes. But for people who were interested in making their own music, Sacred Harp was one of many available forms, and some found their way to it. Many of these people remain only partial participants, singing once or twice a year at folk festivals or conventions but not becoming engaged in Sacred Harp as an independent tradition, understanding it rather as a folk music. Others became dedicated to Sacred Harp itself, building singing communities where they lived and traveling South and to other new singings.

Like most participants in folk revivals, these new Sacred Harp singers tend to be religiously diverse, highly educated (though in many cases underemployed), politically liberal, and most often live in urban areas and college towns. For the most part they do not know each other before they start singing, and do not share religious beliefs. Neither do they have churches with strong connections to Sacred Harp to provide space to sing in, and so singings are held in a variety of rented spaces including churches, folk schools, community centers, and college event rooms, among others.

The meaning of community is therefore very different in different regions, connected to though not identical with church and family in some places and constructed from scratch in others. Being a member of the Sacred Harp community is, then, complicated by the question of *which* Sacred Harp community—the overall body of people who sing in the tradition, a specific local singing community, or some set of people recognized as experts or insiders.

METHODS

Since the bulk of this chapter will be concerned with my methods, I will here only give a brief summary. In addition to semistructured interviews with 24 singers, I conducted extensive ethnographic observation, spending two summers in the Sand Mountain, Alabama, region (in the northeast corner of the state) and making many shorter trips to west Georgia and east Alabama, Chicago, and the Twin Cities of Minneapolis-St. Paul. From 1999 to 2003, I attended 111 all-day singings or multiday conventions. In addition, I attended other events in each of my locations, including local afternoon or evening singings, informal gatherings and convention-sponsored socials following singings, singing schools, and two sessions of a five-day summer camp.

In seeking to understand community dynamics, though, I went far beyond seeing my subjects only at singing events. Even the simple act of going to a convention can involve substantial nonsinging time, such as carpooling on drives of up to three hours each way, staying in the homes of local singers, and, during events to which most participants have traveled significant distances and are staying in hotels, spending evenings with large groups of singers at restaurants and in hotel rooms, talking, singing, and drinking.

Even beyond that, I spent time in people's daily lives. During my summers on Sand Mountain, I had time on weekdays between weekend singings and spent a great deal of it with singers. The first summer I spent in Alabama, I lived blocks from a lifelong singer who had just bought a new house, and I helped her paint her living room and do yard work. Then and during other periods of fieldwork in Alabama in particular, I have run errands for singers, babysat their children, helped cook and clean before big singings, and observed them at their jobs. In fact, the time I spent with one man as he worked installing septic tanks led me to write an article on the way he used social networks to make a living without advertising (Clawson 2005).

These activities, and others like attendance at major life events such as weddings and funerals, give me valuable perspective on the lives of singers and make me closer to being a full part of their community rather than an occasional observer whose presence is cause for changes in behavior and routine. It leads also to a give-and-take relationship, to relationships in which I could reciprocate for help with my research such as helping me gain access to singers I do not know well, not as an explicit exchange but as part of the flow of a friendship in which both parties do for each other occasionally.

Experiencing the nonsinging lives of Sacred Harp singers also revealed more about the place of Sacred Harp in their lives. An interview subject answers the questions asked; if those questions center on a specific topic, that topic may become more central in their accounts of daily life. Similarly, Sacred Harp singers will be disposed to talk about Sacred Harp singing in each other's presence. Going to their homes and jobs provides a different context, one in which they may be more likely to talk about different things.

Most Sacred Harp singers do, indeed, have lives that are otherwise very full, with jobs, families, nonsinging friends, churches, and hobbies. But Sacred Harp is also very clearly embedded in their lives, not simply a persona they adopt in the presence of other singers. They have pictures of other singers in their homes, songbooks given pride of place on bookshelves, e-mail addresses and license plates that refer to Sacred Harp, and children who incorporate Sacred Harp into their make-believe games. Sacred Harp may be only one of several activities or identities in people's lives, but it is clearly not an identity that is casually donned around other singers and shed in their absence, and the depth of my fieldwork allows me to consider this aspect of their participation in a way that interviews alone or even participant observation that began and ended with the singing events themselves would not do.

THE FIELD

Becoming Part of the Community

> We advocate neither distance nor immersion but dialogue. The purpose of field work is not to strip ourselves of biases, for that is an illusory goal, nor to celebrate those biases as the authorial voice of the ethnographer, but rather to discover and perhaps change our biases through

interaction with others. Thus, an "I-you" relation between observers and participants replaces a "we" relation of false togetherness and an "I-they" relation in which the I often becomes invisible. (Burawoy et al. 1991, 4)

"Neither distance nor immersion but dialogue." This elegant formulation ought to be the guiding principle of any ethnographer. In the case of one working in a community to which they claim some membership, avoiding excessive immersion is the constant challenge—whether the illusory immersion Stoller details or what we might call "going native" by absorbing our subjects' values at the expense of analysis.

The paths into Sacred Harp communities taken by me and by Dana, the anthropologist mentioned in this chapter's opening vignette, are instructive. I began with a moment of immersion, and my abiding struggle was to avoid too fully seeing myself or being seen by others in this light. Dana, on the other hand, started her research intent on maintaining professional distance, a distance that was steadily broken down. In the end, we conducted our research from similar positions.

In a sense, any Northern singer beginning to sing in the South is a fieldworker, an outsider arriving in a community and deciding on a balance to strike between distance, immersion, and dialogue. Southern singers, like many often-studied populations, have an established way to understand and evaluate the participation of outsiders. It is common for new Northern singers to travel to Southern singings to absorb the tradition from people who have been singing Sacred Harp all their lives and whose families have been singing for generations. Some allowances as to behavior and appearance are typically made for such travelers during their first trips, but there is an expectation that travelers will actively work to adjust their own behavior to Southern practices.

The visitor who does not do this after a few trips South will not be chastised or overtly shunned, but the relationships and respect available to them will diminish. The established nature of this role—that is, of the new Northern singer who adapts to Southern singing practices—provides a template, one that can potentially garner a new singer significant approval from Southern singers and dedicated Northern ones alike. Even this approval, though, could not be mistaken for membership in a particular community of singers. Membership requires participation in the community's activities, and it depends on relationships with the individual singers of that community.

I first sang from *The Sacred Harp* some six years before I began my formal fieldwork, though by the time I first attended a Southern singing I was already planning to study some aspect of Sacred Harp, and during my early trips South I was actively considering possible topics. My status was therefore always complicated—on the one hand, unambiguously a Sacred Harp singer, but on the other, one with ulterior motives—and it was further complicated by the question of what exactly *insider status* means in this context. Since the music is defined by participation, anyone can lay claim to the title of Sacred Harp singer, but because it is a *community* form, one can be an insider in one local singing community and very much an outsider in another; for instance, a pillar of the Chicago singing community may be but is not necessarily an insider in the Minneapolis singing community.

At the start of my research, I was an insider in the overall Sacred Harp community in the sense that I knew its basic traditions, such as at what times during a day of singing prayer is held or breaks from singing are taken, and I knew the music (though from the perspective of someone with no formal musical training). But I was not an insider in any of the specific communities I chose to study, and in Alabama and Georgia my outsider status was clearly marked by my speech and my appearance: in addition to lacking a Southern accent, I did not wear the makeup characteristic of most Southern women singers, color my hair, or wear similar clothes. By contrast, I was culturally very similar to many of the Chicago and Minnesota singers I would study; yet it was Sand Mountain, one of the Southern communities, in which I came closest to insider status and which is therefore my focus in this chapter.

But beyond this background as someone who cared about the music itself, I had an unexpected and undesired moment of entry into the Sand Mountain community. I first attended a singing there in September 1999, with three friends. In January 2000 we all attended another singing at the same Sand Mountain church. In March, my friend Karen made the decision to spend the summer in Birmingham, Alabama, living with another singer and singing every weekend. In June, the weekend before she was to move South, Karen died of heart failure stemming from a congenital defect. The singers at Liberty Baptist Church, where we had sung in September and January, offered a place for Karen in their cemetery, and she was buried there at a funeral attended by many local singers and church members. This event, and her tombstone in the cemetery, became significant reminders of the depth of the ties between singers from different locations. My own grief, the experience of shared grief with singers in that community, and the fact that I was now tied to the church through the presence there of my friend's grave verified my commitment to Sacred Harp and to that community in particular.

It also made an analytical difference to me. On several occasions during my fieldwork periods, I sang at the funerals of people I had never met. As a fieldworker, I would have agreed to do this as a fieldwork opportunity, to see these practices up close and to show my willingness to participate. But I did so knowing that many of the people I sang with would do the same and sing at the funeral of someone *they* had never met, simply because of shared membership in a broad national community. This amplified my understanding of the commitment my subjects felt.

While I entered the field with this personal connection, and with the aim of acting in ways that would preserve my ability to function in the Sacred Harp community after leaving the field and publishing my work, Dana decided to study Sacred Harp based on a media account of the music and before she had ever attended a singing. Having only attended a handful of Northern singings, she moved to Alabama to study the music and the community with the aim of maintaining strict professional distance and objectivity. I stayed with her shortly after she arrived, and when I suggested carpooling to a convention two hours away with local singers, she said she preferred not to do so because it would entail narrowing that distance between herself and her subjects. When the man who had, at my request, found an apartment for her to rent for the summer dropped by unexpectedly, she became uncomfortable. In her first weeks of study, she did not lead songs at singings—one of the crucial markers of participation in the music—and instead spent significant parts of each day standing at the back of the room, videotaping the proceedings.

This determined distance dropped away quickly, though. Within weeks she was carpooling to singings, spending time at singers' houses, and going to concerts and amusement parks with them, and in the three years since she has kept up strong social ties with a number of people she met that summer. Her initial self-definition as a researcher along with the fact that she began interviewing people quickly after arriving in the area did nevertheless mean that people were likely to see her more as a researcher than they did me. And this in turn led to people giving her (and not me) the stack of instructional materials I commented on at the start of this chapter.

As this example suggests, how often, how insistently, and by what means you disclose your status as a researcher will affect how your subjects see you. Although I have always regularly told people that I was engaged in research—when introducing myself to new people, when answering questions about my occupation or about where and how often I sang—my behavior was, for the most part, that of a community member. The conspicuous exception was when I was recruiting people to be interviewed and interviewing them. But otherwise the only visible reminder that I was doing research was my occasional note-taking during a day of singing or while carpooling home from a singing.

No matter how often you *tell* people you are doing research, what will most make them remember it is *behavior* that differs from standard behavior in the community. Dana's early behavior—both things she did do, like videotaping, and things she didn't do, like leading songs—cemented in people's minds that she was *studying* Sacred Harp. Although she went on to participate in the community herself, and to form close personal relationships with many singers, this initial self-definition set her researcher status in people's minds in a way that mine never was.

The Dialogue

The researcher's own self-definition is therefore crucial to how they are understood by their subjects. Simply wanting to be accepted in a community is not enough to ensure that you will be, of course, but holding yourself aloof is certain to prevent acceptance. It is also important to understand that your participation must take place at at least two levels: Reasonable adherence to community norms and participation in community activities is necessary, but so are individual relationships.

Participation in community norms can be linked to individual friendship, in fact; it is likely to be friends who tell you directly when or how you may be violating those norms. As I became friends with Sand Mountain Sacred Harp singers, for instance, and engaged in extensive informal talk with women there, I changed my appearance to better meet their standards of modest dress (particularly for singings, where, as I have noted, church dress and behavioral standards typically apply).

Such transformations represent an important decision about your identity as a fieldworker. Are you costuming yourself, dressing a particular way as an instrumental means of gaining acceptance, or are you adopting that style on a deeper level, taking it out of the field with you? The same question can of course be asked of a number of other topics, such as what music you listen to or what food you eat. In asking these questions of self-identity, I advocate returning to Burawoy's words and seeking dialogue.

What is at stake need not be a literal dialogue of words but rather one of dress or cultural style.

In this case, while I did adapt somewhat to Southern dress standards at singings themselves, I quickly learned not to take this attempt too far. Doing so felt like a form of drag—one or two dresses I bought diverged too far from my own style and soon ended up in the back of the closet—and I drew certain lines beyond which I would not change my self-presentation. At the same time as I refused to travel the full cultural distance between myself and my research subjects, though, my personal style in other situations migrated somewhat toward my fieldwork style. There was a constant dialogue, between myself-as-sociologist and myself-as-singer, of being changed by my work without signing myself over to it entirely. It was also a dialogue with my subject-friends, one of whom, for the first time, hired a woman to do physical labor after I volunteered to help him install septic systems on a few occasions and demonstrated strength and willingness to work.

Taking the concept of dialogue more literally, I had very serious conversations with some of my subjects precisely about our differences. In the broad community context, at singings, I behaved as a member of the community, but an important way to prevent "false togetherness" was to have my differences understood by at least some people whose membership in the community was uncomplicated and complete. As a Northeastern liberal among white Southerners, race and the civil rights movement were important topics around which to both articulate difference and to engage in dialogue.

Prior to traveling to sing, my mental geography of the South was defined by the history of the civil rights movement. Then, on my second trip to Sand Mountain, I went with a group of people to the only wet town in two dry counties. That town turned out to be Scottsboro, a near-mythic name from high school and college history classes as a result of the Scottsboro Boys. A few months later I found myself in Anniston, Alabama, where the Freedom Riders were ambushed. As the historical geography was replaced by the personal geography, I had a series of conversations with Southern singers about those issues. Those conversations marked me as other, as someone with my own suspicions of and prejudices against white Southerners. But in confronting such a potentially difficult issue, my research was enriched in several ways.

I found, as Brooke Harrington has argued with regard to Michael Schwalbe's study of the men's movement, that even the fieldworker participating in a community benefits not just as an individual but as a researcher by acknowledging moments of disagreement.

> Schwalbe positions himself at crucial moments in the study as a catalyst, eliciting reactions from other participants. Rather than using himself as a source of data, as in some recent ethnographic accounts, Schwalbe enters the account only to generate data from others. This self-placement in the text allows him to retain credibility with readers by emphasizing his independence from the group in which he is immersed. (Harrington 2002)

In the field, my conversations stripped away a level of doubt. Some Northern singers I have spoken to who travel South regularly and consider some Southern singers to be friends but have not had explicit conversations about race continue to wonder if there is an ugly racist side to their friends. While my conversations about race in several cases established without doubt that someone had views on race significantly to the right of my own, and even ones that I would consider racist, I also learned that, with few exceptions, the people with whom I had these conversations consider "racist" to be a particularly bad quality and do use it as a pejorative label. I learned that they are very conscious of the change in their own views over time—most strikingly, one man said of his family having an interracial family as weekend guests that "fifteen years ago, we wouldn't have done it, but we've changed."

In a somewhat ironic way, the fact that I had had those conversations with some of my closest friends/subjects provided me with a verifier of my status—enough of an insider that some would engage in casual racism around me (always in nonsinging contexts), but enough of an outsider that such racism was usually accompanied by some recognition of my discomfort, from a verbal acknowledgment to a wink or an eyeroll. These moments simultaneously told me that I was trusted enough for the caution maintained around most visiting Northern singers to be dropped *and* that I had held to a distinct identity, steering clear of "false togetherness."

Dialogue with your subjects, in other words, can be one of the most valuable ways to elicit views of their context that go beyond the most commonly accepted ones, to get a slightly different angle in someone's response to a challenge. To community members and outside readers alike, it marks you as Other, not completely bought into the norms or ideologies of the subject community. As Harrington further argues, it can open up analytical moments, not only strengthening your position as a careful, un-immersed ethnographer but broadening or deepening your understanding beyond your subjects' own comfort zones.

Writing

Looking back at the negative reception that her book *Fisher Folk: Two Communities on Chesapeake Bay* received from its subjects, Carolyn Ellis resolved that:

> I will not assume that the people about whom I write won't have access to my materials or that they won't be interested in them. . . . I know now that pseudonyms hide little. . . . Insiders often can identify, or think they can identify, the individuals concerned (Punch 1986, 46). (Ellis 1995, 88)

Researchers have an absolute obligation to analyze subjects to the best of their ability; researchers with human subjects may face backlash from those subjects; and researchers who have extraresearch relationships with their subjects have a special burden in balancing their roles. In "Emotional and Ethical Quagmires in Returning to the Field," Ellis (1995) recounts lessons learned from underestimating her subjects' awareness of her work and their negative response to it, illustrating some potential danger zones and the discomfort of failing even if you only intend to revisit your subjects as a researcher and not as a friend.

Questions of confidentiality and anonymity figure in the writing stage of any work with human subjects, particularly qualitative work, and much more so when those subjects know each other and share a community. A researcher doing an interview study in which few if any of the people being interviewed know each other can change not only names but occupations and other details to disguise their subjects' identities. As long as the changes made do not substantially alter the subject's demographic characteristics, they can provide anonymity without disrupting the analysis. It is much more difficult to change such information for a study in which almost all of the subjects know each other and in which details like occupation or family composition are relevant to how the person is located in and interacts with the community.

Whether a person grew up singing Sacred Harp, was raised around it but rejected it for years as an adult before returning to it, or first heard it as an adult; whether their family members sing; whether they travel to sing often or only do so in their local community—all these things are enormously relevant to any mention of them in an analysis of singing communities, but they are also characteristics other members of those communities could use to identify who a pseudonym refers to. In fact, most of my subjects were happy to be identified in most instances; their participation in Sacred Harp is something they are proud of. Without that, my task would have been much more difficult. A researcher wanting to study any close-knit community should therefore think carefully about what degree of anonymity they will need to provide to make their subjects feel safe and whether that degree of anonymity will disrupt their ability to portray and analyze the community accurately. Some projects may not be possible, or research questions may need to be changed to accommodate such concerns.

One issue faced in the writing process that is closely related to the question of whether subjects understand you primarily as a community member or as a researcher is the question of why you know what you know about them. Some significant amount of personal information and gossip came my way because people were not thinking about me as a researcher in the moments they told me those things. Even the people who were most aware that I was studying Sacred Harp clearly assumed that I would put that aside at times and interact purely as a friend, and of course I did do so. But the inescapable fact is that when I stepped back into research mode, I did not suddenly un-know the personal information I had learned. While I would never explicitly refer to clearly personal information, my knowledge of it definitely informs my analysis at some points. In addition, there were gray areas in which I was unsure whether a piece of information had come my way as a researcher or as a friend—conversations, for instance, that touched both on my work and on intimate topics.

In Carolyn Ellis's recounting of her subjects' anger at her book, much of the anger stems from her deceptive practices such as failing to disclose that she was in fact doing fieldwork and secretly tape-recording conversations. These are obvious ethical violations. But people also felt betrayed by her use of information that she had been told as a friend. Ellis had participated as a community member during her research but described it this way: "[I always] remembered that I was a researcher (an awareness I had been taught was important) and, without this role, I doubted I would have gotten as involved with the Fishneckers as I did" (1995). The price of this betrayal was facing anger from people she did care about but who were not part of her day-to-day social or professional world.

In deciding what and how much to write about such things, the question of power comes to the fore, as Michael Burawoy notes.

> Being sensitive to power inequality doesn't remove it. Although many of us had considerable loyalty to the people we studied, and revised our papers in the light of their comments, nevertheless in the final analysis what we wrote was outside their control. (Burawoy 1991, 5)

While this remains undeniably true, writing about a community to which you belong, and wish to continue to belong, adds a twist. You are vulnerable to social pressure from people with whom you want continuing (and positive) relationships. While what you write is "in the final analysis . . . outside their control," their response can affect you. In my case, if I anger too many Sacred Harp singers with what I write, then singing—an activity I love—potentially becomes too uncomfortable for me to continue, and other researcher-community members may face similar sanction—that is, not merely anger but life-altering rejection.

This knowledge swings the pendulum from the tradition, to which Ellis's *Fisher Folk* belongs, of researchers caring too little about their subjects' feelings and dignity to the other extreme of caring too much and producing weak work as a result. For this reason, regular reminders that you are a researcher and will be writing and publishing about your experiences are an important first step, prophylaxis against anyone being surprised to find themselves portrayed in writing. Assiduous attention to accuracy should be a primary concern of any scholar—but wanting to be able to face your subjects later may add weight to this concern. I also saw my ability to use people's real names as necessitating the compromise of sometimes using completely anonymous quotes in cases when someone did not want their name associated with a comment that was critical of others in their community, or of other singing communities.

In another discussion of Wacquant's *Body and Soul*, Robert Zussman writes of the importance of going beyond insider accounts even where a pure insider account is possible.

> If the task of sociology in general or field work in particular were simply to represent groups in ways recognizable to themselves, then we would be content to stop with insider accounts. But field workers aspire to something more. In particular, we often want to place our findings in a social context that may itself be invisible or, at best, only very partially visible to insiders. And we almost always want to place our findings in the conceptual or theoretical frameworks of our own discipline. That ability to move back and forth between a specific observation and a

wider context and between the empirical and the conceptual is what constitutes the special competence of sociology. (Zussman 2005, 206)

A fieldworker studying and participating deeply in the same community may have to work particularly hard to maintain the visibility of the social context under study while at the same time also achieving special insights from that community membership. Always, balance is the key: balancing one's identity as a researcher and as a participant; balancing sincerely felt friendship with the need to write about those friends in a professional manner; balancing disclosure of researcher status with ethnographic unobtrusiveness; balancing adherence to community norms with willingness to critique them when they are in violation of other values you hold. Again, as Burawoy suggests, dialogue is key. The best way to find balance is not to derive rigid rules about what to do or not to do but rather to be thoughtful and always willing to question yourself, your subjects, your own research question and design, and your academic discipline itself.

NOTES

The author would like to thank Eszter Hargittai, Joan Walling, and the anonymous reviewers of this chapter for their comments. This draws on dissertation research funded in part by the Louisville Institute and the Princeton University Center for the Study of Religion.

1. Many of the churches at which Southern singings are held do not believe in seminary education for ministers, who are drawn from the community and apprenticed after feeling a call to preach.

REFERENCES

Burawoy, M., A. Burton, A. A. Ferguson, K. J. Fox, J. Gamson, N. Gartrell, L. Hurst, C. Kurzman, L. Salzinger, J. Schiffman, S. Vi. 1991. *Ethnography Unbound.* Berkeley, CA: University of California Press.

Clawson, Laura. 2005. Everybody Knows Him: Social Networks in the Life of a Small Contractor in Alabama. *Ethnography* 6 (2): 237–64.

Ellis, Carolyn. 1995. Emotional and Ethical Quagmires in Returning to the Field. *Journal of Contemporary Ethnography* 24 (1): 71, 88.

Harrington, Brooke. 2002. Obtrusiveness as Strategy in Ethnographic Research. *Qualitative Sociology* 25 (1): 56–57.

Stoller, Paul. 2005. The Presence of the Ethnographic Present: Some Brief Comments on Loïc Wacquant's *Body and Soul. Qualitative Sociology* 28 (2): 197.

Zussman, Robert. 2005. The Black Frenchman. *Qualitative Sociology* 28 (2): 206.

THE CHALLENGES OF IN-DEPTH INTERVIEWING WITH DISADVANTAGED RESPONDENTS

JOAN WALLING

The sociologist Deirdre Royster recently observed that "even the most carefully designed study cannot anticipate the obstacles—perhaps more gingerly described as surprises—of the field or 'real world'" (2003, 44). In fact, it seems safe to say that the one thing a researcher *can* count on in field research is that few things will go as planned. When teaching qualitative research methods to undergraduates, I stress the fact that one cannot start a project too early—yet every semester students are surprised and frustrated when their projects are delayed by countless canceled interviews, late respondents, and sometimes even populations who simply cannot be contacted for study. "If I have this much difficulty contacting a college football coach, how am I supposed to believe that anyone really does interviews with an even harder to reach population?" Shea, a senior sociology major, asked me one day. "What are some strategies I can use to get the attention of that football coach?"

It is no secret that some populations are harder to reach than others, and in fact some of the groups that are most interesting to social scientists are the least accessible. With impoverished populations in particular becoming less "visible" to the everyday observer (Newman 1999), researchers struggle to gain access to, for example, single mothers working multiple jobs, people too poor to own a phone, or young urban men who live with extended family. The problem of access is one that has been discussed by numerous researchers, but there is little consensus on a dependable, over-arching strategy (Lofland and Lofland 1995, 22–28). Sometimes researchers simply accept their limitations—those who conduct telephone survey research, for example, have to resign themselves to the fact that they will not be able to include the perspectives of populations without a telephone. However, more often than not, a researcher can eventually put together a reasonable sample, and even learn from unexpected limitations or changes to the plan (Royster 2003, 44).

Once respondents are contacted, research difficulties do not necessarily wane—disadvantaged populations also require a certain amount of knowledge and sensitivity if researchers are to bridge the cultural gap between their own research-centered culture and that of a population both unfamiliar with research and in a strained relationship with authority more generally. In this way, the challenge Shea faced with his university's football coach was not really so different from the challenge that another researcher might experience with disadvantaged populations—both respondents must be convinced that the researcher is trustworthy and that his or her project is important enough to warrant a sacrifice of the respondent's valuable time. As researchers, we depend on our respondents for our success and must interact with them effectively to ensure that we not only get the data we need but treat them with sensitivity and respect.

My dissertation research draws on in-depth interviews conducted by myself and others in 2001–2 with 166 low-income respondents receiving aid from various sources. The sample included people from diverse religious and ethnic backgrounds, as well as non-English speakers. In this chapter I describe that research experience in order to highlight issues and concerns that many researchers face as they gather qualitative data from disadvantaged populations. I also discuss some of the challenges of establishing trust with disadvantaged respondents, particularly when addressing sensitive personal topics.

While this chapter is based primarily on my dissertation research, my broader research interests have brought me into contact with several disadvantaged populations and various sensitive interview topics (such as religion or money—or in some cases, both), and so this chapter also draws on experiences I gained in the course of other academic research projects and during my brief stint as a nonacademic researcher.

THE RESEARCH PROJECT

Let me begin by describing in some detail the research project from which I will draw most of my conclusions in this chapter. The three years of research that were the focus of my graduate work centered on how care is received and interpreted differently depending on who gives it. I studied respondents who had recently received some kind of aid from religious, governmental, or community-based social service agencies. My respondents were drawn almost entirely from low-income populations. My research addressed the question of self-worth and how it is experienced and negotiated by those who are marginalized in the American culture of self-sufficiency. In particular, I looked at how care recipients sustain feelings of dignity and self-worth in the face of a culture permeated by the idea that self-sufficiency is a necessary condition for that self-worth.

Part of the reason that these caregiving episodes are so powerful for recipients is the cultural context in which they take place. In his book *Acts of Compassion*, Robert Wuthnow (1991) explores the idea that the American ideal of individualism is at odds with ideals about helping and caring for others that Americans also hold. In a similar vein, my research argues that while caregivers struggle with an ideal of individualism that tells them they should look out for number one instead of focusing on the needs of others, that same individualism tells recipients that they should be able to make it on their own, without help from anyone, no matter what the situation. Like givers, recipients navigate and negotiate these competing ideals to develop a sense of self-worth that includes depending on others to some extent while validating their own individualism.

The findings from my dissertation work address the larger issue of how recipients interpret caregiving as a whole. While differentiation between organizations is examined, what emerges from this research is not an argument about government organizations being more or less helpful than faith-based ones but rather the importance of the cultural context of care and the way it informs recipients' interpretations of themselves as worthy of that care. In this chapter I will discuss the methods I used to conduct research in this context and how I explored sensitive issues such as money, religion, family, and feelings of personal worth while working with a disadvantaged population unfamiliar with this type of research.

RESEARCH INTERVIEWS

Because most other studies have focused on caregivers, volunteers, and altruists, my study looked mainly at recipients of care, using in-depth interviews to determine how they interpret and receive care differently from different types of givers. I used an in-depth qualitative interview method in order to represent accurately the points of view of the recipients of care. In order to protect fully those who helped with this research, names of both agencies and respondents were changed.

In analyzing in-depth interviews, I drew on a rich tradition of qualitative research in sociology. This method is especially well-suited for revealing information about the ways in which respondents understand the meanings of their behavior and the behavior of others. The advantage of an in-depth interview is that respondents are allowed to use their own language to talk about their experiences and their thoughts. Many of the questions used were open ended; respondents were always encouraged to give specific examples and to explain their answers thoroughly. They were encouraged to talk as much as they would like, to use their own words, and to tell stories.

Respondents were asked a number of questions about how they perceived, interpreted, and responded to the care they received from different sources. I used standardized questions in order to provide a strong base for comparison across respondents. The interview questions were formatted in advance, and there was little deviation from the questions in the interviews—the questions were worded in the same way each time so that a difference in response could not be attributed to changes in question wording. Interviews with recipients included three main sections; in the first section, respondents told the basic story of how they were helped by an organization—what the problem was at that time, and how the organization helped to alleviate the problem. In the next section, respondents were asked about their ideas and feelings about that experience. This section included questions like, "Do you feel that your basic outlook was changed by this experience?" and "Why do you think this person helped you?" In the final section, respondents were asked more difficult or probing questions, such as questions about their religious beliefs, about agencies they think might be untrustworthy, and about their biggest challenges in life. The harder or more personal questions were saved for the end of the interview so that respondents would feel more comfortable telling the interviewer the full range of their thoughts on the topic, which was important in providing the highest-quality data.

Respondents whom I identify as "recipients of care" were helped in many different ways, from shelter in a time of homelessness, to food stamps, to drug rehabilitation programs. Some were simply offered assistance with day care or food from a food pantry; others were given counseling or direct financial assistance. Since the purpose of my study had more to do with recipients' own ideas about having been helped in a time of need, I cast a broad net concerning the type of help the respondent received. Most respondents nevertheless told traditional stories about having been helped in just the ways that we expect from social service organizations—basic necessities like food, shelter, and clothing. While some were also given counseling or emotional support, this was usually accompanied by material help.

When questions in the interviews referred to specific religious beliefs or texts such as God or the Bible, the question was modified for other religions (e.g., the Koran for Muslim respondents) and kept as a Christian reference for those who said they were not religious. Over half the respondents reflected the U.S. cultural and historical tendency toward Christianity, with Catholics forming a large part of the respondent group. We know that low-income Americans are often Catholic, so this is not surprising. Following the general trend in the area where the study was conducted (Lehigh Valley, Pennsylvania), there are also more Lutherans and Moravians than would be expected in other areas of the United States.

My experience was that most people were happy to be interviewed, had a good experience with the agency that provided help, and were eager to tell the story of how the agency had helped them. However, it seems quite possible that they may have been less eager if my research team had been less prepared for the challenges they would face in interviewing a disadvantaged population. While most respondents were happy to tell their stories, they did pose a number of challenges (explicit and implicit) to the interviewer. After first describing the context of my research, I will address some of the challenges I encountered most frequently in working with disadvantaged populations: these include establishing trust with low-income respondents, working with non-English-speaking respondents, covering sensitive topics with respondents, and doing research during sensitive times in history.

RESEARCH CONTEXT

While many studies that draw on data from low-income respondents focus on large metropolitan areas, my study examined the social service context of the Lehigh Valley, in Pennsylvania. Understanding their physical context is critical to understanding disadvantaged respondents, and respondents in the Lehigh Valley are no exception. Located in northeastern Pennsylvania, the Lehigh Valley includes the three towns of Bethlehem, Allentown, and Easton. Historically, the Lehigh Valley has been an economically productive area, producing many successful and well-known businesses, including Bethlehem Steel, Mack Trucks, Daytimer, and Binney & Smith (creator of Crayola crayons). The success of these and other businesses made the Lehigh Valley the third largest market area in Pennsylvania, but today, most of these companies have closed their doors in the Lehigh Valley.

One of the most economically devastating closures was that of Bethlehem Steel. The communities that make up the Lehigh Valley have suffered economically since Bethlehem Steel closed. The steel mill had been one of the largest in the world, employing more people than any other company in the area. When Bethlehem Steel closed, it did so slowly, first downscaling, then closing its doors altogether. The trouble started with the first oil crisis in 1973, culminating in the major closings that occurred during the mid-1980s and the final factory closing in 1998. This economically devastating event was important enough to the community that it still informs their talk about practically anything having to do with the Lehigh Valley. While community leaders always sound hopeful about the revitalization of the economy, and while unemployment is now decreasing in the area, there has been a significant loss of morale.

The Billy Joel song "Allentown," written in 1983, characterized the Lehigh Valley in this way: "In Allentown they're closing all the factories down. Out in Bethlehem they're killing time, filling out forms, standing in line." At the time Joel wrote the song unemployment rates were at their peak in the region—12 percent (Hall and Hall 1982; *Morning Call* 2003). Because of its depressed economy, the Lehigh Valley has initiated and maintained many different types of service organizations in order to care for residents in need. For that reason, the Lehigh Valley provided opportunities to examine the service relationship under circumstances that have not been examined in previous studies; in particular, unlike large metropolitan areas, the Lehigh Valley community supports a relatively self-contained system of social services, making it possible to examine the specific relationships between recipients and providers of social service in much greater detail than is typically possible.

RESEARCH SAMPLE

More than half of the respondents were identified through a survey of 2,077 people living in low-income neighborhoods in the Lehigh Valley in northeastern Pennsylvania. This 2002 survey, called the Lehigh Valley Trust Survey, was conducted between January 16 and March 20, 2002, among randomly selected residents from the lowest-income parts of the Lehigh Valley. The objective of the survey was to obtain information from a representative sample of lower-income residents living in a sufficiently concentrated geographic area so that contacts with specific service agencies could be examined. To achieve this objective, the 15 inner-city census tracts with the lowest median household incomes according to the 1990 U.S. census were identified as the target population. The population includes 50,773 persons living in 18,819 households in Lehigh and Northampton counties, of whom 17.9 percent were receiving public assistance, 10 percent were unemployed, 8 percent were African American, and 28 percent were Hispanic (Wuthnow, Hackett, and Hsu 2004). Out of this survey, a subset of respondents were identified who had contact with social service agencies and who were willing to participate in an in-depth interview. These are the same respondents that Robert Wuthnow describes in his book *Saving America? Faith-based Services and the Future of Civil Society* (2004).

Like the survey respondents, all respondents in my study would be considered economically disadvantaged compared to the population of the Lehigh Valley as a whole. Disadvantaged people were targeted as more likely to be recipients of care. Wuthnow, Hackett, and Hsu (2004) note that the median family income of those they surveyed was $26,364, compared with $49,848 for the larger metropolitan statistical area; the unemployment rate was 9.2 percent, compared with 4.6 percent; the percentage with incomes below the poverty line was 36.4 percent, compared with 9.5 percent; and the proportion of households with children that were headed by single parents was 46.8 percent, compared with 25.4 percent. The respondents in my study have similar demographic characteristics.

"WHAT ARE THESE QUESTIONS REALLY FOR?" ESTABLISHING TRUST

"Can I ask you one question?" Seventy-one-year-old Elsie Wicks, a retired switchboard operator receiving help with her medical bills, interrupted her interview suddenly, with a note of suspicion in her voice. "Sure," the interviewer replied. "OK," said Elsie. "These questions that are more of a personal nature, what are they *really* for?" In my dissertation, Elsie's question is mentioned briefly, and the readers are assured that she is given a "brief but honest answer" (Walling 2005, 83). However, in any real-life interview this question can hover in the background, even for the majority of respondents who are not as brave as Elsie and never come right out and ask the question in the back of their minds.

What *are* the questions "really for"? It is more difficult to answer Elsie's question than one might think. One of the first things we learn as field researchers is that the researcher should try to avoid biasing respondents— and giving respondents real information about the project often results in bias. Aside from taking care not to ask leading questions, researchers know that they hold a certain amount of power over respondents in the interview context, and that this can affect respondents' answers. Interviewers control the pace of the interview; they can cut off a long story or probe for more information on a sensitive topic. While respondents can cut off the interviewer at any point, as long as they continue to participate in the interview, the researcher is in control. Especially when there is another active power dynamic, such as gender or social class, the relationship with the interviewer can make respondents eager to please—without even realizing it, respondents will try to say what they think the researcher wants to hear. While outright deception is used in some social science research scenarios, many sociologists feel that deception is not absolutely necessary in their research and try to respect respondents by giving them a true, though often abbreviated or vague, description of the research project.

Despite this effort to be honest, most respondents realize that they do not have the whole story about the research, whether it is because interview questions are not always completely consistent with the interviewer's explanation of the project or because the explanations given are vague and unspecific. Furthermore, when it comes right down to it, the vague answers the researcher gives are only partly about avoiding respondent bias. On the one hand, the researcher herself does not always understand the full purpose of the research until it is complete—research projects evolve and grow as data are gathered and new literature is read. In addition, researchers know that respondents do not necessarily want a seminar on the project—most research stems from fairly technical origins and can be difficult to explain succinctly to those outside one's field.

On the other hand, even if one did set out to explain the entirety of one's research, it is difficult to know what telling the "whole truth" to a respondent would entail. Even researchers who think they are going undercover find that they actually are not pretending as much as they think they are—as Barbara Ehrenreich notes in her "undercover" journalistic account of waiting tables in *Nickel and Dimed*, "There's no way . . . to pretend to be a waitress: the food either gets to the table or not" (2001, 9). Similarly, Natalie Allon finds, in her research of a singles bar, that those she observed did not consider her research agenda to be a particularly significant deception. "I was single and drinking and so a member of the scene just like anybody else. They said that everybody in the scene had ulterior motives and mine happened to be research" (1979, 68–69). Therefore, while researchers might consider it important to be honest with respondents, it is not always easy to know how to carry out that intention.

Unlike Elsie, most respondents do not come straight out and ask about the interviewer's hidden motives—but that does not mean they are not wondering. As researchers, there are things we can do to establish trust with the respondents whose lives we interrupt and who so generously give their time to our projects. Assuring them of confidentiality (and following through on this) is important. However, there are certain groups of respondents who have reason to be less trusting of interviewers and often require more than just assurance of confidentiality before their trust is gained. In the following sections, I will discuss the unique challenges of establishing trust with low-income respondents and non-English-speaking respondents, as well as the role of trust in interviews that deal with sensitive topics like money or religious faith.

BACKGROUND: WHY SOME DISADVANTAGED POPULATIONS MISTRUST AUTHORITY

To illustrate the challenge of establishing trust with disadvantaged respondents, I will first outline some of the concrete concerns disadvantaged respondents might have about participating in research and then go on to talk about the role of commonality with respondents in establishing trust. Low-income respondents may be less trusting of academic researchers than their middle-class counterparts because of their inexperience with academic research, their unique relationship with authority more generally, and their greater vulnerability in general.

Aside from explaining one's specific research project, a researcher should also expect to explain the idea of academic research more generally in certain cases. A respondent who has not attended college would not necessarily have had any reason to come into contact with academic research, and in fact the term *research* might mean something very different to a respondent coming from a disadvantaged context. Until the respondent understands the researcher's overall role, it is difficult to establish trust. When we think about what *research* means in a popular context, we think of detectives or private investigators "researching" a crime, we think of medical research, we think of journalistic exposé on shows like *20/20* or *Inside Edition*. Even Indiana Jones, the exception that proves the rule of social science research in popular culture, is only loosely linked to an academic context—a link that is rarely made explicit in the movies and could easily be overlooked. Therefore, while academic research is familiar to those of us who read and participate in it daily, there are few cultural images of the academic researcher that will aid a respondent in trying to make sense of the term. Moreover, many popular images of research conjure up either an intimidating picture of the "research subject" in a dangerous lab-rat type role (such as Beaker, a familiar character from the Muppets) or a sinister picture of research as necessarily investigating something criminal or unethical. "When you first called me I thought, 'why am I being researched—am I in trouble?'" one respondent admitted with a laugh as we sat down to begin the interview. At times, I found it more helpful to describe my position as a student writing a paper rather than a researcher writing a book—most respondents have helped their own children or others with school projects (such as family trees) and find this image more accessible, and ultimately more accurate.

In addition to unfamiliarity with academic research, disadvantaged respondents might mistrust the researcher because of their group's unique relationship with authority more generally. Sociologists who study impoverished urban populations, in particular, have found that disadvantaged populations have few reasons to trust those in authority over them (Anderson 1999; Conley 1999; Massey and Denton 1993). From impoverished neighborhoods' lack of police presence to disability checks that fail to come in time to be of help, the relationship of the poor with those in authority is tenuous at best. Researchers will find that this relationship is not limited to government and police authority; even the researcher as an authoritative middle-class presence might be considered suspect. Brenda Beagan's research on medical students shows that students with a working-class or impoverished background are most likely to resist socialization as a doctor, in part because of antielitism. Her research even shows that their own families often consider them less trustworthy because of their middle-class affiliation with medicine (2001). Similarly, Royster finds that her trade-school graduate respondents trust her more when she minimizes her affiliation with the elite university Johns Hopkins (2003). Because of this unique relationship with authority and the middle class, researchers should avoid an authoritative tone and expect to earn the trust of respondents, rather than being awarded trust as a matter of course.

A final concrete reason for disadvantaged respondents' hesitations about trusting an interviewer is their vulnerable position in society. I recently thought about taking part in a wrist pain study conducted by the physical therapy department of my university. The experimental treatment would be done with lasers of varying colors and would last three weeks with the possibility, but not certainty, of wrist pain reduction. In contemplating participation in the study, I took two precautions. First, I researched laser treatment online to make sure that it was, in fact, a safe experimental procedure. Then, semiconsciously, I thought about the legal action I might take if the experiment turned out to be harmful. Both steps would be much more difficult for a disadvantaged respondent contemplating participation in research. The disadvantaged respondent enters an academic research context with very little to safeguard her against abuse or misuse of the information—without time and resources needed to investigate the institutions and techniques of the academic researcher, and without money or connections to take legal action should something unethical or libelous occur, the disadvantaged respondent must rely on her own careful interaction with the researcher as her sole protection from harm.

In attempting to overcome these obstacles and establish trust with respondents it is helpful, I think, for a researcher to contemplate her own commonalities with respondents. Many have written about the ideal balance between researching as an "insider" versus an "outsider," or "Convert" versus "Martian," in Fred Davis's terms (1973). The debate centers around whether it is more important to identify with respondents in order to truly understand their perspective (the "Convert" approach) or to maintain a scientific objectivity from which analysis can more easily flow (the "Martian" perspective). Most often, the consensus is that a balance should be achieved, although there is some debate about where that balance might lie. Although every researcher's goal is, as quoted by Laura Clawson in her chapter in this volume, "neither distance nor immersion but dialogue," that place is difficult to find, and researchers disagree as to the side on which one should err. Some researchers actually become so enmeshed in their respondents' way of life that they consider respondents' churches, schools, and community organizations their own (e.g., Patillo-McCoy 1999). A researcher who takes this strategy may find herself identifying with respondents without realizing it, as Clawson herself acquires a slight Southern accent when talking to or about the working-class Southern respondents mentioned in this volume, a habit that helps make her respondents comfortable with the depth of her involvement in the community.

Researchers show identification with their respondents in order to draw on the respondent's knowledge as an "insider," but they also make the respondent more comfortable, which, considering the importance of respondents to researchers, could easily count as an end in itself. While the pros and cons of the insider or outsider approaches are often considered for the researcher, few young researchers think about what the respondent might prefer. Though some respondents like to be the "teacher" for an outsider looking in, in my experience most prefer the insider approach, where they can feel that the researcher understands their perspectives.

In my research, I have found that identifying areas of commonality with respondents is both important and useful. For me, studying people in the Lehigh Valley came relatively easily. The way people talked about Bethlehem Steel felt familiar to me—I grew up in a mill town myself, a town much smaller than Bethlehem, Pennsylvania, but similarly dominated by one manufacturing industry, a paper mill that residents simply called "The Mill," though many community institutions bore its proper name. My dad, both my grandfathers—even my mother and grandmothers for a short time—worked at The Mill. I remember seeing *Roger and Me*, the Michael Moore documentary about displaced autoworkers in Flint, Michigan, for the first time in college and feeling a chill even in the warm library classroom—that could be *my hometown*, if Crown Zellerbach ever closed its doors, I thought. In my interviews with low-income respondents, then, it was relatively easy for me to see them not as a "disadvantaged population" but as individuals who have been affected harshly by the events of economic history; individuals who, but for the luck of the draw or divine providence, might have been employed in the steel mill and sent their daughter to Princeton University while my own uncle or father could have easily been in my respondents' shoes.

I have found that even if I am not interviewing a group with whom I can easily identify, it helps to find some commonality with my respondents or even, in the case of a large data set (as in the case of my dissertation, which employed professional interviewers), to make sure interviewers have at least some small amount of common ground with respondents. Stephanie, the researcher who showed me around the Lehigh Valley, conducted many of the interviews in the area, and as a resident herself she could identify with respondents on those terms. The interviews I conducted myself were mostly with recipients of care given by churches—as a regular church attendee, I think this connection helped me make respondents feel comfortable.

INTERVIEWS WITH LOW-INCOME POPULATIONS

Researchers can gain amazing insights from interviews with low-income and impoverished respondents, but there are challenges to this type of research as well. The old adage about treating others as you would want to be treated is a good guideline, but it also helps to understand the unique perspective of low-income respondents. When I started to interview low-income respondents I found that, more than anything, a researcher needs patience in order to work with this particular disadvantaged population. Low-income respondents were more likely to show up late, to forget an interview, or to change their minds about the interview, once scheduled. This was not because of any personal failure on the respondents' part to prioritize the interview or to keep commitments. In fact, at one point I was both shocked and grateful to find that Tim Smith, a single father who received free day care from his church, had scheduled his interview with me in his four hours off between two ten-hour shifts at a local convenience store. Other respondents "fit me in" in similarly heroic ways as they juggled multiple jobs, child care, care for relatives, and limited time with children and spouses. As a researcher, I found it helpful to keep in mind that the world of low-income respondents is at once unstable and inflexible. Jobs, child care, and transportation are not necessarily to be counted on at any particular time. At the same time, costs for missing an opportunity with any of these elusive resources are much higher than our personal experiences as academics might prepare us to expect.

The most common cause of missing an interview, among my respondents, was the opportunity to pick up some extra hours at work. People usually had very little advance notice about these opportunities, and almost all felt compelled to take them, either for fear of a punitive employer if they refused or because they really needed the extra money. Usually these extra shift opportunities occurred while the respondent was already on the job, and many respondents felt unable to call from work to let me know they would be missing the interview. (This research just preceded the ubiquity of cell phones.) The second most common reason respondents missed or were late for interviews involved transportation problems. Low-income respondents rarely have reliable cars, sometimes share one car between several working adults in the household, or depend on public transportation that is not always reliable. On more than one occasion a respondent asked me to drive her somewhere after the interview because of transportation problems.

Many interviews were also delayed because of problems with child care—a sick child, a relative who said he would watch the child and then was not able to, or problems picking up or dropping off the child at an activity. I found that transportation of children to and from different activities was much harder for my respondents, since they often drove children to school to avoid undesirable school districts, and because of this, extracurricular activities were also further away from home. Even though most interviews were done in the respondents' homes, there were often issues that involved child care either before or after the interview. One respondent with a disabled child rescheduled the interview several times because a specially trained person had to be present to watch the child while she spoke with me.

As a researcher in this context, I found it helpful to be ready for anything. More than once, I kept an eye on a respondent's child while she answered the phone. I also brought in trash cans, fed the cat, carried in newspapers—I even fixed a toilet at one respondent's house.

I was not often worried about safety during the interviews. Whether this was because of intuition or inexperience I am not sure. I usually conducted interviews in respondents' homes during daylight hours, although a few were after dark and some were in public places. The advantage of a public place (safety, easier to find) is offset considerably by the fact that tapes of the interviews do not come out nearly as well. On the one or two occasions when I felt funny about a respondent after talking on the phone, I would sometimes convince a friend to accompany me to the interview and wait in the car or at a nearby park or coffee shop.

Safety was a more serious consideration in my nonacademic research work in some of the most impoverished areas of New York City and Los

Angeles. On these trips, I was always accompanied by a colleague and fellow researcher. Despite the rough reputations of the neighborhoods we visited, out of forty interviews we left only one house without conducting the interview, and we generally felt that those inhabiting the neighborhoods with such bad reputations simply did not have much to live on and for the most part wanted a safe, attractive neighborhood just like everyone else (Patillo-McCoy 1999). The only house we did leave was actually not in a "bad" part of town at all, but a cheerful looking suburb. However, when we arrived at the house we felt fairly certain that the respondents were using some kind of controlled substance—the man we were supposed to interview could not form a coherent sentence, and his mother seemed incapable of speech as well. They were not able to confirm their own identities and did not remember the scheduled interview (despite the fact that we had called that morning and had spoken with someone who did confirm the appointment). On this occasion, my colleague Alex and I both instinctively felt that we should leave the premises immediately and did not need any discussion.

It may sound trivial, but one piece of advice never provided in research methods books is the simple fact that getting to the interview is often more taxing than conducting the interview after one arrives. For the longer academic interviews I usually budgeted three hours (my interviews ranged from 90 minutes to one five-hour interview), and I found that I could not complete more than two per day without exhaustion setting in. Working in the nonacademic sector, interviews with low-income respondents were much shorter, between one hour and 90 minutes, and teams of two interviewers often did seven interviews in one day, taking turns at the primary interviewer role. More interviews would certainly have been possible if it were not for travel and navigation time. However, driving, parking, and, most important, not getting lost are even more stressful when working with low-income respondents. Not only are streets, apartment buildings, and trailers less well marked than the locales of their more affluent counterparts, but safe, convenient parking is more difficult to find, and a wrong turn can lead to some nerve-wracking moments.

INTERVIEWS WITH NON-ENGLISH-SPEAKING POPULATIONS

Some of my dissertation interviews with recipients of care were conducted in Spanish in order to accommodate Spanish-speaking respondents. These interviews were then transcribed and translated into English. In my nonacademic research work, as well, about half of the interviews in my project were done with Spanish speakers from Mexico, Guatemala, Ecuador, Argentina, and El Salvador. I did not conduct these interviews myself, since I am not fluent in Spanish, but I often accompanied the interviewer to Spanish language interviews—my Spanish is good enough to catch the general idea of what was being said, and I took notes about the respondents and their environment.

Often the Spanish-language interviews were less rich than other interviews; respondents spoke less and were not as forthcoming with stories. This could be because of the language barrier, or it might be the result of different cultural norms about how much one says to strangers about personal problems. People who grow up in the United States are likely to be familiar with a therapeutic perspective in which talking to strangers about problems and even having these sessions recorded is a normal and usually helpful thing to do. Even if respondents have no personal experience with this kind of therapeutic exercise, it is depicted in movies and on television shows so they have some frame of reference for this type of interaction. It could be that Spanish speakers are more likely to be wary of this setup or consider it rude to talk about problems with a stranger.

However, although these interviews were usually not as long, they are still a valuable source of data because they provide some idea of these respondents' perspectives even from their shorter answers to questions. It was in the Spanish interviews that I saw the most extreme versions of both poverty and success. These were the interviews where respondents talked about losing everything when their downtown Manhattan businesses were forced to close after 9/11, while their Anglo counterparts drew on insurance, family resources, and other savings. "My family doesn't understand," was another common complaint. "I make a lot of money here, but they don't understand that it also costs a lot to live here. I send them almost everything—I try to live simply." The small apartment of this respondent contained two folding chairs, a card table, and a mattress on the floor.

As this quote illustrates, the Spanish-speaking respondents were more likely to think of themselves as interdependent with their extended families and communities. Recent immigrants in particular talked of sending money home not just to spouses and children but also to community members. One woman told us about sending money back to her hometown for a medical surgery needed by a mere acquaintance. While she felt proud to have been asked for the money, she also felt a little resentful, since she noted that many people assume she has a lot of money because she lives in the United States, and that it is not culturally appropriate to decline when they ask for something. Other researchers have also found this to be true for low-income respondents, even those native to the United States (Stack 1974), since one of the only effective strategies against poverty is interdependence and sharing within a community.

In my experience, trust with non-English-speaking respondents is often harder to establish. Cultural signals don't always translate well, and the language barrier itself leaves respondents with less understanding about the project than their English-speaking counterparts. There is no easy way around this challenging situation, but treating respondents with respect and keeping your eyes open for opportunities to make them feel more comfortable can go a long way. These respondents' perspectives are so valuable (and so difficult to collect) that even a shorter interview can provide important insights about a relevant research question.

COVERING SENSITIVE TOPICS

When attending a dinner party with people one wants to avoid offending, common wisdom says to avoid topics of religion, money, sex, or politics. However, as social scientists these are some of the most interesting research topics. How can we address these issues with respondents, who are strangers to us, when these topics aren't even considered appropriate topics of polite conversation among friends and family?

During my employment at a Manhattan-based research firm, I traveled with co-researcher Alex to the most impoverished neighborhoods of New York City and Los Angeles. While the neighborhoods we visited have reputations for being dangerous, and we saw more than our share of illicit activity on these trips, the research topic would have been just as sensitive in the most bland suburban neighborhoods. Our in-depth interviews were conducted for a large national company known for its money transfer service, and we asked questions about every aspect of money—from how much people earn and how they spend it, to who controls the household purse strings. Money is an especially sensitive topic for low-income respondents, particularly those who receive aid and might be worried that someone is checking up on them (Zelizer 1994).

Similarly, the respondents I talked to during my dissertation research were asked to speak about three sensitive issues—not only about money, but also about their ability (or inability) to care for themselves, a sensitive topic for self-sufficient Americans (Wuthnow 1991), as well as their own religious faith and how they think about religious people. Elsie Wicks's query about what the interview questions are "really for" came about at a particularly sensitive point in the interview—a point when she noticed that the questions were "more personal in nature." Sensitive topics raise questions about the research in general, and the more sensitive the topic, the more likely a respondent will carefully guard what she says.

In both of these projects, I found that there were certain strategies that worked well for reassuring and putting respondents at ease. One strategy is to make an initial show of trust in the respondent—even a simple confession such as when your birthday is, particularly when it is personal in nature, can be disarming in an interview situation. Alex had a policy of accepting any kind of drink or refreshment offered by respondents in order to show that he trusted them. Showing one's own insecurities can also be a good strategy—admitting that you are inexperienced at operating the tape recorder or that you got lost on the way to the house are often good ice-breakers, although it is also important to appear competent.

Of course, there are always exceptions—some respondents simply refuse to say much more than a sentence or two, no matter how much an interviewer prods. One 17-year-old resident of a housing project in Manhattan who supported himself, his mother, two aunts, and a cousin would say little more about his relationship with money than simply, "I like money—it works for me." When pushed to give an answer about how he feels toward the family members who depend so heavily on his teenage labor, he refused to say anything but "I'm glad I can help them." In this situation a researcher thinks, surely he must feel more than that! Surely he sees teenagers on television (which played loudly in the background for the duration of the interview) and notices a difference between their problems—whom to ask to the prom, getting in a fight at school—and his own all-too-adult existence. Yet getting more than a vague sentence or two from Juan about his relationship with money was very difficult.

Sometimes a respondent like Juan will open up midway through the interview. The trigger, I've found, is usually something that is off topic but relates to the interview tangentially; noticing something around the house such as a picture, a card, or even a favorite television show can spark a conversation that will make you as a researcher seem more human to the respondent. Sometimes asking a question that is a departure from the interview guide, especially when your tone lets the respondent know that you are just asking as a person who cares, not as a scientist, can result in conversations that ultimately turn out to be very relevant to the research topic after careful analysis. For example, Juan may not want to talk about money, but he might be willing to describe his family members, or to say how he thinks *other people* think about money.

Besides silence, another way for a respondent to stonewall an interviewer whose topics are too sensitive is with persistent off-topic talking. One respondent I was interviewing about his relationship to money refused to talk about anything but his bitter custody battle for his four-year-old daughter. He had a narrative that was quite set in his own mind, perhaps because of rehearsals for a time when he would tell the judge, and this narrative took about three hours. While Alex and I tried everything we could think of to get him to return to the topic, we eventually decided that this was the story he felt was most relevant to any question in his life right then, and we decided to respect his decision to talk exclusively about the custody battle. While a researcher can try to bring the topic back around, or even, in some cases, say directly, "We're getting off track, here—I really want you to talk about x," some respondents seem unable to do so. A researcher should remember that this in itself is, in a sense, data—it tells a researcher what types of concerns the studied population has and which ones tend to override any other topic. Sometimes this kind of story will come after the interview is finished. I am convinced that a researcher should, when possible, sit and listen to the respondent's postinterview story. From one perspective, it might turn out to contain useful data. From another perspective, it is the researcher's way of saying, "I appreciate your talking about my topic. Now, I'd be glad to talk about what *you* feel is important."

Finally, researchers should remember that collecting data about sensitive topics is sensitive not just for respondents, but also for interviewers. As respondents told me their stories about having received care from others— often unconditionally, often in the nick of time, often above and beyond what they had been expecting—many started to cry. To my surprise, I cried right along with them. I went to a trailer park to interview a man with cancer who had been laid off from his job and did not get his disability pay for a full seven months after he was diagnosed and confined to bed. "Imagine seven months with no paycheck—no money at all, nothing!" he said. As this man told about the generosity of his neighbors, he told me how a man, a "tough guy" two trailers down, came over and put his car keys on the kitchen table saying, "Take it as long as you need it." As he told the story, the three of us (his wife was in the room) became so emotional that the transcription of the tape reads, "can't hear—7 minutes." In my interviews about money the last question was always, "What are you going to do with the $20 from doing this interview today?" (referring to the incentive money). A man sharing a tiny apartment with six other men said, "I will send it to my daughter in Guatemala—her baby has a fever and they have no money for medicine—I hope it's in time. I've never seen him, and I'd like to someday." Moved to action, Alex and I took all the cash we had and added it to the incentive money.

WHEN THE WORLD BECOMES SENSITIVE—INTERVIEWING POST-9/11

While money and faith are admittedly sensitive topics, a researcher may also at times find herself in a situation where the overall atmosphere is sensitive—as if the whole world is on edge, emotionally, because of a particular public attitude or historic event happening at the time. Examples could include such events as a natural disaster, war, or political upheaval. In the midst of my dissertation research, the 9/11 terrorist attacks occurred. Of course, I could discuss at great length what this might mean for people who were talking to me about faith-based organizations and how they felt about self-sufficiency, independence, and receiving help. Any researcher knows that the events of 9/11 had a significant impact on the way Americans think about faith, survival, and security, and this must have affected my interviews as well. However, at the time, it was the day-to-day research details that concerned me, rather than theoretical predictions about respondent bias. I had interviews scheduled on 9/11, 9/12, and the rest of that week in 2001, all with respondents located about an hour from New York City. The practical question I had as a young researcher was simply, "What should I say to these respondents?"

It seemed obvious that I should call respondents and cancel the interviews on 9/11 and 9/12, but how long should I continue this after the disaster? Was 9/13 too early to return to a regular schedule? Would it seem disrespectful to expect a respondent to keep an appointment for 9/14? For 9/15? And how should I begin the conversation when calling respondents on the phone to either reschedule the interview or to remind them of an interview the next day? How would I know if this respondent was grieving the loss of a friend or loved one, or if he or she was one of the many in the area who felt moved to join the civilian relief effort in downtown Manhattan?

For the most part I did not have to be the one to make the decisions about all of this. Several of the ten respondents scheduled for interviews that week called me to let me know when they felt comfortable rescheduling the interview. In the cases when I did call, I said something to the effect of, "I know this has been a very emotional week for everyone in this area—I'm not sure if you remember the interview we had scheduled for Thursday, but I wanted to let you know that I can reschedule or go through with the interview, whichever you prefer." My rule of thumb was to expect that respondents who had scheduled interviews for the week of 9/11 would want to reschedule. For respondents scheduled for interviews during the following week, I called with a reminder that I thought was fairly sensitive, assuming they could do the interview but letting them know that I understood if they wanted to reschedule.

There was only one respondent that I was unable to contact. Her interview was scheduled for 9/12; I left a message on her voice mail, both before the interview and several times afterward. She did not show up for the interview and I was never able to contact her. I have always hoped that it was simply a problem of jammed phone lines and lost voice mail (those who were in the New York area at the time might remember how difficult it was to contact anyone then) and not a personal tragedy. Perhaps the events of 9/11 made her change her mind; maybe she decided to give her time to things really important to her instead of taking time out of an already busy day to do interviews with academic researchers—I will probably never know.

On the other hand, several respondents actually said they felt more like talking because of the events of that week. "I was nervous about the interview before," a mother of two who worked in a local retail clothing store told me. "But now I feel like everyone should get their story out there—you never know what's going to happen in your life and you've got to take opportunities when they come along." Respondents who did keep their interview appointments shortly after 9/11 seemed more open, and on average talked a little longer than other respondents. In the days and weeks that followed 9/11 respondents were quicker to cry, more emotional, and, surprisingly, more sensitive to me as an interviewer. They were more likely to ask me about my degree, my research interests, and my family. At some point early on in our interaction, they usually made a hesitant inquiry as to whether I had lost anyone in "the twin towers," as the disaster was being called before it became known simply as 9/11. This gave me the chance to ask them the same. I heard quite a few stories of people who had narrowly escaped—I didn't interview anyone who had lost someone close to them in the attacks.

CONCLUSION

I am not sure who coined the phrase "expect the unexpected," but I would not be surprised if he or she happened to be a researcher. The one thing researchers can count on is that things will not go as planned—whether it is due to terrorist attacks, language and cultural barriers, responses to sensitive interview topics, or a combination of all these and more. In fact, this is precisely why researchers go to "the field" for their data—because we find out new things that we did not necessarily expect. In the field, we turn real life into data—and real life tends to be messy.

When we as researchers encounter populations unfamiliar to us—from low-income respondents to recent immigrants—we are gaining valuable new information and insights. Listening to respondents and trying to see the world from their perspective is the most important thing to keep in mind. Beyond that, a researcher should think about establishing trust with respondents and making sure the research truly is in the respondent's best interest in order to get the best data possible. Respondents, like researchers, have complex lives with busy schedules, relationships that must be protected, and highly nuanced views of the world. When a researcher is studying any population that is unfamiliar to her, but particularly disadvantaged respondents, she should keep in mind her own position of power, from the respondent's perspective, and keep an open mind about how the respondent might interpret her words and actions. Through this added sensitivity and flexibility, the researcher gains a greater ability to access and interpret her subjects' thoughts and ultimately obtains richer data.

NOTE

Many thanks to the Fetzer Institute, the Sage Foundation, the Center for the Study of Religion at Princeton, Insight Research Group, and Azusa Pacific University for their financial contributions to research projects mentioned in this chapter. Thanks also to Eszter Hargittai, Bob Wuthnow, Laura Clawson, Joan Linsenmeier, Richard Christopherson, Natalie Searle, Tina Walling, and David Linsenmeier for their helpful feedback and intellectual contributions.

REFERENCES

Allon, Natalie. 1979. The Interrelationship of Process and Content in Field Work. *Symbolic Interaction* 2 (2): 63–78.

Anderson, Elijah. 1999. *The Code of the Street.* New York: W. W. Norton.

Beagan, Brenda L. 2001. "Even if I don't know what I'm doing I can make it look like I know what I'm doing": Becoming a Doctor in the 1990s. *Canadian Review of Sociology and Anthropology* 38 (3): 275–92.

Conley, Dalton. 1999. *Being Black, Living in the Red.* Berkeley: University of California Press.

Davis, Fred. 1973. The Martian and the Convert: Ontological Polarities in Social Research. *Urban Life* 2 (3): 333–43.

Ehrenreich, Barbara. 2001. *Nickel and Dimed.* New York: Metropolitan.

Hall, Karyl Lee Kibler, and Peter Dobkin Hall. 1982. *The Lehigh Valley: An Illustrated History.* Woodland Hills, CA: Windsor.

Lofland, John, and Lyn H. Lofland. 1995. *Analyzing Social Settings.* Belmont, CA: Wadsworth.

Massey, Douglas S., and Nancy A. Denton. 1993. *American Apartheid.* Cambridge: Harvard University Press.

Morning Call. 2003. Forging America, the Story of Bethlehem Steel. December 14. Bethlehem, PA.

Newman, Katherine S. 1999. *No Shame in My Game.* New York: Vintage Books.

Patillo-McCoy, Mary. 1999. *Black Picket Fences.* Chicago: University of Chicago Press.

Royster, Deirdre A. 2003. *Race and the Invisible Hand.* Berkeley: University of California Press.

Stack, Carol. 1974. *All Our Kin.* New York: Harper and Row.

Walling, Joan. 2005. The Power of Receiving: Finding Moral Meaning in Care-Receiving Episodes. Dissertation, Princeton University.

Wuthnow, Robert. 1991. *Acts of Compassion.* Princeton: Princeton University Press.

Wuthnow, Robert. 2004. *Saving America? Faith-based Services and the Future of Civil Society.* Princeton: Princeton University Press.

Wuthnow, Robert, Conrad Hackett, and Becky Yang Hsu. 2004. The Effectiveness and Trustworthiness of Faith-Based and Other Service Organizations: A Study of Recipients' Perceptions. *Journal for the Scientific Study of Religion* 43 (1): 1–17.

Zelizer, Viviana. 1994. *The Social Meaning of Money.* Princeton: Princeton University Press.

ONLINE SURVEY

Instant Publication, Instant Mistake, All of the Above

GINA WALEJKO

Developments in information and communication technologies have led to new forms of communication and personal expression. For example, today many adolescents and adults spend time interacting with others via online video games (e.g., see Williams and Xiong in this volume). Others use social networking Web sites to keep in contact with peers, foster new friendships, find significant others, and even develop professional connections. The past several years have also seen the rise of blogs on a diverse array of topics, from personal diaries to politics and technology (e.g., Adamic and Glance 2005; Drezner and Farrell 2004; Singer 2005).

From a social scientific perspective, users of online communication technologies offer researchers interesting populations to study. Scholars can gain easy access to large samples and, with help of online surveys, can ask these users attitudinal and behavioral questions. For example, what do political bloggers think about the mainstream media? Are young users of social networking concerned with privacy? Add to this the ease and relatively small cost of online survey software, and the junior researcher might begin to see a recipe for instant success. (*Start with 1,000 bloggers. Add equal parts Web questionnaire and Stata. Stir. Bake for one year in a 90-degree graduate student office.*)

Unfortunately, the allure of online surveys often masks the difficulties and trade-offs that they entail. For the most part, researchers have surveyed populations of interest located in the "real world" with offline modes such as mail, telephone, and face-to-face data-collection techniques. The Internet challenges researchers to rethink established standards of constructing sampling frames, creating questionnaires, and contacting samples. Furthermore, certain characteristics of these new forms of online communication complicate the process of quantitative research. For example, how does a social scientist interested in studying "the most popular bloggers" operationalize such a project? Should this measurement be based on blog aggregator Web sites (which ones?), Web page traffic (hits, visitors, or page counts?), or neither? This chapter will explore the challenges that arise when doing survey research on Internet-based populations, discussing in depth the complications that arose during one specific study of bloggers and ending with a list of lessons learned.

THE 2007 ACADEMIC BLOGGER SURVEY

Given my interests in survey methodology and Internet use, I decided to execute a survey of academic bloggers. Blogs are online publications usually consisting of Web entries or short articles to which visitors may post public comments either on the Web site itself or on their own blogs elsewhere. Blogs have become increasingly numerous, and, in 2008, the blog-tracker site, Technorati, followed almost 113 million blogs (2008). I began my research by collecting a list of bloggers who work as professors or researchers in universities, colleges, and research institutions. I then designed an online survey instrument to measure characteristics of this sample, specifically attitudes toward blogging and scholarship, frequency of blogging activities, type of content, their Web use, and technological proficiency, as well as general demographic information. I then administered the survey questionnaire online.

As a new (and somewhat inexperienced) graduate student and researcher, I expected the project to be semipainless. Little could I have known that it would take me nearly three months—or a whole summer—to collect the contact information for my population. However, the intricacies involved in sampling an online population as well as the challenges of balancing coursework and research obligations made the study more difficult than I had expected. What follows is a step-by-step description of the hurdles that I encountered while designing and administering an online survey of academic bloggers. First, I discuss in depth the planning associated with the project including hypotheses and sampling design, questionnaire design and testing, and Institutional Review Board (IRB) approval. Second, I briefly discuss survey implementation including correspondence and list management, technical difficulties that arose during data collection, and the problems that I encountered when calculating a response rate. I conclude the chapter with a list of lessons learned for researchers embarking on similar projects.

PLANNING, PLANNING, AND MORE PLANNING

Our fourth-grade science teachers taught us to develop hypotheses before testing and experimentation. However, we were instructed that these hypotheses must be derived from inductive reasoning and educated guesses. How does a researcher interested in technology create well-informed hypotheses about phenomena that are rapidly changing?

During the planning process of the academic blogger project, it was important for me to keep abreast of what was happening in the blogosphere, especially regarding academic blogs. Even though I was to employ a quantitative survey, an initial ethnographic approach gave me the necessary background to construct the final questionnaire in an informed manner. I read blogs more frequently than ever, and I discussed the blogging phenomenon with fellow graduate students and professors both inside and outside of the classroom. I also made sure to keep in touch with academic and graduate student bloggers who provided insight into the current world of academic blogging. Although I had maintained a blog in the past, I realized how much I had to learn as I planned the sampling design and built the questionnaire for the survey. I am truly indebted to all of the individuals who allowed me to pick their brains as well as those that politely reminded me of recent developments in the blogosphere. ("Gina, when you ask me how often I post, do you want me to include automatic del.icio.us updates or not?")

Research Questions and Hypotheses

A sampling frame is the list or directory of names or other contact information from which a researcher draws a sample (Groves et al. 2004), but developing a directory that includes all bloggers, blogs, or blog readers is nearly impossible. Blog-specific challenges like the large numbers of abandoned and spam blogs add to the difficulty (Li and Walejko 2008). As a result, certain sampling strategies will systematically exclude some bloggers while favoring others. This limits the generalizability of many blog studies and is especially worrisome for those aiming to explore a large, diverse population. For example, if a study only includes English-language blogs, it cannot claim to be a snapshot of the entire blogosphere. However, the pitfall of overgeneralization can be avoided by carefully constructing research questions that take into account the sampling frame used to create the sample.

First and foremost, I realized that my hypotheses for the academic blogger project could not overstep the population that they were to generalize. Throughout the study, I refined my hypotheses, keeping in mind the limitations of my sampling frame and the resulting sample. Furthermore, when writing up the study, I took care not to overgeneralize my results to a broad sample. These actions increased the validity of the study's survey measurements.

In the same vein, although researchers are often taught to create research questions first and develop the "perfect" methodology afterward, the difficulty of measuring and sampling online populations requires us to think of both methods and the operationalization of research questions in tandem. Originally, I was interested in whether or not blogging negatively or positively affects the ability of an academic to obtain tenure, but I realized that an online survey of academic bloggers could not possibly answer such a daunting question. Furthermore, as a graduate student with limited resources, I knew that a large-scale public opinion survey of academics was not feasible. Rather than measure the whole academic population's attitude toward blogging as scholarship, I would only be able to measure self-reported data from scholars who blog. Although this survey would not answer definitively whether blogging had contributed to the tenure and job rejections of several highly published scholars, it would shed light on the relationship between this online activity and academic productivity. Thus, I developed the project's hypotheses while keeping in mind the constraints of sampling an online population using an online survey.

Sampling Strategy

While developing my sampling strategy, I was lucky that much previous research had been done on bloggers (e.g., Adamic and Glance 2005; Drezner and Farrell 2004; Herring et al. 2004), including several surveys (e.g.,

Braaten 2005; Kullin 2005; Miura and Yamashita 2004; Rainie 2005). After reading this literature I learned that, for the most part, researchers had relied on nonprobability sampling techniques to sample bloggers and their blogs. Nonprobability sampling does not allow for statistical control over the collected data, and a researcher risks undercoverage when employing a strategy that neglects to sample all elements in the frame. The term *undercoverage* is used to refer to eligible groups or individuals that are excluded from the sampling frame (Groves et al. 2004). For example, in the case of my study, all U.S. academic bloggers who were neglectfully excluded from my sampling frame would be considered undercoverage.

Although nonprobability sampling remains the easiest way to sample online populations, strategies such as snowball sampling do not offer replicable results, and many samples of convenience suffer from a lack of robustness (Couper 2000). A snowball sampling strategy uses past respondents to recruit future respondents, and such a technique is commonly used to sample blogs because bloggers often know other bloggers. I wanted to avoid the pitfalls associated with such online convenience samples in order to ensure that my results were replicable and valid. For this reason, I attempted to construct a comprehensive list of all U.S. academic bloggers. Because I would be working with a list rather than a snowball sample, I would be able to calculate response rates. In addition, it would provide me with a way to contact nonrespondents.

Originally, I wanted to include all U.S.-based PhD-track graduate students in the sample. When I began to develop my list, I realized that this was not the best choice. As I read the content of several graduate student blogs, it occurred to me that many graduate student bloggers have fundamentally different motivations for blogging than other academics. Furthermore, if I wanted to understand the relationship between my sample and academic productivity, there would likely be a split between the productivity of graduate students and academics at later stages in their careers. After reading more blogs written by graduate students, I decided that this group of university bloggers, although similar to other academics, was best represented as a separate population. For these reasons, I made the difficult yet necessary decision to exclude graduate students from the sample.

In order to organize my list, I operationalized the population of inference along several different criteria. The population of inference is the intended population to which a researcher aims to generalize (Groves et al. 2004). First, I included only academics that hold a doctorate degree and currently teach and/or do research based at a U.S. university, college, or research institution. Nonteaching researchers were also included because they disseminate scholarly information in the same system of publication as professors. Conversely, I excluded "public intellectuals" who have PhDs but are not employed at colleges, universities, or research institutions because they do not work on the same structure of tenure and research publications as university-based academics and researchers. The following is a list of characteristics exhibited by all eligible respondents to the academic blogger survey.

Education	Have received doctorate
Blogger Experience	Currently author of or contributor to a blog
Language	Read English and Write blog in English
Employing Institution	Currently work for United States university and/or Currently work for a United States college and/or Currently work for a United States research institution
Contact Information	Have a publicly accessible e-mail address and Have a valid e-mail address

List Construction

I relied heavily on the Web site *Crooked Timber* to develop a directory of academic scholars who blog. *Crooked Timber* is a popular academic group blog that maintained a record of 521 academic bloggers at the time of list development.[1] Although not regularly updated when I consulted it, this Web site offered the most extensive directory of academic bloggers available online. My first step was to visit each of the 521 blogs listed on this Web site. While visiting these sites, I added the names of all blog authors who met the criteria outlined in table 1 to a spreadsheet that included their e-mail address, the name of their blog, and the site's URL. If I could not determine one or more of these characteristics, I included the individual in the database of academic bloggers in order to minimize undercoverage.

I then implemented a technique that used blogrolls to create a database of over 1,000 academic bloggers. A blogroll is a list of links to other weblogs. It is a common practice for bloggers to link to other Web sites that are related to their own, so I used this organic networking to my advantage. First, I created a directory of sites listed on the blogrolls of 20 academic blogs that I had previously documented. This tally numbered well over 300! I then visited each of these 300 sites, adding all eligible authors and contact information to the original spreadsheet of bloggers. This method produced a larger and more comprehensive database of networked academic bloggers. Although not a probability sample, this technique meant that I worked with a list of academic bloggers, and such a catalog allowed me to keep track of response rates as well as to recontact nonrespondents.

Described in this way, the process *seems* simple enough. It nevertheless took several meetings with professors and many hours reading survey methodology papers in order to come up with the technique. I spent afternoons with both my adviser and a survey methods researcher, brainstorming different ways to sample this online population while taking into account my research questions. Likewise, I read dozens of papers on sampling techniques, both those that discussed elusive or rare populations (e.g., Ericksen 1976, 1997; Faugier and Sargeant 1997; Kalton and Anderson 1986; Lepkowski 1991; Rothbart, Fine, and Sudman 1982; Sudman, Sirken, and Cowan 1988) and those that elaborated on sampling Internet populations (e.g., Couper 2000; Couper 2001; Denscombe 2006; Kaplowitz, Hadlock, and Levine 2004; Lee 2006; Schonlau and Elliott 2002; Schonlau et al. 2004). In addition to publications about sampling in particular, I read several helpful research papers that went into depth on their own blogger and blog sampling strategies (e.g., Adamic and Glance 2005; Hargittai, Gallo, and Kane 2008). By taking advantage of survey research experts in my department as well as reading what had already been written by survey methodologists and blog researchers, I was able to develop a sound sample of U.S. academic bloggers. Unfortunately, I would soon realize that *implementing* such a novel strategy was easier said than done.

Eligible and Ineligible Units

Because my unit of analysis was a blog author, not the blog itself, I needed to obtain an e-mail address for each blog author. Furthermore, I needed to verify that each potential respondent was eligible to participate in the survey. In order to do so, I performed a Web search for the home or departmental Web page of academics who did not supply detailed contact and personal information on their blogs. For example, if a blogger wrote that they were currently a tenured professor at Northwestern University but failed to include an e-mail address, I searched for the person's departmental or individual home page in order to locate the necessary contact information. Conversely, if a blogger mentioned that they were an academic and included their e-mail address on their blog but did not indicate if they taught in the United States, I also searched online for this information. This tedious strategy assured the best coverage although the process was daunting, taking several weeks of slow, monotonous work. Adding the authors of the eligible blogroll blogs to the eligible weblogs from the *Crooked Timber* list gave me 1,320 discrete e-mail addresses of which 1,224 were nonduplicates.[2]

In hindsight, I should have been more careful when collecting these e-mail addresses because 44 percent of the survey respondents turned out to be academics from outside of the United States, graduate students or nonacademic bloggers. As a result, I had to throw out nearly half of the survey respondents who did not meet my operationalized definition. This large percentage of ineligible units, or units that do not belong to my population of inference, may have been due to the fact that I included bloggers whose eligibility could not be determined in the spreadsheet.

Questionnaire Design, Testing, and Implementation

During the process of developing this novel yet tedious sampling strategy, I began to design the academic blogger questionnaire. Fortunately, I was aided by several existing surveys from which I pulled pretested questions. Rather than take the time to develop the instrument from scratch as well as risk the inclusion of confusing and untested items, most of the survey was based on questions developed previously by others. I am also indebted to my adviser, other professors, fellow graduate students, and questionnaire design experts for giving me expert advice on successive drafts of the survey (for helpful questionnaire and question design resources, see Converse and Presser 1986; Dillman 2007; Fowler 1995; Tourangeau, Rips, and Rasinski 2000).

Of the total number of questions, I based more than 80 percent on previous surveys. Web and technology use questions were duplicated from Hargittai's 2007 survey of college students. In its second year, this survey provided me with an extensively tested measure of technology use. I also based several of my questions on the 2004 Pew Internet & American Life Project's Content Creation survey (i.e., Lenhart, Horrigan, and Fallows

2004). In addition to technology use and content creation questions, several of the questions on the academic blogger survey inquired about the type of research performed and amount of funding received by each academic. Nearly all of these queries were based on the 1996–97 National Faculty Survey administered by the Carnegie Commission for the Advancement of Teaching (1997). For many years, this questionnaire has been tested and updated, and today it remains the standard for surveys of faculty. Furthermore, Hargittai had already administered an unpublished survey of academic bloggers (i.e., Hargittai 2004), some of which were open-ended questions on the benefits and drawbacks of blogging. I was able to tweak many of the questions from this survey for use in my own. Having had the good fortune to gain access to the responses submitted to the open-ended questions on the Hargittai survey, I was able to code those answers into related categories that then became the answer choices to questions on my own survey. Taken together, these previously implemented questions were invaluable to decreasing the effort expended toward designing and testing the questionnaire.

Even though many of the academic blogger survey questions had already been tested through previous surveys, it was imperative that the novel components of the questionnaire undergo extensive assessment (see Presser et al. 2004 for testing strategies). For example, it was necessary for me to test several original questions that measured attitudes toward blogging. I also needed to make sure that the survey's skip patterns made sense and that the online survey logic functioned properly. I employed three strategies for testing questionnaires: informal interviews with academic bloggers, expert reviews, and several pretests.

First, in order to better understand the target population for the survey, I informally interviewed academic and graduate student bloggers regarding common practices and their own thoughts on blogging. Furthermore, I took my own experiences as both a blogger and an avid blog reader into account while designing the questionnaire. I used this background information to design the questions that were not based on previous survey instruments.

After these informal interviews, two experts reviewed the survey. The purpose of the expert review was to catch flaws like improper answer choices and invalid questions. I then approached several graduate student peers to pretest and comment on the questionnaire. Following two rounds of expert review and pretesting, I redrafted the survey, again. I then transferred the instrument online using a subscription-based tool that had been recommended to me by others. While online, the survey went through three more rounds of pretesting with both experts and a convenience sample. Were I to do all of this over, I would have tested the survey once more on paper before transferring it onto the Web because updating the survey online was a slower process than making changes to a text document.

While creating my questionnaire, I also wrote up a request for participation that highlighted the salience of the survey topic. Many studies show that well-drafted invitations to participation and prenotifications can increase response rates (Bosnjak et al. 2007; Cook, Heath, and Thompson 2000; de Leeuw et al. 2007; Dillman 2007; Edwards et al. 2002; Harmon, Westin, and Levin 2005; Porter and Whitcomb 2007). Blogging can be a time-consuming and thankless task for academics, and a request to take an e-mail survey is easily ignored by an individual who receives dozens of e-mails each day. Therefore, my request for participation emphasized the importance of understanding the demographics and attitudes of academic bloggers. Luckily for me, there had been much discussion both online and in the *Chronicle of Higher Education* (e.g., Fogg and Aronauer 2005; Glenn 2003; Mooney 2007; O'Neil 2004; Read 2006; Tribble 2005; Vaidhyanathan et al. 2006) about the merits of academic blogging as well as the drawbacks of blogging before tenure. I highlighted these features in the request for participation, and I had both a graduate student and faculty blogger provide comments on this document as well.

Meanwhile . . . Back at the University

During the planning stages of the study, I went through several rounds of Institutional Review Board revisions. It was necessary for me to obtain IRB approval before I began constructing my list of academic bloggers, so I began this process a full year before data collection. The procedure was complicated by the fact that my university did not allow graduate students to be named as principal investigators on any IRB submission, and at the beginning of the summer my adviser at the time had moved across the country for a yearlong fellowship. (On the bright side, it reminded me of the utility of fax machines.)

However, not all my communication with IRB is easy to dismiss with a quip. Because I had decided to use a popular online survey software and database to create the online version of the questionnaire and manage my data, I encountered a major IRB hurdle particular to that methodology. Specifically, I needed to explain to the IRB the details of how the online data would be managed. The online survey tool that I used to collect data is owned by a private business, so obtaining information about how the company protects the data that it compiles was like searching for a needle in a haystack. (Do they remove all personal information associated with each respondent? Do they assign random ID numbers to each respondent? How long does the company keep the data on its server? Does it make backups, and when do these backups get destroyed?) After an afternoon of Web searches and e-mail exchanges, I found the information necessary for me to describe to IRB how the company saves and secures personal information collected during the course of a survey.

IMPLEMENTATION: MANAGING THE FLOOD

By the time that I had finalized the questionnaire, I was afraid that my list of potential respondents had been outdated. To ensure an updated list, I spent a full week of monotonous "couch work" examining each entry in my spreadsheet as well as each blog listed on Henry Farrell's wiki index of academic blogs. I made sure that all e-mail addresses were up-to-date, and when I stumbled upon a new blog or a new blog author, I added them to the master spreadsheet. I also discarded people from the list who no longer met my operationalized definition of U.S. academic bloggers. For example, I deleted individuals who had retired or were now working at institutions outside of the United States. Although time consuming, this final updating of the list was necessary to ensure that I had the most up-to-date list of academic bloggers possible.

And We're Off!

After all of the planning and preparation, it was finally time for me to implement the survey—nearly one-and-a-half years after the study's inception. I launched the survey in mid-May. Although some university faculty would inevitably be busy with finals during this time, I decided that it would be better to begin data collection during the school year rather than the beginning of summer when academics might be on vacation or away from regular e-mail. I chose to administer the survey midweek rather than on a Monday when scholars may be catching up from weekend e-mails or a Friday when some researchers and faculty leave early.

I decided to recontact nonrespondents up to three times over the course of three weeks. Recontacting individuals has been shown to increase response rates in surveys more than any other strategy (Cook, Heath, and Thompson 2000). Furthermore, while I initially contacted potential respondents late on a Tuesday morning, I recontacted nonrespondents at different times throughout the workday and workweek in the hopes that sending e-mails dispersed throughout the day and week would increase their likelihood to participate in the study. Finally, I paid special attention to the subject line of each request as certain subject lines elicit higher response rates than others (Joinson and Reips 2007; Joinson, Woodley, and Reips 2007; Porter and Whitcomb 2005; Trouteaud 2004).

To aid in locating nonrespondents and ineligible units, I changed the e-mail subject line of the third and fourth invitations to participate, urging individuals to contact me if they were not bloggers or academics. This final request was entitled "Invitation to Academic Blogger Survey—Please notify if NOT an academic blogger." This change in wording helped me identify nearly 50 ineligible units.

Fortunately, responses started pouring in. By the end of the first day, around 150 people, nearly one-eighth of the sample, had responded to the survey. Unfortunately, I had received over one hundred bounced e-mail notifications and over 50 e-mails from potential respondents. Most were nice: "Happy to do it. Good luck with the research." Others were honest: "Unfortunately, I can find time to blog but not to answer surveys." Some were downright angry, accusing me of spamming while insulting me as a researcher.

Quickly, I generated a thick skin and responded politely to each e-mail. Before the survey, my then adviser had wisely created a new e-mail address for me. This allowed all e-mail correspondences about the project to be kept on a separate e-mail account. During the three weeks that the survey was actively online, checking my e-mail meant encountering one or two new e-mails from respondents or potential respondents. Each day I received several e-mails regarding the academic blogger survey, and it took me many hours to sort through the nearly 100 personal e-mails that I received over the course of four requests for participation.

Nearly 30 respondents requested that I e-mail them when I tabulated the results of the survey. This interest made up for the small number of negative e-mails that I received and kept me motivated to work on the project over the course of survey implementation. In order to aid in the debriefing of participants and dissemination of the project's results, I also created a Web site on which I would post the results. I included the URL to this Web site at the bottom of my request for participation. I felt that this was the least that I could do for the nearly 350 individuals who took the time to complete the survey.

In total, 105 e-mails, nearly 12 percent of the total, bounced back due to improper e-mail addresses, old e-mail addresses, or server problems. When an e-mail address was returned to me, I deleted it from the master list and searched for the correct one online. If I found another e-mail address for the same individual, I added it. Because the online service that I used did not keep track of bounced e-mails, I was forced to delete each returned e-mail from the online list, too.

Technical Difficulties

To further complicate matters (and as luck would have it), the online survey tool underwent a complete Web site overhaul during the implementation of my survey. Shortly after its launching, I noticed a message at the top of the log-in page:

> From Friday, May 18th at 6:00 PM (PST) until Saturday, May 19th at noon (PST), we will be down for maintenance, in order to upgrade to the new website.

Although the "upgrade" was done in order to make the online service more user friendly, it proved to be a major hurdle during the implementation of the survey. For instead of tweaking small portions of the handy service, the company performed a major overhaul of several aspects of the Web site. Apart from taking the survey offline for eighteen hours, it completely changed the way that they stored e-mail addresses and managed lists. I had become accustomed to the old interface, and I was forced to learn how to manage my online contacts from scratch mid–survey administration. I also encountered several bugs while sending out the second e-mail notification although the company did fix these problems within a few days. Whenever relying upon third-party online services to do research, a scholar must realize that companies constantly update and modify their services. Furthermore, sites can "go down" for myriad reasons. A researcher must be prepared for such obstacles, and it often pays to have a backup plan when collecting large amounts of time-sensitive data.

Calculating Response Rates

The goal of the project was to sample 1,000 academic bloggers. At the beginning of the study, I had sent 1,224 e-mails with a request for participation. Several of these e-mails were automatically returned to me with updated addresses, so 13 new contacts were added over the course of data collection. In total, I contacted each of the 1,237 addresses of which 105 bounced back due to old addresses or server problems. Of the total number of messages sent, 42 people initially responded that they were not bloggers, not blogging anymore, or not academics. In total, 108 potential respondents opted-out of the survey, and only 12 of the 346 total respondents partially completed the survey, hinting at a low dropout rate.

DOCUMENT, DOCUMENT, DOCUMENT!

I end my discussion of sampling and surveying academic bloggers with a note on the importance of documentation at every stage, from planning and implementation to data analysis. Throughout the survey, it was necessary for me to save, update, and organize all aspects of the academic blogger project. If I had handwritten notes during a meeting with a professor or graduate student, I made sure to transfer them onto a Word document, naming the file with the person I had conversed as well as the date. Any updates that I made on the online survey Web site I also saved in a spreadsheet or a document file. Furthermore, I organized all articles and literature review documents in a bibliography file, making their recall relatively easy as well as keeping them organized and accessible.

Although easy to shrug off or take for granted, the importance of documentation cannot be emphasized enough. The academic blogger folder on my laptop contains over 100 files including IRB documents, drafts of conference papers, drafts of the questionnaire, notes, lists of e-mails, and spreadsheets of bounced e-mails. Without proper documentation and organization, these many files would have easily become unmanageable, especially over the course of nearly two years of planning, implementation, and data analysis. Furthermore, the more documentation that goes into the front end of the study, the less work necessary when drafting papers, for many of these details will already have been written.

LESSONS LEARNED

The academic blogger survey provides a case study with which to understand how relatively elusive online populations can be rigorously sampled. Although difficult and time-consuming, *it can be done!* What follows is a list of the lessons that I learned while planning and implementing the survey along with accumulated wisdom from numerous Internet researchers, subsequent research on online populations, and tips from other scholarly resources.

1. Become immersed in your online population. Because online populations tend to change rapidly, you must keep abreast of related technological shifts in order to develop an online questionnaire that effectively measures an Internet-based sample. Likewise, a researcher aiming to survey any population using a Web questionnaire must understand the strengths and weaknesses of the mode through the eyes of their sample. For example, a population with a 50 percent Internet penetration rate should not be surveyed online. Furthermore, a researcher interested in surveying individuals either offline *or* online must understand the population of interest in order to craft survey questions that make sense to potential respondents (e.g., see Williams and Xiong in this volume).

2. Do not expect to generalize from a narrow sample to a broad population. You must understand whether or not the sampling frame honestly covers the population of inference. In most cases, it is better to admit that a sample does not include certain units than use it to account for a broader population.

3. Use characteristics of the online population of interest to help you sample the population. In the academic blogger survey, I relied upon a ready-made online list and used blogrolls as well to develop a directory of contacts. Other online populations and communities organize themselves in particular ways that may aid in the development of your sampling strategy.

4. Do not reinvent the wheel when designing your sampling methodology. Much has been written about sampling various elusive offline populations including homeless individuals (Burnam and Koegel 1988) and Native Americans (Ericksen 1997). Read up on commonly used offline sampling techniques, and think about how to apply these to your online population of interest. Furthermore, talk to experts who have experience designing sampling frames. These researchers will be invaluable resources to anyone with minimal background in designing a sampling methodology.

5. Exclude ineligible units from the beginning of the study. I took great pains to exclude ineligible units from the survey sample, yet 45 percent of respondents were found to be outside my operationalized definition of an academic blogger. If I were to do it over again, I would not have included bloggers that I couldn't identify outright as U.S. academics in the directory.

6. Use previously tested survey questions. There is a reason why some survey questions have been used year after year: they provide accurate results. All demographic questions should be founded on other, reputable surveys. Even when doing research on understudied populations (like academic bloggers), it is possible to draw on published survey questions. Doing your homework will make testing your own questionnaire much easier.

7. Aggressively test an online survey on pen and paper first. When you have a final draft, put it online and retest! Although you may want to test your survey online first, it is easier to get a "locked" print copy, transfer it online, and then make minor changes. It takes more time to update the online portion of your survey than it does a text-based version that can then be transferred online.

8. Keep in mind that an online survey of an online population may confuse an IRB accustomed to offline studies. Just as courts had to adapt laws originally written for "real life" to be relevant to cyberspace (Lessig 1999), IRBs have had to negotiate policies written for the protection of offline individuals to include the safety of our online personae. But it is not immediately obvious how online samples should be protected—especially when one considers that it's not possible in such instances to lock the data in a safe for five years. Be prepared for the IRB to ask questions that are difficult to apply to an online environment (for more on this, see Williams and Xiong in this volume). Hopefully, as studies administered online become more common, these kinds of challenges will diminish.

9. Be ready to answer respondents' questions. For the same reasons that you may have chosen an online survey mode in the first place—convenient, e-mail-based communication—potential respondents are likely to contact *you*. I received over 100 e-mails praising, commenting on, and complaining about the survey. Individuals informed me that they were ineligible units, gave me valuable constructive feedback on the questionnaire, and told me that they would like a copy of the results. In total, I sent nearly 125 personal e-mails to individuals on the list.

10. Document each step of survey administration. If employing an Internet survey, e-mails will have to be updated. Over 100 of the original 1,237 e-mail requests to take the survey were bounced back to me. People will be on vacation, servers will be full, and, unless you only send one request for participation (*not* recommended), you will need a record of these correspondences in order to update your sample's contact information and make sense of what you did at a later point in time. I recommend creating a spreadsheet early and using it often.

11. Expect technological difficulties. Because I chose to administer my survey using a third-party online subscription-based tool, I was tied to the abilities of this program. I was forced to update the Web questionnaire online, which turned out to be a slow and daunting task. It was necessary to keep track of and delete by hand all bounced e-mails because the service did not offer an option that would do this automatically. Furthermore, in the middle of data collection, the company changed the interface of its entire online service, making it necessary for me to relearn how to navigate the site while dealing with the random bug here and there.

12. Save, back up, and take detailed notes. I cannot stress the importance of saving files (and naming them something that you will remember!). Related to this, be sure to back up all of your files, especially those that only exist online such as the data that I collected using the online subscription-based survey tool. The more organization involved in the planning and implementation stages of a survey, the less work you will have to do during the data analysis and write-up portion of your study.

CONCLUSION

Researchers interested in using empirical methods of data collection online must develop sampling methodologies that allow them to generalize to their target population as well as accommodate their research questions. Many of the difficulties associated with sampling bloggers derive from the need to sample a constantly changing, Internet-based population. In an effort to encourage researchers to employ sampling techniques that are suited to both their population of interest and research questions, I have elaborated on my own experience surveying a particular online population. Although it may be impossible to accurately measure all units in an entire population, it is possible to develop a sample (or census) that successfully answers research questions developed for a narrow population of interest.

New, improved techniques for sampling people online will become increasingly necessary as social scientists aim to understand Internet-based communities. A researcher interested in learning more about online populations like MMORPG gamers (see the Williams and Xiong piece in this volume), social networking site users, as well as users of certain Internet sites and services must overcome many of the same problems that I faced when sampling academic bloggers. Researchers interested in surveying offline populations using an online instrument will also run into some of the same problems that I outlined in this piece. Although online communities possess characteristics that make them uniquely difficult to sample, many of the lessons that I learned in my research and that are presented in this chapter apply to researchers of both online and offline populations. In an online world devoid of telephone books, lists of mailing addresses, and concrete residences, rigorously sampling online groups remains a daunting but necessary task.

NOTES

The author is grateful to Eszter Hargittai for helping her with numerous aspects of the academic blogger study including comments on this chapter. She is also thankful to Peter Miller for providing helpful feedback on the sampling design and survey instrument.

1. The Web page has since been replaced by Henry Farrell's Academic Blog Portal wiki available at http://wiki.henryfarrell.net/wiki/index.php/Main_Page.

2. Throughout the chapter I refer to this list as a sample although it may be more accurate to call it a census of U.S. academic bloggers because I attempted to contact all individuals on the comprehensive list.

REFERENCES

Adamic, L., and N. Glance. 2005. *The Political Blogosphere and the 2004 U.S. Elections: Divided They Blog.* Paper Presented at WWW-2005 Workshop on the Weblogging Ecosystem. Retrieved April 20, 2009 from ilyagram.org/media/fetch/AdamicGlanceBlogwww.pdf.

Bosnjak, M., W. Neubarth, M. P. Couper, W. Bandilla, and L. Kaczmirek. 2007. Prenotification in Web-based Access Panel Surveys: The Influence of Mobile Text Messaging versuse E-mail on Response Rates and Sample Composition. *Social Science Computer Review* 26 (2): 213–23.

Braaten, A. 2005. The Great Canadian Blog Survey: A Snapshot of the Canadian Blogosphere in 2005. Electronic version. http://www.blogscanada.ca/down loads/TheGreatCanadianBlogSurvey.pdf.

Burnam, M. A., and P. Koegel. 1988. Methodology for Obtaining a Representative Sample of Homeless Persons. *Evaluation Review* 12 (2): 117–52.

Converse, J. M., and S. Presser. 1986. *Survey Questions: Handcrafting the Standardized Questionnaire.* Thousand Oaks, CA: Sage.

Cook, C., F. Heath, and R. Thompson. 2000. A Meta-analysis of Response Rates in

Web- or Internet-based Surveys. *Educational and Psychological Measurement* 60:821–36.

Couper, M. 2000. Web Surveys: A Review of Issues and Approaches. *Public Opinion Quarterly* 64 (4): 464–94.

Coupei, M. P. 2001. Web Survey Research: Challenges and Opportunities. Presented at the Annual Meeting of the American Statistical Association. Retrieved April 20, 2009, from www.amstat.org/sections/SRMS/Proceedings/y2001/Proceed/00639.pdf.

De Leeuw, E. D., M. Callegaro, J. J. Hox, E. Korendijk, and G. Lensvelt-Mulders. 2007. The Influence of Advance Letters on Response in Telephone Surveys. *Public Opinion Quarterly* 71 (3): 1–31.

Denscombe, M. 2006. Web-based Questionnaires and the Mode Effect. *Social Science Computer Review* 24 (2): 246–54.

Dillman, D. A. 2007. *Mail and Internet Surveys: The Tailored Design Method.* 2nd ed. New York: Wiley and Sons.

Drezner, D. W., and H. Farrell. 2004. Web of Influence. *Foreign Policy* 145:32–40.

Edwards, P., I. Roberts, M. Clarke, C. DiGuiseppi, S. Pratap, R. Wentz, and I. Kwan. 2002. Increasing Response Rates to Postal Questionnaires: Systematic Review. *British Medical Journal* 324 (7347): 1183–85.

Ericksen, E. P. 1976. Sampling a Rare Population: A Case Study. *Journal of the American Statistical Association* 71 (356): 816–22.

Ericksen, E. P. 1997. Problems in Sampling the Native American and Alaska Native populations. *Population Research and Policy Review* 16 (1): 43–59.

Faugier, J., and M. Sargeant. 1997. Sampling Hard to Reach Populations. *Journal of Advanced Nursing* 26 (4): 790–97.

Fogg, P., and R. Aronauer. 2005. Political-Science Professor with Well-Known Blog Denied Tenure; Florida State U. Lures Professor and Entire Research Center from U. of Wisconsin. *Chronicle of Higher Education* 52 (October 21): A8.

Fowler, F. 1995. *Improving Survey Questions.* Thousand Oaks, CA: Sage.

Glenn, D. 2003. Scholars Who Blog. *Chronicle of Higher Education* 49. Retrieved April 20, 2009, from chronicle.com/free/v49/i39/39a01401.htm.

Groves, R. M., F. J. Fowler, M. P. Couper, J. M. Lepkowski, E. Singer, and R. Tourangeau. 2004. *Survey Methodology.* Hoboken, NJ: John Wiley and Sons.

Hargittai, E. 2004. Academic Blogging Survey. Retrieved October 2, 2007, from http://crookedtimber.org/2004/11/19/academic-blogging-survey/.

Hargittai, E. 2007. College Students' Internet Uses Survey. Unpublished document. Web Use Project. Northwestern University.

Hargittai, E., J. Gallo, and M. Kane. 2008. Cross-Ideological Discussions among Conservative and Liberal Bloggers. *Public Choice* 134 (1–2): 67–86.

Harmon, M. A., E. C. Westin, and K. Y. Levin. 2005. *Does Type of Pre-notification Affect Web Survey Response Rates?* Paper presented at the American Association for Public Opinion Research Conference.

Herring, S. C., I. Kouper, L. A. Scheidt, and E. L. Wright. 2004. Women and Children Last: The Discursive Construction of Weblogs. In *Into the Blogosphere: Rhetoric, Community, and Culture of Weblogs,* ed. L. J. Gurak, S. Antonijevic,

L. Johnson, C. Ratliff, and J. Reyman. Retrieved April 20, 2009, from blog.lib
.umn.edu/blogosphere/women_and_children.html.

Joinson, A. N., and U. D. Reips. 2007. Personalized Salutation, Power of Sender,
and Response Rates to Web-based Surveys. *Computers in Human Behavior* 23
(3): 1372–83.

Joinson, A. N., A. Woodley, and U. D. Reips. 2007. Personalization, Authentica-
tion, and Self-Disclosure in Self-Administered Internet Surveys. *Computers in
Human Behavior* 23 (1): 275–85.

Kalton, G., and D. W. Anderson. 1986. Sampling Rare Populations. *Journal of the
Royal Statistical Society* (series A [General]) 149 (1): 65–82.

Kaplowitz, M. D., T. D. Hadlock, and R. Levine. 2004. A Comparison of Web and
Mail Survey Response Rates. *Public Opinion Quarterly* 68 (1): 94–101.

Kullin, H. 2005. BlogSweden 1.0: A Survey of Swedish Bloggers and Blog Readers.
Electronic version. http://www.kullin.net/blogsweden.pdf.

Lee, S. 2006. Propensity Score Adjustment as a Weighting Scheme for Volunteer
Panel Web Surveys. *Journal of Official Statistics* 22 (2): 329–49.

Lenhart, A., J. Horrigan, and D. Fallows. 2004. *Content Creation Online.* Washington, DC: Pew Internet & American Life Project.

Lepkowski, J. M. 1991. Sampling the Difficult-to-Sample. *Journal of Nutrition* 121
(3): 416–23.

Lessig, L. 1999. The Law of the Horse: What Cyberlaw Might Teach. *Harvard
Law Review* 113 (2): 501–49.

Li, D., and G. Walejko. 2008. Splogs and Abandoned Blogs: The Perils of Sampling Bloggers and Their Blogs. *Information, Communication, and Society* 11 (2):
279–96.

Miura, A., and K. Yamashita. 2004. Why Do People Publish Weblogs? An Online
Survey of Weblog Authors in Japan. In *Human Perspectives in the Internet Society: Culture, Psychology, and Gender,* ed. K. Morgan, J. Sanchez, C. A. Brebbia,
and A. Voiskounsky. Southampton: WIT Press.

Mooney, P. 2007. Chinese Dean Demoted over Blog. *Chronicle of Higher Education*
53 (March 30): A44.

O'Neil, R. 2004. Controversial Weblogs and Academic Freedom. *Chronicle of
Higher Education* 50 (19): B16.

Porter, S. R., and M. E. Whitcomb. 2005. E-mail Subject Lines and Their Effect
on Web Survey Viewing and Response. *Social Science Computer Review* 23 (3):
380–87.

Porter, S. R., and M. E. Whitcomb. 2007. Mixed-Mode Contacts in Web Surveys:
Paper Is Not Necessarily Better. *Public Opinion Quarterly* 71 (4): 635–48.

Presser, S., J. M. Rothgeb, M. P. Couper, J. T. Lessler, E. Martin, J. Martin, and E.
Singer. 2004. Methods for Testing and Evaluating Survey Questionnaires.
Hoboken, NJ: Wiley.

Rainie, L. 2005. *The State of Blogging.* Washington, DC: Pew Internet and American Life Project.

Read, B. 2006. Attack of the Blog: When Disenchanted Faculty Members Take to
the Web, Presidents Should Worry. *Chronicle of Higher Education* 53:A35.

Rothbart, G. S., M. Fine, and S. Sudman. 1982. On Finding and Interviewing the

Needles in the Haystack: The Use of Multiplicity Sampling. *Public Opinion Quarterly* 46 (3): 408–21.

Schonlau, M., Jr., R. D. Fricker, and M. N. Elliott. 2002. *Conducting Research Surveys via E-Mail and the Web.* Santa Monica, CA: RAND.

Schonlau, M., K. Zapert, S. L. Payne, K. Sanstad, S. Marcus, J. Adams, M. Spranca, H. Kan, R. Turner, and S. H. Berry. 2004. A Comparison between a Propensity Weighted Web Survey and an Identical RDD Survey. *Social Science Computer Review* 22 (1): 128–38.

Singer, J. B. 2005. The Political J-Blogger: 'Normalizing' a New Media Form to Fit Old Norms and Practices. *Journalism* 6 (2): 173–98.

Sudman, S., M. G. Sirken, and C. D. Cowan. 1988. Sampling Rare and Elusive Populations. *Science* 240 (4855): 991–96.

Technorati. 2008. Technorati. Retrieved August 20, 2008, from http://www.tech norati.com/.

Tourangeau, R., L. J. Rips, and K. Rasinski. 2000. *The Psychology of Survey Response.* Cambridge, UK: Cambridge University Press.

Tribble, I. 2005. Bloggers Need Not Apply. *Chronicle of Higher Education* 51:C3.

Trouteaud, A. R. 2004. How You Ask Counts. *Social Science Computer Review* 22 (3): 385–92.

Vaidhyanathan, S. 2006. Can Blogging Derail Your Career? The Lessons of Juan Cole. *Chronicle of Higher Education* 52 (July 28): B6.

HERDING CATS ONLINE

Real Studies of Virtual Communities

DMITRI WILLIAMS AND LI XIONG

The data-collection methods were real, even if the places weren't. So, when did we realize our research was going to be a little different? Was it the time when one potential research subject said to another, "Cry more, noob!" or the time we were accused of running a pyramid scam? Maybe it was when lawyers shut one study down. Or perhaps it was the time when colleagues passing by our office gave us the *Uh huh, sure you're doing research* look for the fourth time. We knew going into the work that this was "brave new world" territory, but we still didn't fully appreciate exactly *how* brave or *how* new. In this chapter, we will share our experiences and lessons learned in collecting data from online populations. In particular, we will walk through the process, describing the pitfalls of conducting systematic online research with that most difficult of quarry: the anonymous online gamer. And although our methods had to evolve with a changing world, we sought at every step to retain and translate all of the social science requirements that make a study valid and generalizable—to let rigor duke it out with messy reality.

The studies from which we draw these notes took place from 2002 to 2007, and all involved a type of online game known as a massively multiplayer online game, or MMO for short. If you have not seen one, imagine a table top *Dungeons and Dragons* session taking place online—with several thousand people all over the world. Millions of players now populate these games, spending about 24 hours a week online with each other rather than in front of a television (Yee 2006). That bizarre milieu of orcs, elves, accountants, housewives, and broadband connections is our workplace.

The source material for this chapter is based on three major studies that we conducted, each of which generated a large data set that led (or is in the process of leading) to publications in peer-reviewed journals. The first study came from Williams's dissertation and involved the MMO *Asheron's Call 2*. Despite the several ups and downs to be recounted here, that effort was productive (Williams 2002, 2003, 2006a, 2006b, 2006c, 2006d; Williams and Skoric 2005). The second study was a two-part test of *World of Warcraft* (*WoW*) users (Williams, Caplan, and Xiong 2007; Williams et al. 2006), and the third study is an ongoing effort with Sony Online Entertainment that we cannot talk about completely because of nondisclosure agreements (NDAs). No worries. We did not know what an NDA was in the beginning either. (It is a legal document that limits what you can say to people who are not associated with the project or company.)

So let us start at the very beginning. Let us assume that you are an aspiring graduate student or junior faculty member ready to jump into the world of online data collection. You have essentially three distinct phases to plan for. The first is the groundwork phase, which includes figuring out where the data will come from as well as dealing with various bureaucracies and culture clashes within the field. Having fought these initial battles, next comes the actual execution of the plan, including the sampling, recruitment, surveying, and general wrangling of the subjects. Last comes the analysis itself, which we will not cover in much detail since it is available in the papers cited earlier.

PLANNING: SEND LAWYERS, GUNS, AND MONEY . . .

Some social scientists are lucky enough to work with existing data sets. In those cases (e.g., see Freese in this volume), the challenges mostly involve the data not being exactly what is the most relevant or appropriate to their research questions. In our case, the data have almost always been what we wanted. The problems arose from having to justify the data collection in the first place. And here we faced three consistent major hurdles: complying with rules regulating the protection of human subjects, corporate relations, and political considerations.

You Want to Do What?

Institutional Review Boards are a cautious lot by nature. After all, it is their job to safeguard the public from our clipboard-carrying, white-lab-coat-wearing, electroshock-inducing, prison-experimental ways. So who can blame them for starting out with suspicion? Still, our problems were initially less about risk to subjects than about explaining what in the world we were trying to do. Some sample dialogue:

> *Researcher:* We would like to do some experiments on players within on-line games.
>
> *IRB Administrator:* Can we get a copy of the games? Form 17 requires us to have a copy of all audiovisual materials.
>
> *Researcher:* Well, the game is online, you see. I could give you a copy to try.
>
> *IRB Administrator:* Well, where is it going to be played?
>
> *Researcher:* It is online. You see, it's a lot like *Dungeons and Dragons.* Only there are thousands of people playing at once, and people use avatars.
>
> *IRB Administrator:* How will you get all of these avatars in your lab?
>
> *Researcher:* No, the people use avatars when they're online. So, like, the avatar could be an elf or something like that. Oh, and there might be children there. We aren't sure.
>
> *IRB Administrator:* (*long pause*) Um, yeah, can you come back next week? I need to talk to my supervisor about this.

Thus, our first step involved explaining the research, which does not fit into standard categories. We have tried explaining it by analogy, but that can be hit or miss. What it all boils down to is the usual key points of IRB approval: demonstrating minimal risks and informed consent, along with the protection of minors. The first two are relatively easy, but in an era where game playing triggers fears of a Columbine-esque meltdown, protecting children from their evils has become a serious point of concern. Interestingly, we had two very different experiences at two Research I universities. The main problem stems from the Internet's key feature: anonymity. If you cannot verify who the people are, how can you verify that you are including or excluding a particular type of person? After all, subjects can simply lie about who they are. Our advice is to do whatever homework you can about (1) the risks your test imposes and (2) the likelihood of children being present. And we found that interviewing and doing participant observation was the key.

Still, say you know that there will be children present and that you therefore need their parents to sign an informed consent document. How can you be sure that the parents will sign it? At the first university IRB, the administrators took the realistic approach. Knowing that we could not verify the age of the participants or their parents' consent, they granted us a waiver based on the minimal risk of our tests. At the second university, the administrators insisted that we get informed consent sign-offs, even though they knew we could not verify them. We found that the latter offered essentially no protection for subjects and could be explained only as simple bureaucratic rear-covering, but since we were doing something with no risk, we slept fine at night.

The moral of the story is that IRBs are still coming to grips with these approaches, and everyone's results are going to vary. The greatest asset for researchers in this regard is an investigation that poses no real risks to the participants. The essentials do not change online.

You Want Us to Do What?

Because online systems often involve a company operating for profit, working within those systems inevitably means considering a relationship with that company. The upside is that cooperation from the company can make a huge difference in the quality of the study. Imagine if you have the choice between asking people in a study what they did and simply *knowing* it as a result of having access to the company's own data about users' actions. You would of course always choose the latter both because subjects recollect things incorrectly and because they lie (sometimes to make you happy, sometimes due to social desirability, sometimes out of convenience). Online systems offer the possibility of collecting valuable unobtrusive behavioral data (Webb et al. 1966) that are typically much more reliable than what we gather offline in labs. To make it more enticing, a company with data can also derive a perfect sample if you can help lay out the right levels of analysis and stratifications. All you have to do is get its help; but this is precisely where many researchers start making mistakes. We have derived two important axioms from our own histories of mistakes and successes: understand the perspective of the company, and recognize the importance of networking.

Axiom No. 1: Understand the Company's Perspective. It is all very well and good to want to work with some company or agency, but let us be honest here: we essentially want something for nothing. Game researchers tend to approach companies with a cold call simply asking for help. Not only is this poor strategy, it is also borderline inconsiderate. Why exactly should company staffers spend time to help you? They have a boss and deadlines and time pressure of their own. What is in it for them, either individually or collectively as a company? Is it realistic to rely on the goodwill of these people and hope they will get a warm and fuzzy feeling from doing pro bono work? The games industry is famously time pressured. It has become cliché to observe that game developers work horrendous hours and are even known to keep sleeping bags handy at some shops. The working conditions have been bad enough to generate an outcry from the workers, especially at the larger game firms like Electronic Arts (Kline, Dyer-Witheford, and DePeuter 2003). So from the individual worker's perspective, an already overloaded and stressful schedule is an important factor for researchers to consider.

As for the company perspective, game development has changed radically over the past 20 years from garage-based start-ups to publicly traded conglomerate corporate firms. These firms are churning out terrific amounts of game content and manage very tight development schedules. Like most public corporations, they are utterly focused on quarterly progress. They do not think long term and rarely invest in research and development. Simply getting on their radar is difficult to do. And it gets worse: they can run the risk of leaking key business information by working with outsiders, like academics, who want to spread information rather than horde it.

Consider the case of the *Asheron's Call 2* study (Williams 2004). The goal there was to undertake the first longitudinal study of an MMO while also doing the first controlled experiment of any game. In brief, the study followed one group that played an MMO for the first time, along with a matched control group that did not play. Getting that set up required the help of the game's publisher, Microsoft. Through a series of meetings and talks (see Axiom No. 2 below for more on the importance of establishing contacts in the industry), Microsoft's game research division decided to help the project by arranging interviews and helping to sample the players. Over a year of discussions, we established a large study framework, constructed measures, and laid out a sampling scheme. And then . . . it all fell apart and that entire year of groundwork went *poof*. This was because the company decided one day that it would not help us anymore (you will see in a moment that it ended up working out). Outrageous, right? Well, to be honest, their sudden withdrawal of support was due to the researcher's failure to consider the company's perspective.

Many of the measures in the study involved "effects" research, which in media basically means, What impacts does it have on the psychological and social well-being of people? Many of these effects are potentially harmful. The most well known are aggression and violence. In the Microsoft case, the company's lawyers eventually heard of the study and realized that it could be very harmful to them. A large company like Microsoft is seen as having "deep pockets." They are consistently the target of dozens of lawsuits, ranging from the frivolous to the very serious. Now consider the position of a company that has engaged in research that potentially shows that one of their products might make someone hurt someone else, that is, the product is harmful. Suddenly, it is no longer a matter of a game company trying to make fun toys. It is the functional equivalent of the tobacco industry, producing a harmful product and sitting on evidence that proves it. The lawyers took one look at the measures and said good-bye.

Now, as it happens, the contacts for the research were both interested in the study and sympathetic to a year of lost time given in good faith. They immediately donated 400 copies of the game, which let them help from a distance. Those copies became the stimulus for the treatment group in a study conducted wholly outside the company. In the end, the total delay was only about one month, and we dodged a bullet. Lesson learned: if you want inside help, take the other party's needs and perspective into account.

Axiom No. 2: Networking Matters. At an undergraduate orientation session one of us attended, the organizers held a session on the importance of social networking. Meet everyone around you, they said. Remember their names. These people will not only be your friends and enemies during college: they will also be key business contacts after graduation. That otherwise unremarkable freshman might be the public relations representative you need to return your call some day. In retrospect, it is one of the most valuable lessons we have learned. As Granovetter (1974) showed, and as hundreds of social network studies have confirmed since then (Ruef, Aldrich, and Carter 2003), social networks really matter. This is no-brainer advice that everyone already knows, right? So why do researchers not use it? Perhaps academics find this approach distasteful. Colleagues with whom we have shared that anecdote have visibly cringed at its cold-bloodedness. But we are not advocating making disingenuous connections. We are advocating meeting people and listening to their concerns. If you want something, you should know the key people involved.

In our literally networked world, this may be a matter of navigating online spaces like LinkedIn, but we tend to think that the face-to-face route is more effective. Recognizing this, we began attending events where industry people would go, learning about them by reading industry journals and listservs. In our case, this meant small informal gatherings where developers get together as well as large industry events where developers go (Game Developer's Conferences). These events are often expensive, but they typically waive fees for speakers.

Attending these conferences (or whatever the equivalent is in your area of interest) accomplishes several other things. First, it enables you to meet people who can then attach a face to your name when you e-mail them later on. Second, it is a great source of insight and information about how the respective industries work, what their goals are, and what is of interest to them. The first steps in all of our collaborations grew out of conversations at industry events. These occurred variously on panels, on trade show floors, and at social events. In each case, the person from the company was interested in some aspect of academia, and the conversations evolved to cover possible collaborations down the road. It only takes one well-placed person to open the door in a company. That person is more common than one might expect; a surprisingly large number of workers are interested in thinking creatively about what they do and what the bigger picture is.

Finding those people and making a genuine personal connection based on mutual interest can lead to a solid connection later on. Just make sure to get (and have) a business card and to follow up before too much time passes. That connection might be more than a networking opportunity, too. After all, these people are often experts in their areas. In one project, we spent several days scanning through millions of lines of computer logs before a company rep told us that what we were looking at was a debugging log and nothing more. *Oops*. More back and forth with them pointed us to the correct files.

Getting the personal contacts of industry professionals, combined with some knowledge of their world, allows you to make use of something that every relationship should involve: reciprocity. The power of reciprocity is immense (Cialdini 1993). People will help you if you have a genuine interest in helping them. Not understanding this principle is why so many researchers fail to gain the assistance of companies. Calling game developers up out of the blue to ask for their help (and we have heard stories of whining and demanding) shows not only that you do not understand their world, but that you also have no intention of helping them in return. From the game developers' perspective, the motivating factors include the opportunities to make more sense of their existing data, figure out vexing usability problems, and capitalize on the pure PR value that comes from a company saying it is helping university X make the world a better place.

Quite often, the question for the games industry is not whether our calls are worth their time but whether what we want to know as social scientists is relevant to their marketing and computing work. For many game developers, there is no compelling reason to commit scarce resources to understanding the social behavior, psychological well-being, and community culture of their users. They want simple answers about why some people keep playing and others do not. As reciprocating partners then, an important task has been to build and demonstrate advanced, rigorous, and accessible tools that both help them understand who quits the game and why, and help us test our hypotheses. Inevitably, this has also meant each side trying to understand the motivations and lingo of the other.

What Are You Doing?

Our last consideration for planning is a purely political reality check. We haven't come across this consideration in research methods volumes but we think it is worth mentioning. If you are doing something wholly new, it is not only going to be hard to do, it is also going to be confusing to some, even many, people. Your project of blood, sweat, and tears may look like a dilettante's gambit or pure navel gazing to others. Or, it might be threatening to those whose success and worldview depend on the status quo in theory, practice, or topic. Recognizing that, you have to blend both patience and persistence. After all, science needs you to challenge its tenets or it stagnates (Kuhn 1962). But first, consider the possibility that you may actually *be* an arrogant know-it-all who disrespects the establishment for pure ego reasons (this is a bad thing). That is to say, stand on the shoulders of giants rather than chop at their knees. Second, consider that cutting-edge work is high risk/high return, and you really could be doing something crucial (this is a good thing), despite what an established person says. As long as you stick to what is both theoretically and personally interesting to you, you will be better off in the long run, even if some people think that what you are doing is nuts.

We have had senior peers tell us not only that ours were dumb ideas but that we should avoid them or else our careers would suffer. The important consideration in such cases is balancing personal integrity with political reality. The danger is in letting the "brash young researcher" approach overshadow the science. To foolishly call out some senior person (and PhD programs practically train us all to criticize for the sake of criticism) is to open the door to personal reprisals. And here is something that no young researcher understands fully for a few years: it (and this applies to your field, whatever it is) is a small field, and *everyone* knows *everyone* else. Moreover, everyone who knows you will be reviewing your papers, your grant proposals, your tenure case, and your job application. Stick to the science and studiously avoid the personal.

Another odd personal calculation comes from dealing with friends and family outside of the academy. All junior researchers are confronted with the challenge of explaining their work to a layperson. Our work on play practically begs to be not taken seriously. Are we not just screwing around with these games? We live in a society where play and work are treated as polar opposites, so in our case it has been nearly impossible to convince anyone that we have to play games to do our work properly. Each of us has a spouse who has looked at us skeptically more than a few times. The truth is that we do not actually play *as much* as we should. It is the only way to get an understanding of the true context of game playing, and it leads directly to better hypothesis testing, better overall methods, and even better question wording in surveys. But try telling that to our parents, mentors, and colleagues. On the other hand, it is also difficult to justify play as work to our fellow players, whom we often tap for research insights or to be pilot subjects.

DOING THE RESEARCH: WHEN SUBJECTS ATTACK

Traditional social science has always meant covering the basics, and that does not change online. What changes are the pros and cons of the online research environment as compared to offline "real life," or "RL" as gamers call it. The Internet has made some parts of the research very easy, and others extremely difficult. The following section covers the issues we have faced in finding and working with subjects.

Choosing and Motivating Respondents

In doing systematic research on a population, there are always things to shoot for: having a sampling frame as part of the total population, having the correct unit of analysis (Backstrom and Hursh-Cesar 1981) and understanding the trade-offs between different methods (Schuman and Kelton 1985). But there are no U.S. Census data for a virtual world, so drawing a random sample requires either a means of selecting people in a truly random fashion or having the assistance of a game developer. In the case of the ongoing Sony project, we had the company's cooperation and were able to draw a random sample of cases based on any number of variables, but this is a first as far as we know. In most cases, we have had to go it alone, which meant that we could not achieve a perfectly random sample. Thus, the convenience samples we did draw had to be as solid as possible.

In an interview project on *World of Warcraft* players (Williams et al. 2006), we aimed to interview a sample of subjects to understand their experiences in groups of various sizes. This meant having an understanding of the possible ways the population could be stratified. And it also meant actually understanding the game world and its culture. We knew we would never have a perfectly representative sample, so we did the next-best thing, which was to get data points from every possible stratum based on the data we could gather, and then bootstrap inferences about the population at the tail end.

We collaborated with a team of social network analysts who were interested in adding depth to their measures. Their team had developed a way to scrape basic network information from the game world by putting fake characters into the game world and having those characters observe and record who was where and grouped with whom. That gave us basic network maps and a baseline census of players as a starting point. Then, based on playing the game and talking to players, we realized that players should be further broken down by the following: the type of server on which they played, their character's race and class, how central they were in their social networks, of which faction they were a part, and whether they belonged to one of the many different slices of guilds as laid out by the fake characters' census. The resulting sampling frame gave us a list of everyone who had played the game in the past month and how they sorted into our various categories.

That was a basic interviewing project, which could as easily have been the sampling procedure for a survey. What about experimental designs? Consider the bulk of social science games research. The typical study takes place in a laboratory setting where subjects come in and play some game for about 30 minutes (Sherry 2001). This lab-based approach has the benefit of control and rigor. The experimenters can control precisely what the players see. The problem, of course, is that the players are keenly aware that they are in a lab and so are subject to the Hawthorne effect, that is, performing unnaturally because they know they are in a study. And they are probably all sophomore college students. Then there is the problem of the short duration. It has been our contention that a 30-minute exposure generalizes outside of the lab to a 30-minute effect, not something longer. We think that if you want to talk about long-term effects, you'd have to have long-term exposure. But here is the problem: once you get out of the lab you get naturalism and real results over longer time spans, but you also surrender control. We wanted to maintain as much control as possible to negate this problem.

So, using the second *Warcraft* study as an example, our goal was to run a controlled test of the effects of online voice (VoIP) using headset microphones and voice servers (Williams, Caplan, and Xiong 2007). Our best shot at control was to get a decent sample size and then make sure we were matching control and treatment groups as closely as possible. Normally, random assignment to condition covers this. We selected a sample of player groups (see below for the fun of recruitment) and then collected information about them in a survey. Then, based on that survey, we randomly assigned the groups to either a voice or nonvoice condition. But the groups are almost never perfectly even unless you have a lot of participants. And in our case, the unit of analysis was groups rather than individuals. So our unit of analysis led us to have to use a difficult statistical procedure (mixed linear models) to compensate.

Here are some further examples of small things with which we had to deal before they became large things.

We wanted the groups to start the stimulus phase at the same time to maintain control and avoid history effects, but they were not in our lab. In fact, they were all over the United States (yes, even in Alaska and Hawaii). How do you get people to start something all at once all over the country? Our solution in various projects has been to stagger the mailers (containing software, a headset, etc.) we have sent participants so that the people in faraway states get theirs mailed on day one, the people less far on day two, etc. We pretested mailers and mailing times to ensure that the staggering dates were working. Also, it is worth noting that the software, headsets, incentives, and mailing all cost money. We have lowered costs by using donated software, buying lighter mics, removing software from bulky boxes before mailing, and even bribing graduate students with pizza in exchange for stuffing envelopes. Each cost-saving step (e.g., pretesting our mailing packets at the post office) took extra setup work, proving that time still equals money.

Game players, like most research subjects, need an incentive. For our subjects (a very suspicious crowd, we assure you), our offers of money were met with skepticism and even derision (see below). In the *Asheron's Call 2* study, we used the game itself as the incentive since the goal was to find the overall effects of first-time play. Getting a $50 value in the form of a game box was enough to gather several hundred participants. In the voice study, the reward was the free headset and $40 for three waves of survey responses (roughly 15 minutes a pop). And in the current Sony project, the incentive to complete a survey was a virtual in-game item. But here is how you know that money is not everything: Nearly one-third of our 200 voice participants never cashed their checks, and we had difficulty finding takers in the first place. Yet for the Sony project, the promise of the "Great Sun-staff of the Serpent" was enough to get 10,000 players to take the survey within a day and a half.

If a virtual world (or a generic social Web site) works anonymously, any participant could have multiple identities. What's the unit of analysis then? Is it the identity, or the real-life person? Of course, it depends on whether the theory calls for a test of one or the other, but surveying identities is a lot easier than people. Without access to who goes with what identity/ies, you cannot even be certain about your unit of analysis. The inflation factor could be very small, or very large, and not knowing it makes us tentative about our conclusions when the real identities of subjects cannot be ascertained. When we have assigned people to a condition, we get the person, but when we go in blind, we are subject to this problem.

Finding the Subjects

Subjects from virtual game worlds can be recruited in several ways. Each of them requires particular strategies of perseverance and carries a unique combination of risks and rewards. Getting to know all of these is an exhilarating (but often excruciating) exploration of the world our subjects inhabit. At the same time, it is also a self-reflective process in which our relationship to the player communities is constantly rethought, and our research questions reevaluated.

In the voice project on *WoW* guilds, we were determined to recruit subjects on various official and unofficial online forums. After our formal requests for endorsement from the administrators of these forums failed to get any response, we decided to move ahead and post our own recruitment messages anyway. These messages contained a brief description of the project and directed readers to visit our project Web page to sign up. Despite all of our efforts at legitimating the project by offering real-money incentives, we were immediately labeled as scammers by the few gamers who responded to our threads. They threw back downright abuses, threatened to get us banned, or made fun of our incentives ("Can you make the payments in peach schnapps?"). We continuously replied to our own threads with faked answers to nonexistent questions simply to keep the threads alive, without much success in getting real attention and interest from the community. Several more sympathetic gamers offered advice, but such advice was more out of cynicism rather than the willingness to help. A gamer replied, "I feel sorry for the guy. As cool as it would be to do a dissertation on Gaming, especially on *WoW*, the community is sometimes not very forgiving and can be downright cynical." It was a point well taken, but we missed it. Worried that most potential subjects might never have a chance to see our threads, we went on a wild posting spree on all of the 100 or so forums on a daily basis on the game Web site. This brought us more responses from interested gamers but also dropped us into the worst category of netizens—spammers—and ultimately got our account banned in the official community of *WoW*.

Ultimately, it was social contacts and persistence with the game maker that made the difference. After nearly two months of e-mails and back-and-forths with legal departments, the company endorsed our posts as legitimate and "stickied" them to keep them in view. You might think that this would take care of the trolls, but it did not. We still managed to get a mixture of abuse, mockery, and cynical consolation. For example:

- "You call yourself researchers? Buahahahahahahahaha. . . . Take that dictionary, remove the dust carefuly, and look under paparazzi . . ."
- "He's been posting this in many forums for a long, long time now. You'd THINK said survey would be over by now, or they would have their people. I wouldn't trust it."
- "Why is U of I wasting money on a game study?"
- "Seems like it would be a little more plausible for you to use UI's database and website and have the link through there on their Speech Comm or who ever the survey's for website, that way the participants would know they ARE dealing with a UI study, and [not a] a shady 300 pound slurpy junky in his moms basement."

These are not the kinds of comments you get in a newspaper recruitment ad or even on a street corner soliciting subjects, and there is a fine line to be walked in dealing with them. Mostly, such posters are hecklers who should be ignored, no matter how strong the temptation may be to blast them. In our experience, the only time they were worth responding to were when they created misinformation about the study's process or goals that others appeared to have believed. Otherwise, feeding the trolls is a bad idea (Pujol 2006).

The unexpected difficulty in recruiting subjects from online forums shows the dilemma of researchers studying existing online communities. On the one hand, special-interest communities like these develop strong norms of language, behavior, and interactions that make involvement by outsiders difficult. To these communities, academics may as well be snake oil salesmen because they do not share a common set of interests, goals, and practices. Yet researchers often need to maintain distance and neutrality as part of the process, which can unintentionally alienate subjects (Bakardjieva and Feenberg 2001). On the other hand, researchers run a great risk of alienating potential subjects if they do not disclose enough information about the research. This trade-off between respectability and neutrality is difficult to manage since they risk the extremes of priming the subjects or alienating them.

Naturally, the risk of Hawthorne effects varies with the nature of the project. In our *WoW* interviewing project, all our recruitment invites were sent on the in-game chat channels and at times from an avatar actually visible to the invited subjects. We found that simply being "in the game" made a significant difference for how our team was treated by the game communities: they were much more willing to answer questions from a fellow orc waiting outside the in-game city bank than from a relatively cold message on a forum board. This approach was more effective not because it was more rewarding for the players but because the researchers were part of the scenery itself and had clearly taken the time to understand local norms and customs. Here again, playing the game proved invaluable.

Working with the Subjects

For lack of a better term, running online subjects is basically standard customer service—just with customers who can leave at any time without even looking you in the eye. The IRB stipulations on voluntary participation effectively grant them the right to opt out whenever they want, so researchers are left with little leverage in interactions with subjects. In the constant fear of losing one more case, we sometimes found ourselves sounding like desperate telemarketers, pleading, cajoling, and enticing the subjects not to hang up on us. While these rhetorical tactics did play a major part in our dealing with individuals during deep interviews, there were more appropriate approaches in other cases.

In our voice project with *WoW* guilds, all subjects were recruited with the help of their guild leaders, in a form of group snowball sample. We made these group leaders clearly aware of the nature, requirements, and incentives of the study so that they could inform their ranks and serve as a central point for contact information. Some complained that they had no control over their guild mates, but in most cases we found that guild leaders worked as opinion leaders, and that when they cooperated, their rank and file followed suit. It also helped us keep abreast of what was going on or going wrong with a particular group of subjects.

Throughout the project, we bore in mind that our subject groups were particularly volatile, so we tried to adapt to unexpected dropouts and other changes. When there were significant changes in a guild in the middle of the study period, we listened to the whole guild about its current situation. As our subjects were all over the world and from all walks of life, we have had subjects who were dislocated by Hurricane Katrina, deployed to Iraq, or experienced family loss. If the situation was assessed to have little effect on the data from the rest of the guild, we would raise the reward to encourage the remaining members to complete the study. To get these people and their guild mates online at 11:00 p.m. to answer questions like "how much do you like that gnome in your guild?" we felt the need to show a little more patience, consideration, and flexibility than usual.

The last lesson we learned was about feedback. Debriefing is always an ethical and important part of research but, as in the case of other forms of research, we found it was also an important way for us to learn. We built debriefing information and response fields into our post-test survey and gave everyone an e-mail for general comments. These comments continually helped us understand our data and the players' perspectives.

Running remote subjects has been a daunting and complex task, and in many ways harder than running a local lab. But although we gave up the tight control of that setting, we feel that we more than made up for it with the natural settings and higher-quality data that exist outside the lab. In nearly every facet, those data were made stronger by our knowledge of social context that we gained through play and by listening carefully to subjects before, during, and after the data collection.

Surveys That Work

The measures in an online experiment can be behaviors or hard results from the online space if you are lucky enough to be able to collect them. But more often than not, a survey is an important way of capturing demographic and psychographic information. And, if the design calls for a pre- and post-test, that means a repeated measures survey. This raises issues of duration, technical expertise, and question wording.

In most of our experiments, the design calls for surveys before the stimulus and then after it ends. We have still managed to make basic mistakes. One early and obvious lesson learned was that with only a pre- and post-test, there was no way to detect nonlinear outcomes; if the score at time one was 4 and the score at time two was 8, can we know what happened between the two times? The answer is: no, we cannot, and so we have started taking more repeated measures, especially for the week- and monthlong time spans that we are using in experimental designs. But that is an interpretive challenge. So, what about simply administering the questionnaires?

Running surveys online used to be a tremendous technical challenge, but there are now enough good tools out there that the challenge is now confined to the validity issues. The *Asheron's Call 2* survey measures required a complicated cgi-bin script that we would not wish on people we care about. Each page took about four hours of hand-coding that had to be perfect. Now there are professional tools like SurveyMonkey and its competitors that enable good-looking surveys that actually work. Our only real lesson learned from the "old days" (of only five years ago!) is that these things must be piloted for both language and technical mechanics. Using odd file types and transferring results and data between some proprietary formats, Excel, SPSS, and other tools is fraught with data-loss dangers. We have lost whole scales and the occasional subject simply through system errors. We now run a pilot from data entry all the way to analysis just for technical debugging.

The last challenge in the survey design has been learning how to ask the questions, and here is where we will beat the drum of social context one more time. In dealing with gamers, we have learned that they have their own language, shorthand, and culture, and that if we try to either (1) pretend we "get it" or (2) ignore it completely, our data will be unnecessarily noisy. We include a participant-observation step in every design we do now, and one of the main benefits is the way it helps us learn the right words to use. For example, we learned the importance of introductory framing statements in a pilot survey for *Asheron's Call 2*. Our question battery involved how much social support the players received, but it did not specify the source of that support. We wanted to know how much came from online friends, offline friends, and people who were both. We discovered that we had to preface a question with an orienting statement that made sense to them. A recent example with language adapted from the National Election Study was, "Now, thinking about the other real-life people in your guild, would you say that . . ." When we left that statement out, the responses mixed online and off for some, but meant only one of the two for others. In sum, we would have had useless data and would not have known it.

A FINAL THOUGHT: WHAT TO DO WITH THE RESULTS?

We find ourselves in the possession of data and findings on a "hot" topic. Studying something that is popular and part of the public's imagination is a double-edged sword for junior researchers like us. It could mean that our findings are the start of a brand new kind of research, or just the flavor of the month. Either way, there has been a genuine learning curve in dealing with both journals and public opinion.

For peer-reviewed journals, we think the bar for success has become generally quite fair. Editors have gone from being downright antagonistic about games research to actively interested. Five years ago, one editor of a media-focused journal wrote, "This is an interesting paper, but games are not media and so really have no place in [the journal]." This attitude has now largely disappeared among editors, though it seems still to lurk in the hearts of reviewers now and then. So be it. We hope we will remember to be open-minded some day when we are the old guard. What remains are good standards for peer review, and research on new topics should never get a free pass. The fact that developing new measures is difficult is never going to be a good excuse for delivering questionable data. So long as we armor ourselves with rigor and transparency, the rest will take care of itself.

What is a little more difficult to get a handle on is the crucible of public opinion. The results of our work have led to literally hundreds of articles in newspapers and magazines, and to radio and television interviews. This kind of coverage is both heady and dangerous, and we have learned a series of lessons here as well. First, the press will use facts and quotations as they like to fit into a frame that they already have in mind. This means that things we have said appear in strange contexts and are often put in conflict with things with which we do not actually disagree. This has no doubt led to some colleagues somewhere reading the coverage and wondering how we could have said such a thing. Caveat interviewee.

Second is the ego check once again. The research should be about the research, not the researcher. The good news (literally) is that press coverage is a rare moment for an academic to get findings out of the ivory tower and into real people's lives where they might make a difference or even affect policy. The reality check here is that research on new topics quickly becomes research on old topics. Studying "new media" means studying something different all the time. That means the work will always be interesting, but it also means that the methods will constantly shift. This year's MMO and avatar study will be next year's holography or some such thing, with a new set of validity challenges. Keeping the social science methods principles out in front and ready for adaptation is the only real advice possible in an age where change is the norm.

CONCLUSION

In sum, the basic lessons we learned about methods in graduate school still apply in strange online environments even though the details are all different. Yesterday's outlier may be today's haxor (cheater) or noob (first-timer). What is important is to translate the values and ideas into practices that fit the new environment. Sampling, ethics, control, and generalizability all remain, but they have to be used and considered in novel ways. Inevitably, these will involve mistakes and corrections. Step one in minimizing those mistakes is spending time in these spaces to learn the local norms and customs. Just as with more traditional areas of research, mistakes can be minimized with careful planning, pretesting, and by listening to the communities in question.

REFERENCES

Backstrom, C., and G. Hursh-Cesar. 1981. *Survey Research*. New York: John Wiley and Sons.
Bakardjieva, M., and A. Feenberg. 2001. Involving the Virtual Subjects. *Ethics and Information Technology* 2 (4): 233–40.
Cialdini, R. B. 1993. *Influence: The Psychology of Persuasion*. New York: Quill.

Granovetter, M. 1974. *Getting a Job: A Study of Contacts and Careers.* Chicago: University of Chicago Press.

Kline, S., N. Dyer-Witheford, and G. DePeuter. 2003. *Digital Play: The Interaction of Technology, Culture, and Marketing.* Montreal: McGill-Queen's University Press.

Kuhn, T. 1962. *The Structure of Scientific Revolutions.* Chicago: University of Chicago Press.

Pujol, J. 2006. *Structure in Artificial Societies.* Universitat Politecnica de Catalunya, Barcelona.

Ruef, M., H. Aldrich, and N. Carter. 2003. The Structure of Founding Teams: Homophily, Strong Ties, and Isolation among U.S. Entrepreneurs. *American Sociological Review* 68:195–222.

Schuman, H., and G. Kelton. 1985. Survey Methods. In *The Handbook of Social Psychology*, ed. H. Schuman and G. Kelton, vol. 1. 3rd ed., 635–97. New York: Random House.

Sherry, J. 2001. The Effects of Violent Video Games on Aggression: A Meta-analysis. *Human Communication Research* 27 (3): 409–31.

Webb, E., D. Campbell, R. Schwartz, and L. Sechrest. 1966. *Unobtrusive Measures: Non-reactive Research in the Social Sciences.* Chicago: Rand McNally.

Williams, D. 2002. Structure and Competition in the U.S. Home Video Game Industry. *International Journal on Media Management* 4 (1): 41–54.

Williams, D. 2003. The Video Game Lightning Rod. *Information, Communication, and Society* 6 (4): 523–50.

Williams, D. 2004. *Trouble in River City: The Social Life of Video Games.* PhD dissertation, University of Michigan, Ann Arbor.

Williams, D. 2006a. A Brief Social History of Game Play. In *Video Games: Motivations and Consequences of Use*, ed. P. Vorderer and J. Bryant, 197–212. Mahwah, NJ: Erlbaum.

Williams, D. 2006b. Groups and Goblins: The Social and Civic Impact of an Online Game. *Journal of Broadcasting and Electronic Media* 50 (4): 651–70.

Williams, D. 2006c. On and Off the 'Net: Scales for Social Capital in an Online Era. *Journal of Computer-Mediated Communication* 11 (2): 593–628.

Williams, D. 2006d. Virtual Cultivation: Online Worlds, Offline Perceptions. *Journal of Communication* 56 (1): 69–87.

Williams, D., S. Caplan, and L. Xiong. 2007. Can You Hear Me Now? The Social Impact of Voice on Internet Communities. *Human Communication Research* 33 (4): 427–49.

Williams, D., N. Ducheneaut, L. Xiong, Y. Zhang, N. Yee, and E. Nickell. 2006. From Tree House to Barracks: The Social Life of Guilds in World of Warcraft. *Games and Culture* 1 (4): 338–61.

Williams, D., and M. Skoric. 2005. Internet Fantasy Violence: A Test of Aggression in an Online Game. *Communication Monographs* 72 (2): 217–33.

Yee, N. 2006. The Demographics, Motivations, and Derived Experiences of Users of Massively-Multiuser Online Graphical Environments. *PRESENCE: Teleoperators and Virtual Environments* 15:309–29.

HOW TECHNICAL IS
TECHNOLOGY RESEARCH?

Acquiring and Deploying Technical Knowledge
in Social Research Projects

CHRISTIAN SANDVIG

As our five-hour trip entered its eighth hour, we were driving through a Midwestern blizzard on Interstate 94. I had borrowed a university motor pool subcompact that wasn't up to the job, and it slithered through the whiteout with the wipers on high, packed with jiggling cameras, microphones, laptops, and a solid-state recorder. My job was to drive, or at least to try to maintain some forward progress through the snow. My colleague was trying to call our next interview, who had agreed to find us a place to sleep. The cell phone alternated between no signal and no answer. It was late at night, and there was no other traffic.

I had my first government grant and a great sense of responsibility. Everything seemed to be riding on these visits. I arranged a three-state driving tour during Thanksgiving break to interview the most promising members of my sample: groups that build their own alternative communication systems. I was then following sixty groups, and the plan was to select the few that seemed to have produced something truly significant and were near enough to reach by car. We would visit them for a day to tour and photograph what they had built, and we would get them to explain how they did it. Thanks to my own overambitious timetable, we had high expectations, we were pressed for time, and we were short of money.

The next morning, in the bright calm after the storm had passed, we walked through a downtrodden residential neighborhood in parkas and snow boots, taking pictures and recording everything: the community center, the park, the condemned house, the abandoned car, and the wireless antennas. Our hosts worked in a local nongovernmental social services agency, and they knew just what we wanted. No doubt they had been called upon to give this tour many times—certainly a representative from each of their various funders would have wanted one. Looking back on the interview transcripts, I see now that they knew just how to package their work for our research: the tour leader had a doctorate, and in fact everyone in our party had a graduate degree.

The person I will call Dr. Gunn led the project, and he explained all of the good the project had produced. In short, they had built their own wireless communication system for the community, and it had made a difference. But in addition to broad statements about educational opportunity, new jobs, and better quality of life, he also had vivid anecdotes of success. Better still, his stories were fresh, and his technical approach was unusual. If it worked here, it looked well worth replicating elsewhere. It was everything I hoped to write about. I was excited.

Gunn didn't concern himself with the technical aspects, so he turned us over to his employee Veronica, who held a graduate degree in information systems engineering. Information technology infrastructure itself is not usually much to look at—it is typically just a bunch of beige boxes. Nonetheless, I still asked to see parts of the communication network in operation. After some initial ambivalence, Veronica agreed. She led us up ladders, through crawl spaces, and across rooftops to show us how the network functioned. Then it happened: the moment when it all unraveled.

On the top floor of the community center that controlled the wireless system, we walked through a utility closet to get to the roof, passing by a communications patch panel. This was a CAT5 patch panel for telephone and Ethernet, and it looked like they all do: a jumble of color-coded wires and blinking LEDs. We stopped in the corridor for a moment to position the ladder and to try to get the heavy roof hatch open. Since we had stopped, I asked a technical question about how the signal for their network traversed the panel—my question was at the outer limit of my own technical expertise. After I heard Veronica's response, I looked more closely at the panel and noticed that what seemed to be the appropriate section of the rack had no lit LEDs. I asked her about it. She came back to the panel, opened the clear plastic cover, and looked at the racks more closely; then she became more and more nervous. She fished out one prominently dangling black patch cable and plugged it into a port. Soon the dark section was a sea of twinkling green LEDs, just like the rest.

THE PATCH PANEL: THE VALUE OF TECHNICAL KNOWLEDGE

Without a little technical knowledge, this moment has little significance. But what I knew about the technology made me jump. I quickly thought to myself, "How long has that cable been unplugged?" "Why didn't the users complain?" "Why didn't anyone who works here notice before I did?" "What kind of network is unplugged without anyone noticing?" I had to admit that the answer to the last question was, "one that doesn't get much use." That patch panel was the turning point for the visit. The project we were excited about existed only as an idea.

Through careful questioning, we eventually unraveled all of the initial claims that had been made about the project. We had thought it was a project for 200 homes. Then we thought that this was a pilot project for 20 homes that would provide expertise for a larger project with 200 homes. Then it turned out that 20 homes was the "recruiting goal." While the point of the project was to provide Internet access for people who would not otherwise have access to it, all of the users already had access to the Internet through some other means. The few people who had signed up had also quickly dropped out, even though participation was free. After another hour of talking, a team member finally admitted that the elaborate community-wide wireless system currently served just one house. (And that house, apparently, didn't use it enough to complain when the network was unplugged, so no one had noticed that the network was shut off.)

As I reflect on that visit, I feel sure that I would have come away from that project site with a dramatically different view if I hadn't looked carefully at that patch panel. The question I asked about the patch panel owed a big debt to serendipity, to be sure. I don't know what made me think to ask about it, and if I had come on another day the uplink cable might not have been unplugged. Beyond chance, I was also able to ask about it because I knew what a "patch panel" was, I knew how to read the LEDs on one, and I knew just enough about network engineering to be able to ask a network engineer comprehensible questions about routing and backhaul distribution to a wireless network.

This technical knowledge saved me from quite a bit of professional embarrassment. Let me say that Dr. Gunn and Veronica weren't liars; they were very careful that their statements were *factually* true. They were in the business of helping people in a neighborhood that needed a lot of help, and this high moral ground and their own enthusiasm for the project probably led them to present the best possible picture to researchers. They knew that if I produced any peer-reviewed research that cited them as a success story, they could almost certainly convert this citation into more grant money for the project. This "success story" case study is plausibly the article I would have written. By saying this, I don't mean to suggest that Gunn and Veronica are special or corrupt in any way but simply to highlight the transaction that is always in play whenever a social scientist is writing about grant-funded public interest projects, or lending her name to what is sometimes called "evaluation research."

Through careful questions, multiple interviews, and long-term engagement with their project, I may have been able to find out some of what I know now without knowing about the patch panel. Maybe a user (or is it "the" user?) would have sought me out and whispered, "this thing doesn't work for s——t," as happened when I visited a different project on this same tour. Yet the patch panel moment still seems important. By knowing the architecture of their specific network and knowing about the significance of a pattern of lights on a piece of hardware, I knew a crucial thing about their project that they would not have told me. Namely, I knew that it was turned off. This situation led to a whole series of questions that otherwise would not have been raised.

In this chapter I want to discuss that technical knowledge and how I came to acquire it. As a social researcher studying technology without a technical degree, I have spent a long time worrying about technical knowledge. When I was a graduate student, I often feared that I would be unmasked by my interlocutors or colleagues as a fraud. I feared the question that a relative recently asked a friend of mine at a family reunion: "That's what you do? But what do you really know about technology?" (My friend was a social researcher.)

NEW TECHNOLOGIES AND NEW RESEARCH PROBLEMS

Although the research project just described in the introduction was based on the qualitative methods of open-ended interview and ethnographic participant observation (Dr. Gunn's field site was based on interviews only), the issue of technical knowledge is consequential for researchers studying technology using any method. It is easy to believe that a survey researcher writing a questionnaire to measure computer skills would do a better job if the researcher was very skilled at using computers. It seems plausible that an econometric analysis of firm behavior in the semiconductor industry would be better if its authors knew a lot about how semiconductors are produced.

My own research is about communication technology, and it is multi-disciplinary, bridging the areas of law, communication, and science and technology studies (STS). But any researcher who has considered a technology-related project has encountered some form of "the technology problem" that I address in this chapter. My colleagues in communication, sociology, economics, anthropology, political science, and other fields have conducted their own research studies about online communities, e-commerce, blogging, and cellular telephones, and I wager that they have also wondered about the role of technology in these essays.

There is one particular area of scholarship specifically directed to the social scientific study of technology—sometimes called "technology studies"—and it developed from the flowering of science and technology studies in the 1980s (for a review and introduction, see MacKenzie and Wajcman 1999).[1] In addition, there are increasing numbers of studies of technology in all sorts of fields. Some of these are motivated by new developments in information technology (e.g., for a review of the Internet's consequences for several fields of scholarship, see Nissenbaum and Price 2003). The social sciences are awash in what Lewis Mumford and Patrick Geddes have called *technics*.

Despite all of this work on technology, when I was a graduate student I didn't know how to proceed when I wanted to start studying a technological area. If I wanted to write a social science dissertation about the Internet (my first attempt at a topic), how much did I need to know about how the Internet works? I wondered, "Do I need to be able to program my own Web browser or just know how to use one?"

It is true that the problem of acquiring specialist knowledge applies to any researcher: research itself could be defined as the acquisition of specialist knowledge. Any successful dissertation or research project involves finding out a lot about a very narrow topic, not just a study of technology. Yet studying technology has always seemed to me to present unique problems beyond research generally. I will focus on two problems that have always bothered me.

First, all of research is filled with what linguist and sociologist Basil Bernstein has called "restricted codes"—speech that is "played out against a background of assumptions common to the speakers" (1964, 60). I know it is part of my job as a researcher to learn to get inside these codes that are relevant for my chosen topic. But technology jargon, unlike the vernacular of a street gang, is often elaborated somewhere.[2] That is, you can look it up in places like technical reference books and Web sites. Indeed, there may already be university courses about it. This has always presented me with a time management problem. As a beginning social researcher who wanted to study technology, I often wondered if I should really be taking courses in engineering instead. "Maybe I'm in the wrong degree program," I worried.

Second, studying new technology can feel very risky. Certainly good research usually feels risky (see Richards 1986), but because little is presumably known about new technology, it is often hard to say which technological features will have lasting importance. It can be quite difficult to know what to do with technical knowledge even if you have a sufficient amount of it, as it separates you from other researchers in your field unless they happen to be studying your particular technology. This problem is more acute in studies of new technology than for other areas of research. For instance, the popular currency of new and controversial developments in technology (e.g., see Lightman, Sarewitz, and Desser 2003) routinely propels graduate students to begin projects that may be beyond the experience of their advisers or dissertation committee members. Yet if you succeed at a risky study of a cutting-edge technology, you can reap great rewards. While I was a student, I asked a faculty member to advise my undergraduate thesis, and he asked me skeptically in response, "Why do you think this [sarcastic tone] '*World Wide Web*' is so important?" (It was a question I did not answer to his satisfaction. Ultimately, he declined to advise my thesis.)

I do not have the solution to these problems, and to some degree they continue to trouble me. Still, I am going to use this opportunity to present some of my research experiences and my own particular responses to the problem of technical knowledge. My first step has been to recognize that everyone working in a technical area has these kinds of problems.

KNOWLEDGE "IN SOME CASES SUPERIOR"

As a student, I read fantastic scholarly books about technology like Thomas P. Hughes's history *Networks of Power.* These were inspiring, but like book-length scholarship in many research literatures, they often gave no clue as to their methods. To solve my confusion, I turned to reading about research methods (like this book), but I often found formal methods handbooks to be terrifying. For instance, the qualitative methods literature sets a very high standard for what sort of domain-specific knowledge a social researcher ought to have when studying a technical topic. Methods textbooks straightforwardly direct that "good ethnography" in the area of technology requires that "the ethnographer develops near native competence in the technical aspects of the science and technology involved" (Hess 2001, 239). *The Sage Handbook of Ethnography* states:

> The standard of near native competence does not mean that one necessarily could pass, for example, a general doctoral exam that covers a wide variety of subfields in, for example, biology. Rather, the technical competence of the fieldworker tends to be narrow band—limited to specific subfields—where one's control of the literature is equivalent to that of the experts, and in some cases, superior to it. . . . This is a high standard that often requires years of research. (239)

It doesn't seem like the social researcher is getting away with much! I imagine few students perusing the *Handbook* before their fieldwork are very relieved to find that they should "only" aim to best their informants in *some* technical and scientific areas, and not in all of them.

The need for this domain-specific knowledge is also scary because it isn't clear exactly how you should go about acquiring it. I never know how much time in a given research project should be devoted to learning domain-specific technical knowledge. When I spend time reviewing the literature, I am not sure if I should be reading the trade and technical literature or reading more in the social science and theory about related technologies (themselves often quite technical). Any one choice could absorb all of the time I have available.

I found my first great source of relief from these worries when I discovered that some authors admit that they have these problems, too. A variety of these experiences can be found in nooks and crannies of the anthropology of technology, and science and technology studies literature, for instance. Writing about himself, Collins candidly admits that

> [he] has some thirteen hours of tape recorded interviews . . . on a theory of amorphous semi-conductors which he is quite certain he does not

understand, in spite of the knowledge of technical terms and acquaintanceship with the literature which were developed over a long period of interaction. (Collins and Pinch 1982, 21)

Similarly, in the classic *Laboratory Life*, Latour and Woolgar (anthropologist and sociologist) describe the experience of trying to read articles in a related technical journal while performing an ethnographic study of a lab. They wrote: "Many of the terms were recognisable . . . the grammar and the basic structure of sentences was not dissimilar to those he used himself. But he felt unable to grasp the 'meaning' of these papers" (Latour and Woolgar 1986, 75).[3]

In Woolgar's phrase, "the fact that all our analyses are essentially flawed is better celebrated than concealed" (1982, 494). In my own research, I have not usually had the space to elaborate at great length on my methods and their failings. In the area of communications technology and policy, personal reflection or autoethnography is discouraged. But my point here is that even those who do not belong to a school of writing that allows you to admit these moments of confusion are likely to find that it helps a great deal to read others who can.

CREDENTIALING SOCIAL RESEARCHERS IN TECHNICAL TOPICS

Clearly one important goal for a researcher starting out in a technology study is to be sure that the results are not wrong because of some sort of technological misperception. One response to this problem of technical ignorance is to study up before you begin. Attaining the appropriate extra degrees and credentials when you do technical work has always been an attractive solution to me because I sometimes hope that some additional credential would put to rest a nagging impostor syndrome. (As I commented previously, I have always feared the question, "but what do you really know about technology?")

Whenever I considered getting extra degrees and credentials, I would daydream heated academic conference debates that would end with me saying something like, "well, I *do* have a master's degree in computer science!" or "well, in fact I *am* a member of the federal bar."[4]

I never got those credentials, and I now see that those daydreams just are not very plausible. While a technical degree can give you an entry into a professional community or a restricted code, heated debates are not concluded by stating credentials. I will not rule out technical credentials as a strategy, but my own experience shows some of the difficulties with them.

My work is multidisciplinary. My research on Dr. Gunn and others like him is grounded in three fields: (1) communication, (2) law, and (3) science and technology studies. Working in and across these three specific disciplines has made it plain to me that a great miscellany of educational approaches has evolved in the subfields that study technology. Many of these approaches are premised on strange and unworkable assumptions.

Take the study of law as an example. Lawyers, as a group, are enamored of credentials—it is a crime to impersonate an attorney. While there are many technological areas in the law, the area of intellectual property is perceived to be the most technical, and within intellectual property law, patent work is the pinnacle. To work in intellectual property law, a bachelor's degree in any scientific or technical subject is recommended, and some bar association newsletters and career guides suggest that the aspiring lawyer consult the list of approved degrees issued by the patent office.

Even though the list of degrees is intended by the patent office to represent fields that produce patents, the law profession uses the designation in a more general way to suggest technical credentials to anyone interested in intellectual property law (see U.S. Patent and Trademark Office 2004, for the list). That means that in vernacular legal education, students are thought to acquire something in a scientific bachelor's degree that will transfer to any other scientific or technical field. If a student follows the patent office guideline, then the BS in integrative biology specializing in applied animal behavior, the BS in materials science specializing in ceramics engineering, and the BS in physics all essentially serve the same function—to qualify them to think about intellectual property. If their résumés are any guide, intellectual property lawyers often do not work in technical areas that have to do with their technical credentials.

The patent office list wears its science and technology politics on its sleeve, noting that "the following typify courses that are not accepted as demonstrating the necessary scientific and technical training: anthropology . . . behavioral science courses such as psychology and sociology, . . . courses relating technology to politics or policy" (U.S. Patent and Trademark Office 2004, 6). So, for the field of law, while botany and computer engineering both convey a kind of transferable technical-ness, social science does not. This means that of my three-part multidisciplinary research, the legal answer to my question would be that I should absolutely obtain a technical or scientific master's degree before working on technology topics.

Another discipline I identify with is science and technology studies, and technical qualifications have made their way into technology studies programs as well. For example, some undergraduate and graduate programs in STS have a "technical depth" requirement. One BS in Science and Technology Studies requires 8 courses in philosophical, social scientific, and historical perspective and 12 courses in science, engineering, and mathematics, while another BS can only be pursued as a second degree program with a science or engineering major.[5] Although there are few graduate programs in STS, they often encourage earlier degrees in a science and technology related major. Increasingly, the STS answer to my question is then probably that I should get a technical degree.[6]

Other fields have never embraced technical credentialing. My PhD is in communication. A communication researcher (or a sociologist, anthropologist, or economist) studying technology at any level is unlikely to find any technical coursework requirement, even within a declared emphasis like "sociology of technology" or "communication technology."

This situation can lead to paralyzing anxiety for new researchers. It is unlikely to be clear if technical preparation is necessary, or even what ought to be studied. Academic research is a world that revolves around the formal diploma, yet even with a scientific or technical credential in hand a social researcher is likely to still feel inferior when participating in a technical debate or studying a well-educated community of technically trained informants. Even after securing important background knowledge, respect will still go missing. Telling a PhD in a scientific field that you have a BS in that field might get you somewhere, but not to parity.

Although two of my three multidisciplinary homes encourage credentialing, I have found instead that strategic ignorance is far more useful in my own work. That is, I have been happy to be an outsider, and even though this means I make technological mistakes, I use them to learn. While time should be spent studying up on the technical, there is no guarantee that technical knowledge gained in advance will be of much help later. That is why I try to learn all I can about the technology I am studying from my informants. I am wary of technical degrees because they seem unlikely to address my specific research interest or motivation. Using studies of patents, industrial economists once estimated that every year from 5 to 15 percent of all recently acquired technical knowledge that seemed valuable will never be used again (Bosworth 1978). In my own area, communication technology, consultants tell CEOs that they should estimate the useful lifespan of any particular technological skill as two years (Varma 2005).

UNDERPREPARED AND INSECURE

I don't have any technical or scientific degrees. I have always had an interest in computers, and I taught myself how to program them, with some help from my father and my college roommates. I later became good enough at it to work as a programmer, but this is the extent of my technical experience. When I started my first large research project after my dissertation it was to be about nontraditional and "grassroots" communication infrastructure. I was fairly sure that my practical experience with computers would help me, but I was wrong.

Like the *Handbook* quoted earlier, the methodological essays that focus on my own subfield of interest (communication technology and infrastructure) have sometimes urged academic researchers to be just like engineers: to build their own computer networks or to at least enter into detailed technical conversations with system designers that aim to shape technical characteristics of computer networks (Harrison and Stephen 1999, 237). Half of my dissertation committee was technically credentialed in some way, and a few prominent social scientists in my area of technology research (communication technology and public policy) are technically credentialed as well.[7] The main result of this background was that when I spoke to my interlocutors during fieldwork, I often felt unprepared, and I worried that at any moment I might be unmasked as a dilettante or amateur. This happened even when (later on) I knew all about the technical aspects we were discussing.

At first, the more I started to learn about my new chosen research topic, the more worried I became. Undefined acronyms multiplied through my notes like virulent weeds. Since my research was about "wireless computing" and I knew something about computing, I hoped my expertise would be of help, but the subdomain of wireless turned out to have almost nothing to do with computer programming. I could write a computer program, but my discussants sometimes had a background in radio frequency (RF) engineering. The material I came across related to computing was all about routing algorithms and protocols, something that I had no experience with.

I spent some time finding my feet. First, I realized that since I was studying the newest of the new, I needed a way to stay up-to-date on new developments so that I could be a more competent interviewer. I figured this out when one of my interviewees asked me what I thought of a wireless product that had been released just the week before. He referred to it by acronym, and I had no idea what he was talking about. I was surprised to find that he expected me to know what he meant and to have an opinion. I used a news clipping service to solve the first problem. A clipping service now automatically sends a daily list of news stories that contain the technical terms that are of concern to me (later, this service became available for free from Google).[8]

Next, I looked for books that matched my lack of expertise. Although some of the things that I wanted to understand for my research were current general debates in the technical literature of network engineering, I had to work my way up. I started instead by reading how-to guides for practitioners that dealt with specific problems, such as the O'Reilly guides (see Gast 2002).

Finally, I started reading blogs and visiting online communities related to the interests of my participants. Any domain of technology is likely to have an associated blogosphere. This gave me a big benefit over ethnographers from years past: a sampling of the right blogs represents an informal version of an elite technical discourse, but they are written down and relatively easy to obtain. Commentary on blogs doesn't define terms or explain them, but it does tell you what developments in a rapidly changing field of endeavor are worth paying attention to.

All of this discussion has been about preparation, but what is to be done at the specific moment in the field when your interlocutor says something that you don't understand? Even though it is sometimes painful, I think that humility along with an admission of ignorance is the best route. At first I thought that if I didn't know an acronym or have an opinion on a new technical debate that my interlocutors would lose respect for me. On the contrary, one benefit that social researchers have is that in the transaction that is social research, technological populations are often happy to be studied, and to our interlocutors this demands only that we social researchers know about social science.

Let me explain in more detail. Just as Dr. Gunn wanted to show off his project to make it more likely he would receive grants in the future, even technocrats far outside the evaluation research and grantmaking sphere are often happy to be studied. Aside from Dr. Gunn, I also visited a group of antiestablishment technology activists. This group built their own communication systems in part by stealing from established systems in a variety of ways. Some of them could be quite difficult to work with. For instance, a few of them went only by pseudonyms and refused to be recorded. Some wouldn't sign consent documents with their real name. Even though this group had no hope of ever getting a government grant, having an attached social researcher was valuable to them in a way similar to that of Dr. Gunn. It legitimated the group, and it proved to the members that they were doing something important. In short, they wanted to be studied.

To live up to their expectations, I didn't have to have any technology expertise, I just had to know how to study it. My technologist interviewees certainly didn't expect me to have knowledge "in some cases superior" to them—for if I did, why would I be following them around asking them questions anyway? I also learned to recognize my role and to see that when dealing with technologists, my esteem was a kind of currency I could trade with them. When I speak to research participants working in a technical area, I spend this currency when I act in ways that reassure them that their technical work is important.

THE ADVANTAGES OF IGNORANCE

My lack of preparation became an advantage once I began to treat the technical knowledge embedded in my data analytically. That is, one year into the project I finally figured out that a coherent subset of my respondents were in the same boat that I was in. While people like Veronica and Dr. Gunn may have been way ahead of me in their knowledge of the technological systems I was studying, since we were all working on an area of very new technology, everyone was constantly learning.

Thinking about my own deficits provided a point of entry to interview questions and research about technical skill itself. If as a researcher I want to study the phenomenon of open source software (see Weber 2004), I should ask the question: how do people get to be skilled and accepted participants in open source software?

In new and multidisciplinary areas of technology this can uncover a surprising wealth of new ideas and research directions. To take just one minor example, in the course of one conversation I was stunned to find that all of my interlocutors had the same worries that I did. In the area of wireless communication technology, some technologists that I interviewed were moving from wired communications to wireless, and they constantly felt inadequate. They were worried about that same question, "What do you really know about technology?" Others had experience in radio but felt un-prepared in the area of computing. Still others had experience in comput-ing but felt unprepared in radio. Another one wanted to work on the busi-ness side of wireless, but he saw his technical degree (instead of an MBA) as a big liability. A programmer wished he could work "closer to the ma-chine" at a different level of abstraction that he did not (yet) understand.[9]

I am far from the first to mine the resource of my own technical igno-rance. A number of famous studies of science have used a technically unin-formed person as an analytic model to understand what is going on during their fieldwork (see Lynch 1982, 506–9; Latour and Woolgar 1986, 43–90). This is a version of the "anthropological stranger" familiar to any reader of anthropological work. In it, "practical disability is turned to methodologi-cal advantage, and it becomes a resource for critically examining the taken-for-granted practices which make up . . . ordinary work" (Lynch 1982, 509).

My learning process was the same as that described in the literature. As one example from science and technology studies states,

> the social researcher . . . entering a new domain initially understands neither the banter nor the technical terms pertaining to some new piece of science being investigated. After a painful period the inferences in others' conversations start to become clear and eventually it becomes possible to begin to join in . . . what were once "interviews" then be-come "conversations." (Collins 2004, 128)

The important thing about this process for me was the need to stop and question the "taken-for-granted practices." It would be entirely possible to learn all about wireless networks without pausing to reflect on why some things were "normal" and some things were "problems."

Unless technology studies students are instructed to take science and technology classes with an outsider's mentality, requiring credentials or coursework from them is depriving them of this experience. In a technical project, "being able to claim prior membership in the field can open many doors, but not without also adding special burdens. . . . the question of po-sitioning sometimes shifts from figuring out how to get in to figuring out how to get out" (Downey and Dumit 1997, 28).

To return to one of the fields that most evokes debate about the value of technical knowledge, let us again consider science and technology studies. While some scholars in science studies are scientists and some are not,

Collins writes, "practicing scientists are not, in virtue of their scientific knowledge, noticeably better sociologists of their respective domains than those who have not practiced the science" (2004, 128).

If sociologist scientists are not "noticeably better" than nonscientists in science studies, this begs the question of what role, exactly, technical knowledge plays in carrying out a social research project on a technology-related topic. Rather than "knowledge" and getting enough of it, the crucial thing seems to be what Downey and Dumit (1997) above called "positioning." Successful scholars of technical topics may or may not be technically trained, but they all need to know how to identify the audience for their research and learn to position themselves with respect to this audience. In the social sciences, this is an audience of social researchers. In every study of technology I have to get "inside" or "close" enough to have some connection to the new artifacts and practices that I want to study, be they blogs, wireless systems, or software. But to succeed I have to learn about the technology while still staying far enough "outside" to write articles that appeal to social researchers. To further explain this idea of positioning yourself with respect to your audience, I will consider what it is that audiences want out of new technology research.

POSITIONING: ". . . NOW THIS IS WHAT YOU SHOULD TELL THE GOVERNMENT . . ."

The word *technology* used to be interchangeable with the phrase *the useful arts* (Cowan 1997, 204). I always wanted to study technology topics in my own research because I wanted my work to be useful. There are many ways that this can happen in as many kinds of scholarship. If my findings helped anyone think interesting thoughts about my topic, that would be useful and I would be satisfied. Yet the study of new technology itself adds a pressure to be useful that nontechnological research projects do not share. It is not just that I want my research to matter to someone, but also that if I am studying technology—especially *new* technology—it is a safe bet that many audiences will expect a kind of usefulness that I cannot offer them. I will try to explain what I mean here by using another situation in my own research as an example.

As mentioned earlier, Dr. Gunn and Veronica needed my research because a favorable peer-reviewed article could be converted by them into more funding for their project. That kind of possible transaction is one way that research can be useful. In addition, in social scientific studies of technology most readers relate to the technics under discussion in a number of important ways that differ from other kinds of claims to usefulness.

For studies of widespread consumer products, in the simplest case there is the relation of the reader as user of the technology. As a graduate student, when I first presented some of my research findings about wireless communication at academic conferences, some of the responses I frequently received included "I don't do that" or "My wireless network doesn't work that way." The first response is common to all social research.[10] But the second response is telling.

People look to a study of technology to find out how their own technological objects work, as well as how they (or society) work. Ideally, the reader of an article on technology expects or requires some nuggets of technological explanation alongside whatever other goals the research might have. People hearing about my research on wireless networks, I found, often wanted to relate it to their own upcoming technology purchases or their recent problems configuring their own wireless networks.

More important, the ideas and findings presented in social research about an area of technology where little is known have the possibility of affecting that area—this is the "double hermeneutic" framed by Anthony Giddens (1986, 284). For any piece of research, it is hard to foresee whether or not it will end up affecting its object of study. Yet again with technology research, this dynamic means that I am offering a different kind of interaction to my interviewees than I might be in another area of research.

For example, in my study of wireless communication I often told my interviewees that I was studying the law and policy related to wireless. This frequently caused them to divide knowledge into two categories, what was meant for me, and what I was meant to pass along to the domain of law and policy. One interviewee put it succinctly when he said, "The technology works like I just said, but now this is what you should tell the government . . ."

At the time, I found it flattering that anyone would think that the government would listen to me (it did not). However, what I should have realized at that moment was that my interlocutor was looking through me and trying to discern the purpose of my research and to manipulate it. While the previous quote was about policy-related research, when studying the design of technological objects the terrain of the design itself becomes a strange ground for unusual trades and bargains.

Just as the technology users that read my work expected that I be part engineer and explain technology to them in my social research, the engineers I interviewed often tried to use me as a proxy for the user. When I asked them about how something they were building works, they would often reply with a description of how they *wanted* it to work, and not mention how it actually did (or did not). They would assume I was a kind of user or a proxy user. My experience with the patch panel on my visit to Dr. Gunn's project taught me some skepticism, and future interviews taught me more.

RISK AND USEFULNESS: WHAT IS "OFF TOPIC"?

A further example from a study of science will cement this point. Science studies is a useful comparison because science is seen as highly specialized and technical, and to a novice it looks like a hard case for social researchers to crack. But by and large, the scholars in science studies have had a choice as to which scientific topics they want to research. On the one hand they can choose current debates relevant to popular science or science policy, or on the other hand they can choose examples and issues far removed from the personal experience (or interests) of most general readers.

Social studies of science have done an admirable job in both domains, but technology studies usually tend to emphasize the former—the study of well-known or everyday technology that is self-evidently relevant to a large number of people. Invariably when a research project is meaningfully about technology it is also likely that some manifest consequence or feature of the technology motivated the researcher's initial interest.

The classic Latour and Woolgar study *Laboratory Life* investigated a biology laboratory and subsequently wrote about the construction of scientific facts, yet they intentionally selected a "minor episode" (1986, 106) of science to analyze. For example, among other facts, they chose to study the construction of thyrotropin-releasing factor (hormone), or TRF(H), a topic surely far removed from the interests of most readers of this paragraph, much less their paragraphs.

Although I do not know for sure, my guess is that when they attend professional meetings, it is unlikely that their colleagues ever ask questions like "What do you think of TRF(H)?" "Is TRF(H) a valuable industry I should invest in?" or, "How well does Salk run his lab?" If they had been asked those questions, I think they would be right in saying that they were off topic, and that this explanation would be accepted by most reasonable members of the audience. After all, *someone* cares about TRF(H), but not the audience for social studies of science. To them, it serves only as an example of a broader theory about scientific knowledge.

My own technology-related projects have concerned things that a large number of people use or talk about. The popular or manifest understanding of the technology will not go away, and this frequently drags me into uncomfortable epistemological positions. These often revolve around prevailing expectations about technical knowledge.

In the early 2000s, a colleague of mine who studied the Internet parodied the questions she receives at conferences and professional meetings as: "Internet: Good or Bad?" While many others (most notably Winner 1993) have highlighted the moral imperative for scholarship to be engaged with worldly consequences, the problem here is more about the unavoidability of that engagement and how to manage it.

In my own research on wireless, people ask me questions like these all the time: "What do you think of WiMax [a new wireless technology standard]?" "Is wireless broadband a valuable industry I should invest in?" "How well does Dr. Gunn run his project?" When I started out as a researcher, I sometimes got into trouble when I forgot that these questions ought to be more like questions about TRF(H). That is, I should have remembered: Who cares about TRF(H), or about WiMax? They are only examples that are supposed to teach us something about an underlying theory or process.

HYBRIDITY: "WILL MESH NETWORKING ACTUALLY WORK?"

At the beginning of this chapter, I used my encounter with the patch panel to demonstrate the value of technical knowledge in my own work. In this section, I will use my encounter with another technological situation, mesh networking, to demonstrate the harm of technical knowledge, or at least its complexities.

In 2004 I coauthored a conference paper with two of my research participants (Sandvig, Young, and Meinrath 2004). The paper concerned recent developments in wireless Internet routing, which were at the time a matter of extreme excitement among a small group of experts. I presented the paper at a research conference in Washington, DC. The conference is important in this research area, and I felt the stakes were high.

I was happy to coauthor with my interviewees for a number of reasons. First, I liked them. Second, I had been told by the methods textbooks that in this day and age the goal is collaborative participatory research. I do not steal insights from my subjects like a bandit and publish them under my own name. Instead, we work together using participant validation and collaboration to make a difference in the world. It all sounds naive and a little foolish when I type it out here, but those were my motivations. I should also mention that this may have been a way to make up for that still nagging feeling that I still lacked important technical knowledge. If I coauthored with a skilled engineer, maybe I would become more like one, I reasoned at the time.

After I presented my paper to a full audience, the first question I received was, "Will mesh networking actually work?" This question was, for me, dumbfounding, because I knew too much about it and I cared about the answer. Looking back, maybe I should have been able to see this as a question similar to, "TRF(H): good or bad?" where the obvious answer is then, "I'm sorry but that question is not about the topic of this paper."

But because of my well-meaning collaboration, I knew too much for a social researcher. You, dear reader, do not have to care about mesh networking just as you are not expected to care about TRF(H). (Feel free to skip to the end of this paragraph if you do not like jargon.) I knew that the question referred to a style of network routing, and specifically to an ongoing debate in network engineering concerning the likely efficiency of multihop, self-configuring wireless networks. I could tell from the context that the questioner also meant to include some ideas about business models and forms of social organization for mesh networking that were a hot topic at the time. The questioner also surely wanted to know if the networks would scale, because small testbeds were already well established—the real question was one of scale. I think they also wanted to know what routing protocol showed the greatest promise in this context. And the idea, I thought, was not to ask me about a way of meshing that was only good for one kind of networking efficiency. The holy grail for network research at the time was a protocol that would solve the entire problem, not one part of it. This is called a "general solution." I will stop here, but there were more background and further parameters beyond these.

All sorts of colorful episodes from my fieldwork flashed behind my eyes because this question came up all the time among my informants, and it was a topic of much debate. I had recently sought out the advice of a colleague of mine—an esteemed senior professor of network engineering—and asked him about the debate. He had explained to me that in a recently published article he had constructed a mathematical proof that demonstrated that such a network was impossible, but I could not follow the math. A few months earlier, I had a conversation with a very well-respected networking pioneer who had related his attempts to solve these problems in research funded by the Defense Department in the 1970s. He told a vivid story of his attempts to solve the problem by driving panel trucks in groups all around local roads and pretending that they were tanks. (He said that he had never managed to solve it.)

In sum, I had accidentally become a hybrid. I did not know enough to be a technical expert, but I knew too much to stick to my proper place and insist that the question was off topic. This hybridity is dangerous. Too much focus on the technical side and the two paragraphs preceding this one could have gone on for pages—which too many social studies of technology do. They mistake their own aims and turn into technology textbooks, magnifying that portion of their text where they are most likely to make embarrassing mistakes.

CONCLUSION: THE IMPORTANCE AND DIFFICULTY OF EXPERTISE

At the beginning of this chapter, I mentioned that Dr. Gunn and Veronica may have hoped I would produce a positive case study that they would be able to convert into more grant funding. After the previous example of wireless meshing, another kind of transaction that is often not talked about in the practice of research might be clearer: the way that technical knowledge and external credibility are exchanged whenever a technical domain with important consequences is written about by a social researcher.

It is worth again asking the question given in the title of this chapter. How technical is technology research? Or, what is it that a social researcher needs in order to participate in this transaction of expertise? I hope the examples in this chapter have made clear that there are many possible routes to take. To sum up my own strategies, I would first say that thinking seriously and analytically about expertise is a critical step in a technical research project—and not expertise as the researcher's problem but as *everyone*'s problem.

This advice is useful even in technology projects that are not about expertise. If you plan to interview political bloggers and investigate their effect on elections, it is worth at least pausing briefly to puzzle about how they learned to blog, and to consider the implications of different paths to blogging and computer skill on outcomes like the form of blog they produce. Obviously all technology studies will not have expertise as the object of their theories and conclusions. But even when expertise is not the quarry I am chasing, I think I have written better interview questions and made more sophisticated analytic points as a result of thinking about technical expertise as an enmeshing system that all of my interlocutors are a part of with me.

Next, I have learned to follow my influences and embrace ignorance—my initial place in this system—as a research strategy. Rather than seeing knowledge about technology as one peak I must conquer on the path to the greater summit of an exemplary social study of technology, I recognize that I am offering my interlocutors a different gift of legitimation and respect. Technical knowledge, on this climb, isn't a set of acronyms and operations I have to memorize by rote, but a system I have to weigh with a critical eye. Not so much, "What does this acronym mean?" as "What does this acronym mean to them?" As I have tried to explain, this has led me to be skeptical of technical credentialing and technical depth requirements for social researchers, even though they are increasingly common in some disciplines.

Even then, all technology researchers must still fear making an elementary technical mistake for which they will be called to the carpet. I have tried to avoid this kind of mistake by remembering my position with respect to the audience for social research. While my readers, if there are any, may hope for technical knowledge in a social research article about technology, it is my role to minimize my own exposition on technological topics, as they usually just are not the point. Yet the process of this kind of research changed me into an uncomfortable hybrid researcher, part techno part social. As a result, it is impossible to avoid having a stake in technical points that would otherwise seem to be off topic.

Finally, it has always helped me to remember that I am far from the first person to be struck by these dilemmas. Returning to Woolgar's quote that "the fact that all our analyses are essentially flawed is better celebrated than concealed" (1982, 494), I have just celebrated some of my own flaws and worries, and I hope this will in turn confirm Woolgar's conclusion—that some research is better as a consequence.

NOTES

This material is based on work supported by the U.S. National Science Foundation under Grant No. 0546409. The author would like to thank Hope Hall, Rayvon Fouché, and Eszter Hargittai for their advice and support.

1. Despite the word's appearance in the title of this chapter, in keeping with this book's focus I wish to avoid an extensive review of the many definitions for *technology*. For a beginning, see McGinn 1978.

2. In addition to restricted codes, Bernstein proposed that there might be a special kind of "elaborated code [that] . . . facilitates relations between objects" and serves to isolate scientific topics from nonscientific speakers (1964, 65; see also 65, n2).

3. Admittedly, this was a study of science and not of technology.

4. That is, qualified to practice law before a federal court in the United States.

5. See http://sts.stanford.edu/BS.html and http://web.mit.edu/sts/students/undergrad/.

6. At least, if you read the curricula in STS as a guide.

7. My own doctoral adviser, François Bar, holds a Diplôme d'Ingénieur Civil. A member of my dissertation committee, Robert E. McGinn (author of McGinn 1990), holds an MS in mathematics. A few prominent scholars in my field have acquired technical credentials. For example, Robin Mansell became a chartered electrical engineer fourteen years after receiving the PhD in communication and long after she turned to technical topics (e.g., Mansell 1993).

8. See http://www.google.com/alerts.

9. The idea of reflecting on expertise has been one of the important preoccupations of science studies scholarship in recent years (see Collins and Evans 2002, 2003; Jasanoff 2003; Rip 2003; Wynne 2003).

10. It is sometimes called the ecological fallacy.

REFERENCES

Bernstein, B. 1964. Elaborated and Restricted Codes: Their Social Origin and Consequences. *American Anthropologist* 66 (6, part 2): 55–69.

Bosworth, D. L. 1978. The Rate of Obsolescence of Technical Knowledge—A Note. *Journal of Industrial Economics* 26 (3): 273–79.

Collins, H. M. 2004. Interactional Expertise as a Third Kind of Knowledge. *Phenomenology and the Cognitive Sciences* 3:125–43.

Collins, H. M., and R. Evans. 2002. The Third Wave of Science Studies: Studies of Expertise and Experience. *Social Studies of Science* 32 (2): 235–96.

Collins, H. M., and R. Evans. 2003. King Canute Meets the Beach Boys: Responses to "The Third Wave." *Social Studies of Science* 33 (3): 435–52.

Collins, H. M., and T. Pinch. 1982. *Frames of Meaning*. London: Routledge.

Cowan, R. S. 1997. *A Social History of American Technology*. London: Oxford University Press.

Downey, G. L., and J. Dumit. 1997. Locating and Intervening. In *Cyborgs and Citadels*, ed. G. L. Downey and J. Dumit, 5–29. Santa Fe, NM: School of American Research Press.

Gast, M. S. 2002. *802.11 Wireless Networks: The Definitive Guide*. Sebastopol, CA: O'Reilly.

Giddens, A. 1986. *The Constitution of Society: Outline of the Theory of Structuration*. Berkeley: University of California Press.

Harrison, T. M., and T. Stephen. 1999. Researching and Creating Community Networks. In *Doing Internet Research: Critical Issues and Methods for Examining the Net*, ed. S. Jones, 221–42. Thousand Oaks, CA: Sage.

Hess, D. J. 2001. Ethnography and the Development of Science and Technology Studies. In *Sage Handbook of Ethnography*, ed. J. Lofland and L. Lofland, 234–45. Thousand Oaks, CA: Sage.

Hughes, T. P. 1993. *Networks of Power: Electrification in Western Society, 1880–1930*. Baltimore, MD: Johns Hopkins University Press.

Jasanoff, S. 2003. Breaking the Waves in Science Studies: Comment on H. M.

Collins and Robert Evans, "The Third Wave of Science Studies." *Social Studies of Science* 33 (3): 389–400.

Latour, B., and S. Woolgar. 1986. *Laboratory Life: The Construction of Scientific Facts.* Rev. ed. Princeton: Princeton University Press.

Lightman, A., D. Sarewitz, and C. Desser, eds. 2003. *Living with the Genie: Essays on Technology and the Quest for Human Mastery.* Washington, DC: Island Press.

Lynch, M. 1982. Technical Work and Critical Inquiry: Investigations in a Scientific Laboratory. *Social Studies of Science* 12 (4): 499–534.

MacKenzie, D., and J. Wajcman. 1999. *The Social Shaping of Technology.* 2nd ed. New York: McGraw-Hill.

Mansell, R. 1993. *The New Telecommunications: A Political Economy of Network Evolution.* London: Sage.

McGinn, R. E. 1978. What Is Technology? *Research in Philosophy and Technology* 1 (1): 179–97.

McGinn, R. E. 1990. *Science, Technology, and Society.* New York: Prentice-Hall.

Nissenbaum, H. F., and M. E. Price, eds. 2003. *Academy and the Internet.* New York: Peter Lang.

Richards, P. 1986. Risk. In H. S. Becker, *Writing for Social Scientists: How to Start and Finish Your Thesis, Book, or Article,* 108–20. Chicago: University of Chicago Press.

Rip, A. 2003. Constructing Expertise: In a Third Wave of Science Studies? *Social Studies of Science* 33 (3): 419–34.

Sandvig, C., D. Young, and S. Meinrath. 2004. Hidden Interfaces to "Ownerless" Networks. Paper presented to the 32nd Annual Telecommunications Policy Research Conference (TPRC) on Communication, Information, and Internet Policy, Arlington, VA.

U.S. Patent and Trademark Office. 2004. General Requirements Bulletin for Admission to the Examination for Registration to Practice in Patent Cases before the United States Patent and Trademark Office. Washington, DC: U.S. Patent and Trademark Office. http://www.uspto.gov/web/offices/dcom/gcounsel/oed .htm.

Varma, R. 2005. "Aligning Training with Business Goals." *Express Computer.* Mumbai, India. September 19. http://www.expresscomputeronline.com/20050919/ technologylife01.shtml.

Weber, S. 2004. *The Success of Open Source.* Cambridge: Harvard University Press.

Winner, L. 1993. Upon Opening the Black Box and Finding It Empty: Social Constructivism and the Philosophy of Technology. *Science, Technology, and Human Values* 18 (3): 362–78.

Woolgar, S. 1982. Laboratory Studies: A Comment on the State of the Art. *Social Studies of Science* 12 (4): 481–98.

Wynne, B. 2003. Seasick on the Third Wave? Subverting the Hegemony of Propositionalism: Response to Collins and Evans (2002). *Social Studies of Science* 33 (3): 401–17.

ON UNEXPECTED EVENTS

Navigating the Sudden Research Opportunity of 9/11

KAREN ALBRIGHT

One of the greatest joys of social scientific research comes from discovering—and seizing—uncharted territory. Scholars are forever trying to do this in one form or another, most typically by identifying gaps in the literature and then building careers dedicated to filling them. When it comes to breaking new ground, however, there may be nothing that can compare to the thrill (and challenge) of pursuing a sudden research opportunity. Capturing an unexpected event and harnessing its research potential in a social scientific framework requires quick thinking and action: researchers in such instances must work on unusually uncertain terrain, navigating without the benefit of temporal perspective.

The uncertainty of the terrain is further compounded by the lack of clarity regarding how exactly to go about such research. This is due, in part, to the difficulty of generalizing about sudden research opportunities. Not only is their timing impossible to predict, but they come in varying forms and contexts. Think, for instance, of the social and economic devastation following Hurricane Katrina, or the political and media backlash following the criticism of George W. Bush by the country music group The Dixie Chicks. Both are excellent examples of unexpected research opportunities that have resulted in intriguing social scientific analyses (see, e.g., Elliott and Pais 2006; Rodriguez, Trainor, and Quarantelli 2006; Rossman 2004), but they are also very different in substance and scope. Further, the suddenness of such events does not always enable application of the standard logico-deductive model favored by many in the social sciences, which can make the process even more difficult and uncertain. Nonetheless, there is a great deal to be gained from pursuing research on an unexpected event, and this chapter is devoted to providing some guidelines to help you do just that.

How you go about crafting a project from an unexpected research opportunity, of course, depends on the larger context in which that opportunity has emerged. If you have been looking for a test case for a phenomenon that you have already studied or have been planning to study, and this unexpected event fits the bill, consider yourself lucky; serendipity has smiled on you. Because you will already have developed relevant research question(s) and identified appropriate theoretical framework(s) with which you can arm yourself as you move into the field, your investigation will likely be able to proceed in a relatively straightforward way, more or less following the aforementioned logico-deductive model. If, however, you do not yet have enough expertise in this area to know which theoretical frameworks would be most appropriate for your project—if, in fact, you were caught so unprepared by this research opportunity that you are not even sure what your research questions are—a different sort of experience lies ahead. Because the latter experience is typically much more difficult to navigate than the former, this chapter will focus on how researchers can seize research opportunities for which they lack preexisting questions and frameworks.

Throughout the chapter, I will draw on my own experience with a sudden research opportunity: a project on the aftereffects of the September 11, 2001, attacks on New York City, which I began, along with several colleagues, as a graduate student in the Department of Sociology at New York University (see Abrams, Albright, and Panofsky 2004). The events of September 11 (hereafter referred to as 9/11) could not possibly have transformed my scholarly horizons more suddenly; indeed, had I been asked on September 10 about my interest in the domestic effects of terrorism, I would likely have indicated little curiosity. Just a day later, however, both my professional and personal interests were transformed as I, along with my colleagues, began the laborious, consuming, and often frustrating process of trying to study this sudden and emergent event. In sharing here the lessons we learned along the way, I hope to help you minimize the frustrations you may encounter when pursuing similarly unexpected research opportunities.

In keeping with my research on 9/11, the chapter will primarily emphasize the gathering of original data using qualitative, rather than quantitative, methodologies, though it is certainly possible to gather quantitative data from sudden events as well (see, e.g., Rossman 2004). I will also, at times, reference some of the methodological practices advocated by proponents of grounded theory, which proved helpful to our project. Grounded theory refers to the development of theory from research grounded in data, as opposed to the deduction of testable hypotheses from existing theories (see Glaser and Strauss 1967; Glaser 1978, 1992; Strauss 1987). Though it was not developed specifically to aid in handling sudden research opportunities, its principles and, especially, its methods can provide an excellent road map when taking on such a project. Grounded theory's emphasis on facilitating emergence provides guidelines that are systematic enough to help construct some order out of chaos, yet also flexible enough to incorporate investigators' need to continually adjust, adapt, and reconceptualize their analyses according to the emergent data (see Charmaz 2006 for a comprehensive overview).

In the pages that follow, I discuss some of the benefits and challenges of collaborative research, review the immediate decisions and other preparations that need to be made before you enter the field, and offer guidelines for gathering, analyzing, and writing up data. You should keep in mind that although these steps are rather neatly cordoned off into discrete sections, there will be a significant amount of overlap between them in practice, particularly between data collection and analysis. Before we begin, however, it is worth considering whether pursuing a sudden research opportunity is the right decision for you.

THE CHALLENGE OF SUDDEN OPPORTUNITY: TO PURSUE OR NOT TO PURSUE?

Prior to taking on the challenge of a sudden research opportunity, it is important to consider the state of your past and current research experience. Do you already have other research projects started? Have you brought any projects to completion? If this is your first real research project, you, too, should consider yourself lucky: there are few things as thrilling and as rewarding as finding a topic in which you are intensely interested and immersing yourself in it, and you are about to do just that. Though suddenly encountering such a research opportunity is not without difficulties, your experience will likely be one from which you will get much satisfaction, and it may well set you down a career path that brings you great fulfillment. If, on the other hand, you already have some research experience in another area, your trajectory may not be so straightforward. If you are currently involved in one or more research projects, you should think seriously before adding another project to the list, especially if you already feel overwhelmed by your current commitments.

As compelling as the event in question may be, you need to make some hard choices about what you can reasonably accomplish—and by "accomplish" I mean, of course, *finish*, since that is ultimately the only thing that really counts in research. Jumping into a new project when you already have a trail of half-finished projects behind you is perilous business, particularly when the new study is not conceptually or empirically well defined from the outset. Indeed, doing so virtually guarantees frustration and/or paralysis, if not failure itself. This is especially true if the research experience you already have lies in topics that are largely unrelated to the event in question, because that means you will be starting from scratch in more ways than one. If this is the case, then you have some serious thinking to do. Indeed, you must ask yourself a very important question before proceeding: namely, *should* you proceed at all?

As you ponder your answer, there are a few things to keep in mind. Like it or not, you have a finite amount of time and resources, just like everyone else. If you are already balancing work on two or three projects, you likely do not have much time to breathe—or concentrate—as it is. (And keep in mind that a "project" in this case does not only refer to a separate *research* project. You should also consider any teaching responsibilities, coursework requirements, and so on as projects for accounting purposes here.) As mentioned earlier, you need to concentrate on what you can feasibly and reasonably bring to completion. Weighing yourself down unnecessarily is simply not a good strategy for moving forward. Besides demanding a great amount of time and resources, managing multiple and disparate projects can also wreak havoc on your sanity and your professional identity. Though this point is often easy to overlook with all the emphasis on (and expectations for) multitasking these days, most people are not actually very good multitaskers, and particularly not when the tasks in question require thinking, conceptualizing, theorizing, and/or analyzing. It is simply hard to do these things well when you are constantly jumping from one project to the next. Trying to do too much comes at a cost: you can wind up wearing yourself out and still have too little to show for it.

On the other hand, as long as you are not already overcommitted to other projects, getting involved in a study that fascinates you is an excellent way to find meaning in your work. Though some people are able to work well without becoming especially invested in the substance of the undertaking, spending time on something that feels meaningful is likely to be vastly more rewarding and enjoyable. Being deeply interested in your subject and having the time to fully explore that interest is one of the surest paths to success: you will be much more committed throughout the process and much more likely to see it through to completion. Because you will be investing more time, energy, and thought in the project than you might in one about which you care less, your chances of discovering something truly interesting are also greatly increased. Further, by combining good social science with the ability to seize the moment, you can construct and contribute insights that are not only valuable but likely unique. Beginning your research as close as possible to the actual occurrence of the event—that is, jumping on the opportunity as soon as you can—not only is invigorating but provides you with an uncommon vantage point as you collect your data. Though such a vantage point can also present problems of perspective, its potential is unparalleled. Indeed, it is possible that your research will turn out to be one of the defining works on this event, and, for that reason, you may have carved out a nice niche for yourself simply by being in the right place at the right time—and, of course, by being daring (or is it foolish?) enough to act on your interest.

Ultimately, of course, only you can decide whether or not to pursue a research opportunity; only you know your own research experience and agenda, as well as the weight of the other responsibilities you have. For those of you who have decided to proceed, the rest of this chapter is devoted to helping you figure out how to do so.

THE COLLABORATIVE EXPERIENCE

Once you have determined that you do, indeed, want to pursue this sudden research opportunity, you will need to decide whether you will collaborate with others or go about it alone. Sometimes, of course, that decision is not only yours to make; opportunities may present themselves in specific ways. That was certainly the case with my research on 9/11, which began rather inauspiciously and at the invitation of someone else. In the next few pages I describe briefly how our collaboration came about and offer some pointers designed to help you make your own collaborative experience more generative and gratifying, should you choose to go that route.

A couple of days after the attacks, Dr. Heinz Steinert, an Austrian professor visiting the NYU Department of Sociology for the 2001–2 academic year, sent an e-mail to all of the graduate students in the department in which he proposed that anyone interested in developing a research project about what had happened meet that weekend to talk about it. In retrospect, it is perhaps telling—and likely indicative of the state of discombobulation that many New Yorkers found themselves in immediately after the attacks—that such an invitation came from a non-American visitor rather than a resident New Yorker. I certainly was not thinking clearly, to say the least. While I was preoccupied both emotionally and intellectually with the meaning and impact of the attacks, I doubt that it would have occurred to me for some time to channel my preoccupation in a scholarly direction if I had been left to my own devices. Nonetheless, the appearance of Heinz's e-mail in my inbox was very welcome—and intriguing. This, it seemed, would be an excellent way to channel my interest in the situation in a constructive manner. Not surprisingly, I was not alone in thinking this. When I reported to the meeting, I found a handful of other graduate students with similar ideas. Though we were all rather shell-shocked from our various individual experiences on 9/11, we were also very keen—indeed, anxious—to get involved. Heinz then led us in a discussion about how we might be able to gather data on the event, and together we worked out a plan, which I will discuss in more detail in the following sections.

As is often the case with collaborative projects, however, there would be a number of changes to the group's roster, even as the research itself moved forward. After a few weeks of working intensively on the project, several of the graduate students in the group decided to drop out—an understandable decision, certainly, not only because of the time commitment required during this frenzied early period but also because many of those students were at very early stages in their graduate program and thus also had to deal with a number of other pressing course requirements. Besides Heinz Steinert, then, this left just three of us on the project: Courtney Abrams, Aaron Panofsky, and, of course, myself. We four continued to gather and analyze data, meeting weekly or biweekly for the rest of the academic year. However, by the end of 2001, Heinz's interests and style had diverged somewhat from Courtney's, Aaron's, and mine, and, though we continued to share our collective interview data and to engage in many fruitful and enjoyable discussions, it was understood that Heinz would pursue his own work on the subject (see Steinert 2003), while the three of us would work as a separate team.

Thus, by the end of 2001, we had entered what could aptly be described as the third, but "main," phase of the project: the three of us were now fully responsible for what would become of our research. Though professors would occasionally read and comment on drafts of our work, for the first time in each of our respective academic careers there was no longer a more experienced adviser holding our hand(s); it was up to us to figure out how to make something out of our research—and how to balance it with the other demands of graduate school. We were all busy: I, as a fifth-year graduate student, was beginning to collect data for my dissertation research in addition to finishing up work on another major project. Courtney and Aaron, both in their third year, were finishing up their required coursework and beginning to think about their dissertation proposals. Nonetheless, we were committed to this work, even quite consumed by it, and for at least a year it took center stage in our academic careers.

Collaboration between equals is a vastly different experience from collaboration between people of differing ranks (e.g., between a student and a professor). In the former case, it is much less clear who is in charge and how the labor should be divided; because there is no preestablished status order, it is up to each group member to negotiate a working relationship that is both productive and pleasant. Though decisions about division of labor are all too often made tacitly, the collaborative experience will generally be a much smoother one if such practical issues can be broached openly early on in the process. For example, all members of the research group should share up front what they think their scholarly strengths and weaknesses are and what they feel they will be able to contribute to the project (both in terms of skill and time). Doing so will not only provide everyone in the group a better idea about who should take the lead on which tasks but will make it more probable that each member will feel as if she or he is part of a real team, rather than a ragtag group of people joined loosely by a common interest. This will be an important feeling to maintain. The last thing you want is for one member to become resentful, as dealing with resentment can make working on a project miserable for all involved as well as diminish the final product. Thankfully, Courtney, Aaron, and I managed to keep the channels of communication open and, thus, avoid such a predicament without too much difficulty.

However, while getting an idea of who might be better at some tasks than others is both logical and necessary, you should take care to avoid letting that knowledge translate into tacit assignment of roles that will remain static throughout the project. For example, you do not want to stick one person with the thankless task of always being the group's copy editor, even if she or he is particularly gifted at it. Not only can resentment (and boredom) build over time, but establishing rote roles may even diminish the final product. Collaboration in general, and perhaps especially collaboration between equals, is more than the sum of discrete and specialized tasks. At its best, it is a synergistic experience that results in the enhancement and/or expansion of each individual's talents as well as in fine work. Thus, instead of assigning roles for the duration of the project (or just passively allowing them to evolve), assign roles for each specific task or step in the project, and try to keep them at least somewhat varied.

Of course, taking such steps to divide the labor equitably may also introduce problems when it comes to the issue of authorship. If everyone contributed more or less equally, how do you decide the order in which your names should be listed? The optimal solution to this dilemma is the alphabetical listing; Courtney, Aaron, and I opted for this upon publication of our first article. Alphabetical listings should be accompanied by a footnote that states clearly how the order was determined, since without this information the first author may benefit unfairly. Another solution to the authorship issue is an agreement to rotate first-authorship if you plan multiple publications (this is a particularly good option if each collaborator has a particular idea for a publication that he or she is willing to lead). You may also want to take into account any immediate needs of each collaborator. For instance, if one coauthor is approaching the job market, a first-authored publication sooner, rather than later, might be particularly helpful for that person.

In addition to sharing responsibilities (and credit) fairly, the key to a successful collaboration is to keep things out in the open, making sure to talk about issues as they come up and collectively deciding how to proceed. Set goals and time lines for the project together and early. Although these will no doubt change as the project itself changes, it is important to establish what you are aiming for both collectively and individually and to start to plan how you can achieve it. Setting some clear and time-specific goals (e.g., "By April we will have finished collecting all of the surveys") will provide you with a straightforward means of determining your progress. Doing so will also add structure to the research process and clarity to your own expectations, both of which are particularly welcome on the uncertain terrain of sudden research. Of course, you will be helped greatly in your efforts to maintain both equality and communication among members if you keep your group relatively small. Collaboration between approximately two to four people is ideal. When more than four people are involved, distinct tiers of workers are more likely to develop, roles typically become more narrow and specialized, and the nature of the dynamic becomes significantly different.

Though the frequency with which you meet will depend on your other responsibilities and the stage of your research, setting regular and purpose-driven meetings is extremely helpful in making progress on your collaborative research project. Courtney, Aaron, and I found that meeting at least every two weeks played a key role in maintaining our momentum; indeed, for much of our collaboration, we met weekly or near weekly. However, we did not typically keep to a set day and time. Instead, at the end of every meeting, we would reflect on the tasks we had set for ourselves, estimate the time we thought it would take us to accomplish those tasks, and then set the next meeting for as soon as possible after that.

Given that our meetings typically lasted at least several hours at a time and that the meetings continued at this pace and intensity for more than a year, we also sometimes grew tired of each other. However, those periods of interpersonal fatigue were, under the circumstances, surprisingly few and far between. The three of us had been in overlapping social circles prior to the commencement of our collaborative work and genuinely liked each other—and, somehow, that bond only strengthened as our work went on and we learned each other's strengths and weaknesses. We were extraordinarily lucky in this respect; indeed, had we liked each other less, our research might not have come to fruition. That does not mean that all collaborators will or even should develop close friendships, of course. Sometimes better work is done between people who have some emotional distance. In our case, however, our work was sustained by and largely strengthened from our interpersonal rapport. That said, in some respects, we might have gotten along *too* well: our friendship sometimes made it difficult for us to rein each other in and to coax action or product from endless discourse. In hindsight, we would have benefited considerably had we made a concerted effort to be more explicit about the purpose of each meeting and to keep our chitchat to a minimum (at least until the end of each meeting). In the end, our relative lack of discipline in these areas probably added several months to the project.

Ultimately, however, despite—or perhaps because of—our tendency to chat, the fact that we were collaborating helped keep us engaged and energized for the duration of the project (occasional down days excepted, of course). Though we sometimes got sidetracked by the force of our own dialogic process, working collaboratively helped us avoid procrastination and kept us from feeling completely overwhelmed with the uncertainty of our project. (Or, more accurately, having three of us on the project meant that it was never the case that *everyone* was completely overwhelmed at the same time.) Collaboration forced us to face the work and to develop and engage our ideas—arguably the biggest and most fundamental research challenges. All in all, then, the collaboration propelled us forward and enhanced immeasurably both the research itself and our experience doing it.

PREPARATION

Whether or not you are collaborating, you will have a lot of decisions to make before you head out into the field, and you will need to move quickly. (Again, keep in mind that the following guidelines are designed specifically for research opportunities that come up unexpectedly, rather than for cases when the event serendipitously serves as an empirical test case for theoretical frameworks and/or hypotheses that you have already developed.) The first thing you must do is to abandon the logico-deductive method as a starting point. This will likely be difficult, not only because it has been deeply ingrained in most of us as the appropriate method for research but also because it is rather terrifying to go out in the field without the definition that such an approach provides. Nonetheless, though you will have to frame your findings in these terms later, you need to put that approach on hold for now. You simply do not have the same kind of lead time such a method requires, particularly since at this point you cannot yet know the nature and form of the phenomenon you are about to study. Instead, the priority right now is to start to gather your data.

Before you start the data collection process, however, you have four important decisions to make. Though these decisions need to be made fairly immediately in order to enter the field as soon as possible, be sure to give them careful consideration. They will have a continuing impact on your study from this point forward, despite the fact that the methodological approach I describe in this chapter allows for a significant degree of flexibility. Because of their importance, it is wise to talk these decisions over with others before you act on them. Even if you are involved in a collaborative project, talking out your ideas with people not involved in the project is a good idea. You can use them as a sounding board to help you determine if the choices you are making in the heat of the moment make sense.

1. *What is your motivating question?* You will first need to decide on an initial research question or two that represent (and will remind you of) your basic motivation for going out into the field. Very broad questions are fine at this point; they will almost certainly change or evolve after you develop a better understanding of what is happening in the data. Right now, you just need something with which to go out in the field that can orient the initial data gathering. One way to generate this initial question is simply to ask yourself what exactly is interesting to you about the sudden event. Why are you so motivated to study it in the first place? Be honest with yourself in articulating your interest. Because my colleagues and I entered the field without any particular expertise in the sociology of disaster or terrorism, we did not already possess a theoretical framework that might have primed us for what to look for, what to ask, what to see. Thus, our first—and very broad—aim was simply to better understand what New Yorkers had experienced on 9/11 and during its immediate aftermath.

2. *What will serve as your data?* You will also need to decide on the source(s) of your data. For example, should you conduct interviews? If the answer is yes, whom should you interview? What should you observe? Because you will want your data to be as rich and as comprehensive as possible, and because getting a handle on what is really happening in a given situation is often difficult, gathering more than one type of data and/or utilizing mixed methodological strategies is extremely helpful. However, practical constraints may prohibit this, particularly if you are working alone. You must also think about whether it is important to your project to achieve population representativeness. If your work is qualitative, the answer is typically no, as qualitative research tends to lend itself to deeper, rather than broader, analyses. (Of course, this will also vary according to the nature of your research opportunity: it may be that you only need to interview thirty people to conduct an exhaustive examination of a particularly small or limited event.) In any case, the most important thing to remember in deciding on your data source(s) is that, in accordance with the principles of grounded theory, you should sample with an eye toward theory construction, rather than population representation *per se* (Charmaz 2006). The main purpose at this stage of the research, if not the entire project, is to explicate and understand the more particular circumstances of the event, not (necessarily) to ensure generalizability across the larger population.

Because we were interested in understanding New Yorkers' experiences on 9/11, deciding to gather data through in-depth interviews made a great deal of methodological sense. (Courtney, Aaron, and I later supplemented these interview data with ethnographic data and data from additional narratives, which I will discuss in more detail later, but at this initial stage interviews were the sole source of data.) We also decided that we were most interested in understanding the 9/11 experiences of so-called regular (i.e., nonheralded) New Yorkers, since even in those very early days the media focused almost exclusively upon the special few who were singled out as heroes or victims. We decided that we would simply try to interview as many of these New Yorkers as possible, with an eye toward reaching representatives of a variety of ages, genders, and backgrounds—racial, class, national, religious, educational, and cultural—but without trying to fill specific quotas for any category. Our main requirement was that our interviewees be what we would come to call "bystanders" to the actual attacks; that is, that neither they nor their close relations participated directly in the disaster.

3. How will you access and approach your data? Having determined your data source(s), you next need to figure out how you will gain access. For instance, if you hope to conduct ethnographic observations in a place that is not open to the public, you will need to gather permission from the appropriate authorities to do so. You will also need to figure out a number of practical questions. From what position or perch will you observe? Will you participate in the activities around you in addition to observing them? How often and for how long will you conduct your observations? If you wish to gather information directly from individuals, whether through interviews or surveys, you will also need to obtain their permission to participate in your study. This is typically done by having participants sign a letter of informed consent, although sometimes oral consent can suffice if respondents are not asked to provide their names or other personal details. It is imperative that you check with your Institutional Review Board (IRB) and/or Office of Human Subjects to determine the guidelines they require for obtaining consent. (I will return to the subject of IRBs later.)

You will also need to figure out the practicalities of approaching potential participants. Will they be complete strangers or people you already know? Will you just walk up to them and ask? Will you ask someone else for an introduction? You should take great care to be gentle and respectful in your approach, particularly if the event in question is a sensitive or painful one; after all, while people may welcome the opportunity to talk about the event, they could just as easily find it—or you—taxing or offensive. If your goal is to study a community's response to a sudden event or experience, you should also take care to avoid inadvertently interviewing only the most vocal or activist members of that community (unless, of course, you have specifically determined that those are the people whose perspectives you are the most interested in studying). It is not uncommon for interviewers to fall into this trap, for approaching people to be interviewed can be psychologically difficult, especially when the subject matter may invite a lot of rejection. If this is your experience, you may feel relieved when anyone will talk to you, but you should try to think reflexively (at least after the interview) about who these people are and why they might be so interested in talking with you, especially if you experience more resistance from others. That, of course, does not mean that you should *not* interview them, only that you should also go to greater lengths to approach people who may be less vocal and/or visible.

For our research, we decided to interview both strangers and acquaintances; we were interested in talking to anyone who would talk to us while their memories were still fresh and their narrative about the events of that day had not yet become too practiced. We approached acquaintances either on our own initiative or through snowballing (i.e., using suggestions from other interviewees or acquaintances); we approached strangers we found in public spaces throughout New York City (e.g., local parks, coffeehouses, neighborhood streets, restaurants). In both cases, we approached respondents straightforwardly, told them that we were NYU students researching New Yorkers' experiences on 9/11 and asked if they would be willing to share their experiences. We typically interviewed strangers right then and there; we interviewed acquaintances either immediately or during a follow-up appointment. This simple strategy proved very effective. We encountered almost no one who refused to talk to us—at least, not during the immediate 8- to 10-week period following the attacks, before the window of opportunity presented by the disaster, which functioned similar to a collective ethnomethodological breach (Garfinkel 1967; Heritage 1987) during this period, closed. However, our success was no doubt less a testament to our strategic prowess than to the enormity of 9/11 and New Yorkers' need to process it.

4. What questions will you ask? Finally, if you are conducting interviews or gathering data through surveys, you must construct your instrument. What kind of information do you want to find out from respondents? Again, your questions will likely change or evolve as time goes on and you learn more about the nature of the event you are studying, but you must still put together a list of basic questions from which to start. Though this can be difficult if you still are not quite sure what is of most interest, give it your best shot. For interviews, be sure to construct a considerable number of open-ended questions (only in very few instances will you want respondents to answer a simple yes or no), as respondents' answers will likely suggest subsequent questions to ask and/or new directions to take the project, not to mention indicating which questions should be eliminated. (This, of course, is in contrast to other methodological approaches, where the research is more closely locked into the original concepts.) Be careful that you word questions so that your own preconceived assumptions and perspectives are not discernible to respondents; the goal, after all, is to see respondents' experiences from *their* perspective (or as close as possible to it), rather than your own. Asking respondents if there is anything they would like to add that was not covered in the interview is often an excellent way to expand your own thinking about the project. Such strategies will also allow you to stay open to what is happening in the data, rather than trying to force the data into preconceived categories (Glaser 1978).

In keeping with these points, our interview questions were semistructured; we asked respondents about their experiences on and after 9/11; their feelings and interpretations of the event; their opinions about politics, political figures, and the media; the stories they had heard; and the changes in their everyday routines, as well as anything else they wanted to discuss related to 9/11. While this generally worked well, the fact that our interviews were only semistructured was somewhat problematic when it came time to share and compare our data. Because each interviewer framed his or her interviews somewhat differently—with general topic agreement, to be sure, but still with slightly different questions, foci, and tones—there was not always parity across interviews. While, in the ideal world, we could have dealt with these issues by revisiting earlier respondents and asking them additional questions in follow-up interviews, we were stymied in doing so for two reasons. First, we had interviewed many strangers and in many cases did not have adequate contact information to reach them for a second interview. Second, even if we had had that information, we would likely not have been able to get the data of most interest to us because too much time would have already passed: our interview data reflected a specific moment in time, before the aforementioned breach had closed and when norms were still being negotiated. Thus, a number of interesting angles were suggested in some of our data that we might have explored further in different circumstances but instead were forced to abandon. (Of course, had our interviews been more structured and rigid across interviewers, we might never have gotten a hint of these angles in the first place!) This part of our research experience underscores two key takeaway points: not only should you analyze your data sooner rather than later, something that I'll discuss in more detail later in this chapter, but you should also collect some type of contact information for your respondents if at all possible.

After making these decisions, one thing remains before you can start actually gathering your data: you must obtain approval from your institution's IRB. Though the level of detail that IRBs typically require of researchers (i.e., detailed research plans and complete instruments for review) is often inconsistent with the emergent nature of sudden research, particularly qualitative research, you can still submit a well-thought-out list of open-ended questions that is "sufficiently detailed to convince evaluators that no harm will befall research participants yet open enough to allow unanticipated material to emerge during the interview" (Charmaz 2006, 30). Although IRBs are often accused of slowing projects considerably (and, indeed, they often do), there are ways to try to speed up the process if need be. In the case of a sudden research opportunity, you can—and should—request an expedited review and/or an exemption. Contact the appropriate person on your institution's IRB to explain the immediate nature of the event and ask how you can expedite the process. If necessary, enlist a professor in your department to lobby on your behalf. We were very fortunate in that we received an exemption from NYU's IRB very quickly and could thus go forth to collect our data with very little lag time.

If you have some time to wait until you hear back from your IRB—or even if you do not—this is also a good time to apply for grants. Particularly if your topic of study is a big event, there may be special funding sources available to enable research on it. One potential funding source that should not be overlooked is the internal emergency fund(s) that most universities and many funding agencies have. We applied for and received an internal grant from NYU that was earmarked specifically for research on 9/11, and that was extremely welcome (not to mention a morale booster). However, because it took some time before both that grant and a second grant we received from an external funding agency came through, and we needed to get out in the field immediately, we decided early on to pay for expenses out of our own pockets (e.g., recording devices), save all our receipts, and simply hope that we would be allowed to get reimbursed later. (Many grants do not permit this.) Happily, this strategy worked, and we ended up being reimbursed for all the expenses we incurred up front.

ENTERING THE FIELD

Once you have gotten the go-ahead from your IRB, you are ready to start gathering your data. For this type of project, I advocate a somewhat unorthodox way of structuring your field experience: immerse yourself completely in collecting data for a relatively short, finite period of time, then pause, take stock of what you have gathered, and refocus the direction of the project. In the context of a wholly new and unexpected research opportunity, this is perhaps the most helpful way to conceive of your time in the field. Such a plan incorporates both the need to get a relatively broad initial sense of the event and the emergent data, and the need to then concretize and focus the project.

In the first period of the time line, you should utilize the decisions you made prior to entering the field regarding your data sources, your approach, and your questions, and simply gather, gather, gather. If at all possible, put other projects on hold and concentrate exclusively on this. Though the length of this initial data-gathering period may vary, particularly if you are not able to devote yourself exclusively to this project, approximately two weeks is ideal in most cases. If you have gotten almost immediate approval from your IRB and have moved into the field just days after the occurrence of the event, two weeks should cover the initial, first-stage impact of the event. Even if you are not able to move as quickly, or if your event (or your interest in it) is not as time sensitive, two weeks is still a good amount of time in which to gather broad data. This will provide you with a better idea of what is out there, what can be feasibly gathered, and what data are most interesting.

After about two weeks (or a different amount of time, as necessitated by your other responsibilities and the nature of the event itself) in the field, stop and take inventory of where you are with the project. Of course, you should be thinking critically about your project throughout it, even during the initial data-gathering period, but this is a special turning point in the project where you have the opportunity to rethink the research and to change gears if necessary. From this point forward, you should move back and forth between data gathering and analysis by constantly evaluating which aspects of your data should be treated as major concepts in your study.

After thinking carefully about the data you have collected so far, you may need to reevaluate your questions, your method, and/or your population. Consider: which interview questions are working well and which are not? What are the data telling you? Based on what you know now, is there a subpopulation that you especially want to follow? Be sure to keep in mind that a "subpopulation" does not have to be one of the usual suspects of social scientific analysis (e.g., based on race, gender, or class). For instance, in the case of your event, it might be more appropriate to focus on a group of people with particular experiences during or after that event, as Bryan (2004) did in her study of the impact of 9/11 on Arab Muslims in Jersey City. Similarly, think about the particularly intriguing ideas or topics that have emerged in your initial data and seem to call for further investigation. Now is the time to begin honing your research question(s) into something more specific so that you can avoid collecting conceptually thin data—that is, broad (rather than deep) data that provide you little to no traction on your more focused points of interest. Rather than employing deductive reasoning, then, or even inductive reasoning alone, your work utilizes *abductive* reasoning: you are using the data that you have to begin to develop theories, which you will then test through further data collection. As Charmaz (2006, 103) puts it, "abductive reasoning about the data starts with the data and subsequently moves toward hypothesis formation" (see also Deely 1990; Fann 1970; Rosenthal 2004).

If you are uncertain or insecure about the data that you have gathered so far, you may also want to change or add to the way(s) you are collecting information. In order to supplement our interview data, we began to gather additional material in two ways. First, we collected, read, and analyzed approximately 200 additional personal narratives of 9/11 that we gathered through solicited and unsolicited e-mail, the radio, published sources, and, especially, the Internet, particularly accounts posted on a number of Web sites about New Yorkers' experiences on 9/11 and blog entries on the subject. These additional sources gave us more leverage, although we ultimately used them much less than our interviews and our ethnographic data (described later). Indeed, using additional accounts such as these is often quite difficult, since they are not in response to questions that you have posed and do not necessarily engage your particular concerns. Nonetheless, they may still prove helpful as a check against your own data, to give you a sense of whether something is significantly off or absent from the data that you have collected. If public accounts of the event you are studying are not widely available, you might also consider the possibility of comparing your data with accounts of previous similar events (if applicable); indeed, it will likely be very helpful to consider the similarities or differences between your event and others. At different points in our research, we strongly considered the idea of comparing 9/11 to several other events, including the attack on Pearl Harbor, the London Blitz, and the assassination of John F. Kennedy; however, we could not find narrative data to make an adequate match, and so we never developed this comparative angle further.

Second, we began to treat New York City, especially downtown Manhattan, as an ethnographic site. We visited Ground Zero multiple times, observing its evolution from a mecca of mourning to an organized tourist destination to a sad but fading curiosity and then, finally, to a contested ground for official commemoration and representation. We attended exhibits about the World Trade Center and the events of 9/11; we listened to news reports that charted the city's recovery from the destruction; we noted the length of time before displays of victims' photographs and other forms of spontaneous commemoration were removed; we witnessed the city's reactions when some forms of commemoration, both state-sponsored and organic, returned on the anniversaries of the attacks; we read or watched everything we could find on 9/11 and its aftermath. These additional data proved exceedingly valuable to our research, particularly as a complement to our interview data, as they enabled our extended focus on the structure, range, and intensity of people's experiences and practices, as well as the changing nature of social norms and cultural constructions.

At some point after you have refocused your project and returned to the field to gather data with this focus in mind, it will be time to stop gathering data. How will you know when to stop? The answer to this will vary considerably, of course, but one way to think about it is that the ideal time to stop is when the categories of data that you are developing become "saturated," in the language of grounded theory. This is not necessarily the same thing as repetition of stories being reflected in your data. It means instead that no new properties or patterns emerge as you examine and compare concepts in your materials, nor does the emergence of new conceptual relationships seem likely. A more helpful means of describing this phenomenon may thus be Dey's (1999) term "theoretical sufficiency."

Achieving such theoretical sufficiency, however, is not always feasible. In the course of doing research, you must also face the realities of the empirical world and adjust accordingly; if they accommodate your ideal theoretical sample, you are fortunate indeed. Usually the window of opportunity is only open for a finite period of time, and, when it closes, your data gathering must either end or change. Our research made it necessary to confront the fact that, somewhere between 8 and 10 weeks after the attacks, the atmosphere had changed significantly, especially with regard to talking publicly about 9/11. At that point, it became apparent that a certain amount of "9/11 fatigue" had set in: both acquaintances and, particularly, strangers were no longer interested in talking with us about their 9/11 experience. Though 9/11 would continue to influence New Yorkers' daily lives and communities in many ways, both apparent and not so apparent, it became clear that accessing people's experiences through in-depth interviews was no longer a useful method. After each of us independently noticed this fatigue and reluctance, we discussed it in meetings and acknowledged that it was time to stop pursuing interviews. In fact, we had begun to feel that we were nearing theoretical sufficiency anyway. We had conducted 52 interviews by then, and we knew that attempting to force reluctant interviewees to talk would bring no additional data of value. We decided instead to concentrate our efforts on gathering ethnographic data and additional narrative accounts, as well as carefully analyzing all the data.

We also recognized that the very fact that 9/11 fatigue had occurred, and that the cultural winds were changing, was itself an important piece of data. In fact, this temporal marker added to our growing sense that the most intriguing story went far beyond the relatively static issues of respondents' experiences on and after the attacks or how the attacks had affected, for example, their political beliefs. Thus, our basic research question soon evolved from "What happened?" to "What *is* happening?" In other words, over time we began to realize that the phenomenon we were most interested in was, in fact, *what was happening over time.* While we had begun our research as, in essence, an oral history project about respondents' experiences on and after the attacks, our interviews and our ethnographic observations together (as well as, to a lesser degree, the accounts in our additional source materials) were most engaged with the issue of how respondents were experiencing the social and political changes that were occurring in the New York community over time and how they were interpreting and navigating the process of "getting back to normal." Indeed, what we were witnessing—and capturing—was a *process;* our interview and narrative data had crystallized one precious, but fleeting, moment in time, and our ethnographic data chronicled the reconstruction of "normalcy," with all its attendant hegemonic implications, following that moment.

ANALYZING YOUR DATA

In the methodological approach I emphasize in this chapter, data collection and data analysis are not discrete and wholly separate tasks. As mentioned earlier, your analysis of the data should begin at the two week (or so) reevaluation point and should continue throughout the rest of the time that you gather information—as well as, of course, beyond it. Though there is likely no way that your analysis will be able to keep up completely with the pace of your data collection (nor should it), the important point is that you want to stay as aware of what is going on in your data as possible, and that means starting to analyze the material early. By looking for patterns, key themes, and problems in your data while you are still in the field, rather than waiting until after the collection process is over, you will be much more attuned to what is emerging, whether your methods should be altered or supplemented, and at what point you have attained theoretical sufficiency.

Among the most helpful analytical strategies to keep you attuned to your data are coding and memo writing. Practitioners of grounded theory recommend two stages of coding: first, "initial coding," in which you examine the data very closely (e.g., examining an interview transcript word by word or line by line) for their analytic import, and then "focused coding," in which you select what seem to be the most useful codes from your initial coding to create tentative categories, which will then be applied to other data to determine their larger relevance.

Ideally, initial coding is done from interview transcripts or very comprehensive fieldnotes, so that you have a great deal of detail to sift through (and, certainly, a great deal of care should be taken to capture exact words or phrases used by respondents whenever possible). This is particularly important because one of the things you want to keep an eye out for in the initial coding phase is what are known as in vivo codes; that is, symbolic markers of participants' speech and meanings. These codes represent condensed meanings that respondents take for granted, and thus they offer a window into respondents' worldviews. While they may be new terms, they are more typically general terms used in a fresh or different way (Charmaz 2006). For instance, Anderson (1976; see also 2003) discovered that the labels "regular," "hoodlum," and "winehead" represented different levels of respectability among the group of African American street-corner men he studied; similarly, Eliasoph (1998) noted that the phrase "close to home" was used by volunteer activists to separate "do-able" problems from those that seemed more intractable and, thus, less desirable.

Examining in vivo codes involves recognizing that these words or phrases hold special meaning for respondents and, accordingly, should be unpacked and translated in order to shed light on their perspectives. This is part of the reason that initial coding is the ideal first step in this type of analysis: because it encourages you to examine your data very closely, it also makes it more likely that you will be able to recognize the words or phrases that are used frequently and/or that seem to hold special meaning. Such recognition, of course, is likely to facilitate important insights into respondents' worldviews. In our research, identifying "getting back to normal" as a phrase that was particularly laden with meaning for New Yorkers in the wake of 9/11 was an important discovery, as it highlighted New Yorkers' struggles in a state of disequilibrium and prompted us to seek out what "normal" meant (as well as how respondents envisioned getting back to it). Similarly, we discovered that respondents frequently referenced, both implicitly and explicitly, a "New York patriotism," which allowed them to express affinity with their local community while simultaneously distancing themselves from the more militaristic and exclusionary connotations of national patriotism.

Though our recognition of these (and other) in vivo codes helped deepen our understanding of the data tremendously, we were not exactly disciplined about making distinctions between initial and focused coding— indeed, in practice, we blurred the lines between them. One of the key reasons for this is that not all of us had had our interviews transcribed (yet another problem with the lack of standardization in our approach to data collection during the interviewing stage of the project). Thus, during the first few months of the project, when our weekly meetings were devoted specifically to sharing, discussing, and analyzing each interview, we sometimes worked directly from transcripts, while at other times we worked from very detailed memos that summarized and described the interviews. Initially, this did not seem to present too much of a problem, because we were only focused on getting a general sense of what had happened to interviewees on and after 9/11—the more descriptive oral history part of the project. Later, however, when the project evolved into an investigation of the process of constructing normalcy over time, Courtney, Aaron, and I regretted that all the interviews had not been transcribed. This feeling was particularly acute when we felt stuck; having the ability to code line by line with verbatim transcripts of all the interviews might ultimately have shortened the length of time that we puzzled over the data. In any case, we made do with what we had.

Though we did not engage in initial coding in a particularly rigorous way (i.e., literally going line by line), we engaged in *focused* coding with a great deal of rigor. We pored over both transcripts and memos (and, later, ethnographic fieldnotes) and took note of words and phrases that seemed particularly meaningful or poignant. Over the course of reading and rereading (and rereading and rereading) the data, we took note of concepts and categories that stood out, and then began to write memos about them.

The importance of memo writing as an analytic practice is difficult to overstate. Memos can contain ideas, stories, and explorations of concepts; generally speaking, they should be informal and relatively unpolished. Further, to be most useful, memos should not have a fully fleshed-out purpose, particularly in the initial stages of your analysis. For instance, do not tell yourself, "I have to write a memo on the way that X affects Y"; instead, use the memo to write out your thoughts on an interesting concept that emerged in some of your interviews: why, exactly, do you find it interesting? If it proves to be relevant in your other data, what might that mean for analysis overall? Not only is memo writing an excellent way to expand the analytic work you have done—and should continue to do—with coding, but it is also a great bridge to writing drafts of papers (and writing papers, as we all know, can often be quite terrifying, especially when starting out with a completely blank page). Above all, memo writing provides the opportunity to dialogue with yourself, to get your ideas out and explore them with little to no pressure.

When collaborating with others, memos are also very helpful in allowing you to exchange and develop ideas with the other people on your team. Courtney, Aaron, and I wrote countless memos on numerous topics: sometimes on specific topics that were beginning to emerge in the data (e.g., respondents' political conversions in the wake of 9/11, the ways respondents engaged in commemoration practices and media usage) and sometimes on ideas that we wanted to explore further because we theorized that they could be relevant to respondents' experiences (e.g., religious practices, differences in reactions by gender and race).[1] Sometimes we devoted entire memos just to the analysis of one respondent or group of respondents because we thought that there was something particularly intriguing in their experience(s) that was worth further thought. Our memos were typically one to three typewritten pages in length, though at times they were as short as two paragraphs or as long as six pages.

In the first few months of the project, we wrote memos at least weekly; after the interviews were completed (and after Courtney, Aaron, and I began working solely with each other), we wrote memos with decreasing frequency. After writing each memo, we would share it with the group and together discuss and/or investigate how relevant the ideas contained within it were to all the data (i.e., all the interviews as well as our ethnographic data and supplemental accounts) and if or how the ideas fit into the larger whole of the project. Indeed, here, too, collaborating with others proved to be both a blessing and a curse (though mostly a blessing). Having to constantly discuss our memos with others forced us to work through them in a way that would likely have not been possible otherwise. On the other hand, our discussions often knew no bounds, and, given our multiplicity of ideas and the multidimensionality of the data, we could—and did—get off track very easily.

WRITING IT UP

While the practice of writing memos helps enormously in the analytical process, it is also beneficial in that it forces you to get into the routine of writing. Indeed, doing a little bit of writing on a regular basis is a great way to demystify and depressurize the writing process. Since one of the most common places for scholars to experience paralysis is at the "writing stage," you will be far ahead in the game if you have already started to integrate writing into your analysis before it is time to start writing up your work for public consumption. As with the overlap between data collection and analysis, it is best not to think of the analysis period and the writing period as wholly separate, discrete stages of your research.

Drawing on the memos that you have already written, you should first concentrate primarily on further developing your analysis through writing. That is, do not start out expecting to write an entire draft from introduction to conclusion. Instead, expand your memos; think through your categories; make sure your analysis is sound and coherent. Because it is likely that more than one empirical and theoretical thread will have emerged from your analysis, you will have to consider which of these to focus on in your more formal writing. You will want to pick the thread(s) that best represent your data for the main paper or product; however, if appropriate, you may also want to separate out particular points or findings to further develop in additional publications.

When writing to publish, of course, you will have to (re)structure your work into the standard logico-deductive format typically required by academic journals. "Required formats often presuppose a traditional logico-deductive organization. Thus, we need to rethink the format and adapt it to our needs and goals" (Charmaz 2006, 154). One way to adapt the format requirements to this type of methodological approach is to delay writing the literature review until you have pieced together an original theory that fits your data; though it is often difficult to do this, putting it off is a fantastic exercise because it encourages you to articulate your own ideas first. You will then review the literature after you have developed those ideas sufficiently; indeed, having developed ideas and/or theories will mean that you will be able to focus more clearly and quickly on the relevant research literature. And, certainly, linking your work to a legitimate and interesting social science debate or discussion is very important. Though it is sometimes all too easy to fall into the trap of just being descriptive when working with new and unique data, keep in mind the larger purpose that your research can and should serve. What broader questions does it help to answer? Where does it overlap with other research? What audience are you trying to reach? Ultimately, why is *your* analysis of *this* sudden research opportunity important? (And remember that, in most cases, "because no one has ever written about it before" is not a satisfactory answer.)

As with most tasks, the more you write, the better your writing will be. You should expect to go through many drafts of a paper before you send it out for publication. The process of writing and rewriting helps ensure that implicit arguments are clear and provided with the appropriate context, that the necessary links are made with relevant literatures, that your categories receive critical examination, and that your analytic arguments are supported by data. With each draft, your work will grow more theoretical and comprehensive. Throughout the writing process, it is also extremely helpful to seek and incorporate feedback from others. This might take the form of having others (preferably, both social scientists and non–social scientists) comment on versions of your written work, or it might involve presenting your work in public; ideally, you will obtain feedback both ways.

An excellent place to start presenting your ideas is in smaller talks or conferences within your department. If there is not a regular institutionalized opportunity to give such a talk (e.g., a weekly departmental workshop or an annual departmental conference), you might consider scheduling something yourself to use as a forum for your work. After some practice at these relatively low-stakes talks, you will then be ready to present your research at larger venues (e.g., a regional or national social scientific conference), which will not only help to get the word out about your work but will help further hone your analysis. Remember that, whether the venue is small or large, informal or formal, people are typically very interested to hear about the new and unique data that come from sudden research opportunities. This was certainly the case with our research on 9/11; the topic was interesting to many, and, though we spent much of the first nine months in relative isolation, we eventually gave six public talks on our work, in settings ranging from the semiannual NYU Graduate Student Conference to the annual meeting of the American Sociological Association.

CONCLUSION: LOOKING BACK, MOVING FORWARD

After you make your work available for public consumption—whether through oral presentation, publication, or, preferably, both—it will eventually be time for the project to come to a close. You should be proud of yourself. Not only have you completed a research project successfully (a feat that is hardly a given), but you have persevered under conditions that are particularly conducive to anxiety. Indeed, because of the uncertainty of its terrain and the somewhat nonlinear nature of its methodological approach, scholars engaging in this type of research often feel at loose ends. Learning to tolerate and manage ambiguity and uncertainty is one of the most valuable skills a scholar can develop, perhaps especially when dealing with sudden and emergent data. It was certainly the case that Courtney, Aaron, and I often felt anxious: we worried frequently about the specter of thin data and worried that, despite all our hard work, we still would not wind up with anything worthwhile. We felt especially insecure because we had had to put so much of our other work on hold in order to pursue this research opportunity. What if it did not pan out? What if we did not know what we were doing? What if this project was just a black hole for our time and energy? What if we had made a big mistake?

Ultimately, however, despite the anxiety and the time it took away from my other work, our 9/11 research was among my best professional experiences to date. (I cannot speak for Courtney or Aaron, but I believe they feel similarly positive.) My work on the project brought several additional lines to my curriculum vitae, for which I am of course both thankful and proud. Perhaps even more important, however, it taught me that collaboration among equals can be an extremely rewarding process (if one that also needs to be at least somewhat disciplined), and that getting involved in a sudden research opportunity can be incredibly enriching and enlightening. Not only do you get to discover and explore completely new data, you are forced to react quickly and think creatively to do so, and that can be quite a thrilling experience. The process also provides an extraordinary opportunity for self-knowledge. Though I wish I had appreciated earlier the value of engaging the outside world (for much of those first nine months I felt too protective of and insecure about our nascent ideas to discuss them with others) and known how much care should be taken with those first initial decisions (as discussed earlier, some of the early decisions we made about sampling and transcribing haunted us to some degree), the project turned out to be an overwhelmingly positive experience: exciting, challenging, and deeply engaging.

In order to maximize your experience, however, it is also critical to think carefully about how you can integrate this particular research experience with the rest of your work. What are the links between this project and others that you have already completed? How does your body of work (including this project) link to the research that you would like to do in the future? Even if the similarities between projects are not immediately obvious, they are almost certainly there if you think hard enough—if not substantively then at least in the overlapping reasons that motivated you to study them. For example, though my 9/11 work may not initially seem to have much substantive overlap with my dissertation research on the experience of intergenerational downward mobility, I was motivated to pursue both projects because of my interest in the social psychological experience of individuals in the face of larger social phenomena. It is very important to start to build a coherent narrative about your work that integrates the kind of questions that are of interest to you. Though these questions may change or evolve with time, thinking about them as early as possible will set you more firmly on the path for a successful career as you move forward. As a result, your experience with this sudden research opportunity will not only contribute to your scholarly development, but it will be viewed positively by others who, rather than interpret it as an aberration or a detour from your "real" career, will see it as evidence that you can think on your feet, take initiative, craft an interesting and original project, and engage with the world around you. And they will be right.

NOTES

Many thanks to the Society for the Psychological Study of Social Issues and the Graduate School of Arts and Sciences at New York University, which provided the grants that funded the research described in these pages, and to Stanford University and the Family Research Consortium IV at the Center of Culture and Health in the Semel Institute for Neuroscience and Human Behavior at the University of California, Los Angeles, which provided me with the time and support to write this chapter. I am grateful to Eszter Hargittai for the invitation to write about this research and for the helpful feedback she provided along the way. Last but not least, I will always be grateful to Courtney Abrams and Aaron Panofsky, with whom I shared this very memorable research experience.

1. This latter type of memo writing veers dangerously close to applying preconceived categories to the data, which grounded theorists warn against because the category does not emerge organically from the data itself. And, interestingly enough, these ideas almost always went nowhere. Nonetheless, we found it to be a helpful exercise, both because it allowed us to get even closer to our data—that is, to learn what it *did not* contain as well as what it did contain—and, importantly, because it meant that we could feel secure that we had considered virtually every possible angle of relevance to the project.

REFERENCES

Abrams, Courtney B., Karen Albright, and Aaron L. Panofsky. 2004. Contesting the New York Community: From Liminality to the 'New Normal' in the Wake of September 11th. *City and Community* 3 (3): 189–220.

Anderson, Elijah. 1976. *A Place on the Corner.* Chicago: University of Chicago Press.

Anderson, Elijah. 2003. Jelly's Place: An Ethnographic Memoir. *Symbolic Interaction* 26:217–37.

Bryan, Jennifer L. 2004. Searching for 'the True Islam' in Hostile Times: The Impact of 9/11 on Arab Muslims in Jersey City. In *Wounded City: The Social Impact of 9/11,* ed. N. Foner, 133–59. New York: Russell Sage Foundation.

Charmaz, Kathy. 2006. *Constructing Grounded Theory: A Practical Guide through Qualitative Analysis.* London: Sage.

Deely, J. N. 1990. *Basics of Semiotics.* Bloomington: Indiana University Press.

Dey, Ian. 1999. *Grounding Grounded Theory.* San Diego: Academic Press.

Eliasoph, Nina. 1998. *Avoiding Politics: How Americans Produce Apathy in Everyday Life.* Cambridge: Cambridge University Press.

Elliott, James R., and Jeremy Pais. 2006. Race, Class, and Hurricane Katrina: Social Differences in Human Responses to Disaster. *Social Science Research* 35:295–321.

Fann, K. T. 1970. *Peirce's Theory of Abduction.* The Hague: Martinus Nijhoff.

Garfinkel, Harold. 1967. *Studies in Ethnomethodology.* Englewood Cliffs, NJ: Prentice-Hall.

Glaser, Barney G. 1978. *Theoretical Sensitivity.* Mill Valley, CA: Sociology Press.

Glaser, Barney G. 1992. *Basics of Grounded Theory Analysis.* Mill Valley, CA: Sociology Press.

Glaser, Barney G., and Anselm L. Strauss. 1967. *The Discovery of Grounded Theory: Strategies for Qualitative Research.* Chicago: Aldine.

Heritage, John. 1987. Ethnomethodology. In *Social Theory Today*, ed. A. Giddens and J. Turner, 224–72. Stanford: Stanford University Press.

Rodriguez, Havidan, Joseph Trainor, and Enrico L. Quarantelli. 2006. Rising to the Challenges of a Catastrophe: The Emergent and Prosocial Behavior following Hurricane Katrina. *Annals of the American Academy of Political and Social Science* 604:82–101.

Rosenthal, G. 2004. Biographical Research. In *Qualitative Research Practice*, ed. C. Seale, G. Gobo, J. F. Gubrium, and D. Silverman, 48–64. London: Sage.

Rossman, Gabriel. 2004. Elites, Masses, and Media Blacklists: The Dixie Chicks Controversy. *Social Forces* 83:61–79.

Steinert, Heinz. 2003. Unspeakable September 11th: Taken-for-Granted Assumptions, Selective Reality Construction, and Populist Politics. *International Journal of Urban and Regional Research* 27:651–65.

Strauss, Anselm L. 1987. *Qualitative Analysis for Social Scientists*. New York: Cambridge University Press.

WAT R U DOIN?

Studying the Thumb Generation Using Text Messaging

ESZTER HARGITTAI AND CHRIS KARR

A relatively recent and sudden change in the landscape of American youth can be seen in the growing numbers of people walking around with their heads looking down and their fingers moving vigorously on a gadget. Cell phones have spread widely, and their use for communication through text messaging has taken off considerably. Is there a way for social scientists to benefit from the proliferation of this technology? Can such short messages help us understand human behavior better?

We were in the midst of an unrelated study when we suddenly realized that we could piggyback on it to supplement survey questions with time-diary data collected using text messaging from college students about their everyday activities. The method of data collection that relies on calling respondents has suffered from declining response rates for years, while more traditional time-diary data collection means (e.g., journaling or beeper studies) have posed their own set of challenges regarding logistics and data quality. We were curious to know if text messaging, a new method of communication already present in many people's everyday lives, might allow us to improve on existing methods.

With this in mind, we decided to add a component to a larger study that was already under way with questions that we believed were worth pursuing even if, in the end, our time-diary data collection ended up being exploratory at best. Overall, we had both methodological and substantive reasons to pursue this new work, and given what was already being invested in the larger project, we decided that the marginal costs were worth our time and effort. In hindsight, we are very happy that we had seized this opportunity, and although it took more time—as it always does!—than we had anticipated, we achieved interesting and unique results that were well worth the investment.

At the time we embarked on this research, one of us (Hargittai) was in the midst of working on a two-year project that involved studying adolescents' Internet uses, skills, and participation by means of surveys and in-person observations. The study also had a longitudinal component whereby some participants would be randomly assigned into a training program and then observed again at a later point in time—along with those who had not received training—to test whether the intervention had made a difference in students' online know-how. These parameters meant that some people were already going to be approached for participation more than once. More important, the data that we had begun collecting on respondents could easily be merged with the additional information we were hoping to collect about them through text messaging.

Every methodology has its limitations, and we can only learn so much about any topic using just one method. One challenge of surveys—the main method of data collection in the larger study—is that it is hard to gather nuanced and reliable information about the details of people's everyday time uses. This concern prompted the idea of trying to gather some additional time-diary data from respondents (e.g., Larson and Csikszentmihalyi; 1983, Robinson 1977). However, given students' busy lives and the difficulty in convincing people to participate in recurring studies, the challenge remained: How do we collect diary data from 18- and 19-year-olds who are physically hard to pin down amid their busy college lives?

This age group is sometimes referred to as the Thumb Generation, because young adults spend so much time on their cell phones either calling people in their networks or texting them using the dial pad of their phones. Data that one of us (Hargittai) had collected a year earlier about a similar group suggested that most students in the population of the larger study owned cell phones, and many used text messaging. Accordingly, our belief that texting was a popular activity was not simply based on unsubstantiated assumptions but rather, available data. In fact, a look at the survey responses of the current study's sample made it clear that over 98 percent owned a cell phone and that over 90 percent of those cell phone owners used the device for text messaging. This gave credence to the idea that collecting diary data through the relatively unobtrusive medium of text messaging might yield helpful information. The method would not require researchers and respondents to be physically copresent, and it would draw on an activity in which students are already engaged during their everyday lives using a device they already own and operate.

In what follows, we will describe the various research tasks associated with this project. We will say a few words about the long-distance nature of this collaboration. Next, we offer a full time-line of the research project in order to give a realistic overview of what type of time commitment a study of this sort entails. One's first reaction may be that collecting diary data through text messaging should be fairly simple—that is what we had thought! But not surprisingly, as with any other research project, once one hits the ground, complexities emerge from every direction. Having described the motivation and context of the study, we go on to offer detailed descriptions of the following important components: establishing and setting up the technical and logistical system for sending and receiving text messages, developing and revising a coding scheme, building and refining the coding interface, and finally, collecting the data. We conclude with a discussion of main lessons learned and the kinds of challenges that may be encountered when trying to scale up from our experiences.

LONG-DISTANCE INTERDISCIPLINARY COLLABORATION

While somewhat tangential to the study, one important point we want to get across is that long-distance collaboration is very much feasible in this day and age and that researchers should not be deterred from pursuing a joint project simply because they are not physically copresent. The lead on the overall study was a junior faculty member at the time (Hargittai) on leave from Northwestern University at the Center for Advanced Study in the Behavioral Sciences in Stanford, California. The collaborator on this study (Karr) was in his first year of graduate school in the Media, Technology, and Society PhD program at Northwestern University.

This work cut across academic positions (faculty/student), disciplines (communication/sociology/computer science/psychology), and distances (California/Illinois). Hargittai approached Karr to see if he had an interest in the study and, after a positive response, the collaboration began. We established early on that outcomes would be coauthored assuming similar levels of input from both researchers. Given some of the technical details involved with the project, the interdisciplinary nature of the partnership worked to our advantage. It did pose some challenges especially when attempting to communicate certain ideas through our different disciplinary terminologies (see also Sandvig's piece in this volume). However, frequent communication—mainly using e-mail—helped clarify any confusion in a timely manner. The upside of such group effort is not only that different types of tasks can be addressed quickly internally by team members (i.e., it is not necessary to hire a programmer if a tool needs to be developed), but also that the researchers are very likely to learn about new concepts, terms, and tools associated with the work.

Because one of us was on leave two thousand miles away from the other and from the study location, almost all of the work on this project happened without any in-person meetings. Given this, the experiences described herein are not simply instructive examples of collaboration, but long-distance communication and coordination among multiple people and project components. We want to acknowledge the important role that free online services, such as the videoconferencing tool Skype, play in making such undertakings possible.

Finally, while only two names appear on the byline of this chapter, it is important to note the helpful input from our larger research team members throughout the study. Such expressions of gratitude are usually left for an acknowledgments section, but we consider it an important part of our entire research process worth mentioning in a behind-the-scenes piece of this sort. During the time of this study, the research group for the larger undertaking met weekly to share progress reports and address questions raised by current project specifics. Consequently, the work benefited from all team members' regular feedback. Moreover, much of the coding was done by undergraduate research assistants whose continuous input was very helpful to the project. We address some logistical specifics related to this latter point later in the chapter.

TIME LINE

Before launching into a detailed description of how we approached the various components of the project—from figuring out the technical specifications of our messaging system to recruiting respondents, doing the data collection, and compiling our coding scheme—we want to present an overall time line of the project (table 1). Our goal here is to give the reader a realistic sense of the many behind-the-scenes activities that are an integral part of such a study but that rarely ever see the light of day in publications.

TABLE 1. Time Line of the Project

	Nov	Dec	Jan	Feb	Mar	Apr	May	Jun	Jul
Project idea, first e-mail exchanges	■								
Seeking funding		■							
IRB (supplement to main study)		■							
Securing funding			■						
Taking notes on our methods		■	■	■	■	■	■	■	■
Test of first system (just the co-authors)		■							
Building our messaging system		■							
Building our coding interface			■						
First internal pretest on research group			■						
Constructing and fine-tuning our coding scheme				■				■	
Training coders				■				■	
Fine-tuning our coding interface				■					■
Coding of pretest data (to test coding interface and scheme)					■				
Second internal pretest on research group (expanded group)						■			
Recruitment of respondents					■				
First data collection (15 participants)						■			
Second data collection (20 participants)						■			
Third data collection (21 participants)							■		
Fourth data collection (4 participants)								■	
Compiling full data set								■	
Preliminary coding of study data (to test coding scheme)								■	
Coding of data									■
Write-up of methods									■

INITIAL PLAN OF ACTION

As noted earlier, we approached this project with the belief that it would be relatively straightforward. After all, text messaging is a common activity among college students, and the technology seems fairly simple. How hard could all this be? Those are, of course, famous last words at the initial stage of any project when the researcher almost inevitably assumes that the study in question will be a quick and easy undertaking.

To tackle the methodological issues raised by relying on text messaging, we planned to send automated text-message requests to which respondents could reply. As the section on setting up our system attests, while not impossibly difficult, this process was nowhere near as simple as one might think.

To address the substantive questions, we were interested in collecting four types of data from respondents for each moment in their day when we prompted them for a response.

1. Location: Where is the respondent located?
2. Activity: What is the respondent doing? (multiple activities are possible)
3. Social surroundings: What are the gender and number—if any—of the people with the respondent, and what is their relationship to the respondent?
4. Communication processes: What—if any—communication processes is the respondent engaged in? In particular, is the respondent using any communication media?

This information is in line with episode data collected in traditional time-diary studies (Pentland et al. 1999, 27). However, the difference here is that we had a particular focus on communication processes and digital media use. Moreover, our respondents were constrained by the limitations of the medium. Is it realistic to expect such detailed information from respondents in 140 to 160 characters, which is the message limit imposed by service providers? Although the purpose of this chapter is not to discuss our substantive findings, the results are encouraging. Many respondents shared considerable amounts of information about their whereabouts, allowing us to supplement our survey data with additional details about the role of digital media in students' lives. However, as our notes will demonstrate, gathering this type of information from participants through this restricted medium requires communicating detailed instructions to them ahead of time, and that raises its own set of logistical issues.

SETTING UP THE SYSTEM FOR SENDING AND RECEIVING MESSAGES

We had to keep several issues in mind while considering various technical solutions to our data collection challenge. Our requests were to be received by, and responses sent from, participants' mobile phones. Our "pinging" system—as we called it, in a nod to the practice of sending short messages to networked machines to assess their availability—would have to meet two main criteria. First, we had to automate the process of sending out requests for participant responses. That is, we needed the ability to schedule the requests ahead of time and implement that schedule with minimal human intervention. After all, it is not reasonable for any one person to sit next to a machine and send out requests to numerous respondents every hour for a full day, and it is certainly not a very scalable solution if we wanted to run the study—as we did—multiple times on larger groups in the future. Second, we needed a way to collect responses and store them for later aggregation and coding. Given the various issues that may arise during the study, our system needed to be flexible and extensible so that we could modify it to meet our particular needs. This meant exploring and evaluating competing systems to determine the best fit for our project.

Evaluating Existing Systems for Data Collection through Text Messaging

It is usually best to avoid reinventing the wheel when it comes to various components of a project. Thus, we started by examining a few research systems that were targeted to studies similar to our own in the hopes that we might be able to use them for our purposes. In the end, this process did not reveal any systems that we could adopt for our study though it did help us clarify the needs of our project. We include this part of the process here because it is precisely the kind of detailed description that is never included in project write-ups but nevertheless takes considerable time and effort and therefore must be part of any realistic research plan.

After performing a literature review on related studies, we found a few preexisting systems. We first looked at Momento (Carter, Mankoff, and Heer 2007) to determine if this tool kit for ubiquitous-computing experiments fit our needs. We evaluated its architecture, documentation, and design goals. Its focus on using SMS messaging to communicate with respondents mirrored our own, but we found that it was ultimately a poor fit for our needs. The fact that it originated in the human-computer interaction field meant that it was primarily a tool for simulating interactions on mobile devices rather than a robust and extensible data collection instrument. Momento is an impressive tool for testing and designing mobile software and devices, but we determined that in order to adapt it to our purposes, substantial additional development would be required. Furthermore, Momento's design required much more human intervention to conduct studies than we could provide.

We also looked at the Experience Sampling Program (Feldman Barrett and Barrett 2001), a tool kit for creating sophisticated time-diary studies like the one we were designing. Its study setup and analysis features would have been a good match for our project, but it required that the participants be equipped with customized preprogrammed handheld computers running the Palm or Windows Mobile operating systems. Since one of the most novel components of our study was its reliance on devices that participants already owned, requiring specific pieces of equipment or programs was a significant deterrent. We did not want to be hindered by requirements of particular hardware or software specifications beyond what would be readily available to anyone who has a text-messaging subscription on a regular cell phone plan. Providing study respondents with such devices would be cost prohibitive, and introducing a new device would recreate many of the problems associated with traditional paper-based or beeper diary studies (see, e.g., Pentland et al. 1999; Christensen and Feldman Barrett 2003). For example, respondents would be required to integrate the new device into their daily routine (decreasing the likelihood that the equipment is continuously present), and we would have to retrieve the apparatus at the conclusion of the study (for complexities involved in such undertakings, see Adam, Doane, and Mendelsohn in this volume).

We also evaluated several commercial services for sending and receiving messages, but we found that the services were either too limited, too unreliable, or too expensive (or some combination of these three) for our needs. We investigated a number of other providers, which supply services that avoid problems such as spam filtering, but these services were both too expensive and a poor fit for our needs, having been designed primarily for regular marketing campaigns that either broadcasted one-way announcements or solicited simple responses ("text '1' to vote for the first contestant"). Their pricing models also assumed a longer continuing business relationship than was compatible with our study's time line. Finally, we were mindful throughout this initial process of the need to avoid becoming locked into any single service provider. This was important in case it disappeared, started charging too much, or changed the system in ways that would make it difficult to use for our purposes. Following our strategy, we could switch services without too much setback (both in terms of labor required to update our system and time lost to revising our course of action).

After several weeks of research and investigation, we decided that the best approach would be to create our own system. We had clear goals for it, and this greatly assisted in defining both the scope of the project and the necessary features of the system.

Creating Our Own System

From the beginning, we decided to focus on a simple, yet extensible system that would allow us to develop and deploy it quickly so that we could take advantage of a rapid iterative testing and development process. We decided to run the test using AOL's instant messenger network since it included free SMS integration allowing users to send short messages to mobile phones. We discovered this feature in our prior day-to-day use of the service. Combined with robust open-source libraries that provided access to the AOL network, this was a vital component of our early development and testing. We simulated the study using this system to determine how the software might function in practice. We sent and received messages manually using a compatible instant-messaging client.

We asked members of our research group to act as pretesters. Of course, we did not require these team members to participate, but given that most other people in the research group were involved in doing studies on this same larger project, and given that we have a collaborative atmosphere in the lab, most research group members willingly participated, giving us helpful feedback. We participated in this pretest ourselves as we believed it important to acquire firsthand experience with the method from the perspective of a respondent.

In this simulation, we experimented with the format of the requests, and we evaluated the frequency and content of the responses. By format, we mean the phrasing and structure of the requests that fit within the constrained 140–160 character limit of text messages. Regarding content of the responses, we were curious to see whether we could make sense of the responses and whether they included the type of information we were seeking. As to the frequency of responses, we wanted to know how realistic it was to contact people for feedback about what they were doing on an hourly basis. We also solicited input from the pretesters to gauge how intrusive and demanding the study was from their perspective. We found that participating in the simulation was not excessively laborious and that we were able to collect the kinds of information that we wanted. With this helpful experience under our belt, we proceeded to build the actual system to be used for the study.

We first focused on the immediate task of data collection. We needed an automatic system that would send requests and collect responses for later analysis. To fill this need, we constructed a Java Web application that maintained a schedule of requests to be sent out at predefined times. We created a simple Web-based interface that allowed the manual scheduling of requests, but we also provided a remote application programming interface to be used by external scripts to batch-schedule complete studies.[1] These scripts were typically less than 100 lines of code, and the bulk of that consisted of listing the respondents and their schedules. To further simplify the implementation, we avoided using a relational database server and used a simpler XML file. We chose XML as the storage format since it is an open text-based standard that may be read and manipulated using a wide variety of programming languages and tools. This provided us the widest latitude for the future creation of tools to parse, translate, and manipulate the collected data. Since our application only required a single stand-alone software package, we were able to set it up and host it on a departmental server with very little assistance from the local IT staff. Overall, building this component of the system took less than three weeks of part-time effort. This quick development cycle allowed us to conduct fully functional—that is, automated as opposed to manual compared to our earlier pretest—live tests with lab members and to begin investigating methods for sending and receiving text messages.

As we developed the Web application, we used the AOL network again for the initial testing of the custom-built software. Since we worried that we would be banned for abusing the network if we sent out too many text messages (AOL provides the service for free, and pays the SMS costs on behalf of its users), we began researching suitable replacements for it. A number of commercial firms offered similar text-messaging services, but we found that the services were either too constrained or too expensive for our needs. Many services provided message deliveries but were unable to receive any responses. Firms that provided both the sending and receiving services charged high setup fees for establishing the necessary mobile presence and short code—the five-digit number used to contact systems through text messaging—in addition to charging substantial rates for the continued service and maintenance. We found a provider that offered the features we needed for a reasonable per-message fee, but after testing, we realized it was not sufficiently reliable for our study since the way the provider sent our messages activated the spam defenses on the mobile phone networks.

In the end, we addressed the various issues by creating an in-house solution that used one of our team member's own mobile phone to send and receive messages.[2] We connected this phone to a recycled lab computer that received commands to send and collect messages and communicated with the phone using open-source programs. We had no problem developing a suitable plug-in that connected to this system. We had some initial concerns about the reliability and cost of using a regular mobile phone for this purpose, but this ended up being more reliable than any of the alternatives we previously considered. Furthermore, it was less costly than the other options, even though we used a regular data plan provided by the phone's carrier.

Overall, the creation of this system followed a typical software development pattern. To summarize, in our first live pretest we manually simulated how the proposed software would work in practice. Next, we built the software and tested it using AOL's instant messaging network. A month after the initial simulated pretest, we did another pretest using our first service provider and discovered its reliability problems. We spent several months researching alternative service providers and then building our own homemade text-messaging setup that used our own mobile phone. We tested this configuration of hardware and software and found that it was very reliable. A week later, we went live and started collecting data from respondents.

All in all, the main takeaway message is that researching available tools is important, but one should not compromise core needs of the project just to cut down on some initial up-front investment in tool development. Moreover, continuous testing of the instruments is essential for addressing the various issues that arise during such an undertaking.

DEVELOPING AND REFINING THE CODING SCHEME

As noted earlier, the overarching substantive goal of our study was to get a better understanding of how digital media are integrated into adolescents' everyday lives. We collected diary data with the goal of seeing how often college students in our sample use various digital devices and what types of communication processes they engage in during the course of a day. That is, we were interested in seeing how much time they spend watching television, using the Web, interacting with others face to face, and so on, and how reports about these activities through the text-messaging medium compare to participants' survey responses about their media uses. In addition, we wanted to learn about digital media uses and other communication practices in the context of their other activities. Ultimately, this meant creating a coding scheme that would account for anything anyone might do. Obviously this is a daunting task with unlimited options. We made this task manageable by deciding on the categories of information most relevant for our purposes, and we classified responses by type. We will not get into the specifics of the coding scheme here, but we do want to say a few words about how we developed it and refined it during the study.

Text-message responses had to be coded by more than one person to establish intercoder reliability. We trained two undergraduate research assistants for this task in addition to doing a bit of preliminary coding ourselves. As when we were developing the messaging system, here again we asked research team members to give us feedback about both the tool and any difficulties or ambiguities posed by the messages they were coding (see the next section for details about developing the technical tool we used for coding). We decided to rely mainly on e-mail for communication and a flurry of messages soon flooded our mailboxes. Prompt responses were important so the coders could proceed with their job. We realized that several types of issues were cropping up with some regularity so we decided to take a closer look at the coding scheme as a whole.

We met using Skype and made significant progress. While e-mail can be extremely helpful, it is hard to replace the efficiency that can be achieved in one or two hours of face-to-face discussion about questions of this sort. This holds true even when not all participants are physically co-present. Soon after our initial meeting, we held another meeting and came close to finalizing our scheme with only a few changes left. A few more minor adjustments surfaced in the following days, but before long we were able to finalize the coding scheme.

After these alterations, the research assistants began the coding process again. We made it clear to them that this was in part a methodological project so they should not feel that the time and effort spent on coding that was now discarded had been wasted. It was important for their morale, we believed, that they understood how the feedback they had given us was an integral part of the project, that it was an important part of their job, and that their input was taken very seriously, had been incorporated into the project, and was much appreciated. In fact, it was essential throughout this exercise to let research team members know that we took their comments very seriously and encouraged their contributions.

Despite every attempt to make study participants' responses systematic, the reality of data collection is never as clean and straightforward as one envisions up front. While the majority of the responses we received were sent shortly after the participants got our requests for information, some came in considerably later. This was mainly due to disruptions in people's service (whether due to technical unavailability or a conscious effort to disconnect from the network in some situations, e.g., during class time). Consequently, some responses came in after we had already sent subsequent requests. These cases were usually easy to note since they entailed receiving a quick succession of participant responses that were separated only by minutes as opposed to the standard hour or so difference between messages. These responses were typically sent as a batch when the respondent finally got around to responding to requests missed. We interpreted responses in order (unless the participant specified a time stamp in the message that led us to believe we had not received the messages in order) so overall this did not pose a major challenge.

Another issue we had not anticipated—and one that was not trivial to handle—concerned responses that referenced information communicated to us by participants in earlier messages during the day. On occasion we would receive a message that may simply state "same as before" or "still at work" without further elaboration. In such cases, we may have already possessed additional information about the setting, but we had to decide how to code the entry as it did not itself contain additional information.[3] We decided to add fields to the coding scheme signaling whether the four main types of information had been included in the message itself, even if the information was known to us but not made explicit in the short response.

All in all, this was a very detailed and valuable exercise. Getting the coding scheme right is crucial to a study's success. In particular, it is important not to lose information about the data at this stage. It may be that later in the project we decide to get rid of certain nuances in the data set by collapsing various categories or values. Nonetheless, not knowing all details of potential analyses ahead of time, it is best to hold on to as much detail about the data as we have at our disposal at the initial coding stage. Collapsing and aggregating material is always a possibility later, whereas any information lost during coding remains lost to all subsequent investigations (unless one goes back to the raw data, which is not realistic in most cases given the effort involved).

BUILDING AND FINE-TUNING THE CODING INTERFACE

With the data collection components in place and an idea of what information we wanted to extract from the collected data systematically, we began developing a tool for coding and annotating the responses we would receive from participants (fig. 1). We wanted to be able to create a flexible and user-friendly interface. Since we would have several people working on the coding—on occasion concurrently—we also wanted a tool that was accessible from within a Web browser and could be used by more than one person at a time. This remote accessibility allowed coding to take place from different locations.

To provide a rich interface that avoided the pitfalls of cross-browser incompatibilities, we used Adobe's Flash as our platform. We created a tool that directly imports the data collected by the scheduler and builds an interface that reflects the desired coding scheme. The coding scheme is saved as an XML file that the tool interprets to construct a suitable interface. Components of this interface can be as simple as a checkbox or as complex as a tree view that allows multiple selections. A paging mechanism allows the interface to represent coding schemes of arbitrary length, thereby not imposing a technical limitation on the scheme authors. Again, by using XML, we were able to test and develop the scheme rapidly and iteratively. Had we used an external database or other file format, this would have delayed our development by introducing additional installation and integration requirements. Our format allowed us to add new fields and options by simply updating the file in a text editor. This proved useful when team members recognized that the scheme was missing crucial items that needed to be included.

Since we had previously obtained the Flash software for a prior project, we incurred no costs when creating this interface. However, we should note that unlike the Java tools used to build the scheduler, the Flash tools do cost several hundred dollars, and this should be taken into consideration if money is unavailable. Overall, it took us about two weeks of part-time work to create the initial version of the coding tool.

Once we finished development of the tool, we tested it to learn how

Respondents	Ping and Response Timeline	Swap View

Respondents		Ping and Response Timeline
2007-04-11		*** 2007-04-25 @ 14:29:57: Lecture class, watching movie, 2 friends F, movie projector
2007-04-11		*** 2007-04-25 @ 15:30:3: Cafeteria, eating, 5 friends F, no media
2007-04-11		*** 2007-04-25 @ 17:32:31: Van,listening to music,dad and sister, listening to ipod
2007-04-11		*** 2007-04-25 @ 17:37:3: At home, eating and watching tv, mom; dad; 3 sisters ; 1 brother; 1 niec
2007-04-11		*** 2007-04-25 @ 18:19:33: Home, watching tv, mom 2sisters 1brother, television
2007-04-11		*** 2007-04-25 @ 20:36:20: Home, doing homework,2 sisters mom dad and 1 brother, using computer
2007-04-11		*** 2007-04-25 @ 20:38:50: Home,doing homework, mom Dad 1 brother 2 sisters, using computer
2007-04-11		
2007-04-11		2007-04-25 @ 20:38:50: Home,doing homework, mom Dad 1 brother 2 sisters, using computer
2007-04-11		
2007-04-25		☐ This response is interesting.
2007-04-25		☐ Has notes
2007-04-25		Notes
2007-04-25		
2007-04-25		
2007-04-25		☐ Delete this response.
2007-04-25		Reason for deletion
2007-04-25		
2007-04-25		
2007-04-25		☐ Merge this response.
2007-04-25		Reason for merge
2007-04-25		
2007-04-25		
2007-04-25		☑ Did report social surroundings
2007-04-25		☑ Did report location
2007-04-25		☐ Public location
2007-04-25		☑ Did report activity
2007-04-25		Page 1 of 7 Save - +

Fig. 1.   The Web-based coding interface

well it met our needs. As described in the previous section, we trained undergraduate research assistants, and using data collected from our pretests, we started coding responses. There are always aspects of coding—both at the substantive and technical levels—that are impossible to predict without putting a tool into action. Input from the research assistants started coming in soon after we started this exercise, and we promptly made changes to the interface to address the various concerns having to do with both the usability of the tool and the coding scheme (whose compilation we described in detail in the previous section). We received another round of feedback at a later stage in the project when we moved on to coding responses from the actual study. Again, we responded promptly to all suggestions. That round led to some more elaborate changes to the system such as, for example, the addition of a tree-view widget to facilitate navigation between coding options.

All in all, having our own interface to code the responses worked out well. We were fortunate to have a team member (Karr) who had the necessary expertise to implement the interface. Something similar could likely be achieved by hiring someone part time. In addition to the added financial cost, the downside of such a solution, of course, is that the person would not be available as readily and promptly as a member of the research project. Based on our experiences, it is worth having such a customized platform. With the refinements suggested by the research assistants who were using the interface the most, the tool helped speed up coding considerably.

DATA COLLECTION

Getting IRB Approval

Before we could proceed with going in the field, we had to obtain permission to do so from our Institutional Review Board for Human Subjects (IRB). Since we were piggybacking on an existing project that had already obtained IRB approval, we submitted a revision request to the already approved study. It turns out that gaining approval for a revision to an existing project can be much quicker than starting up a new study. This makes sense since the board will have already reviewed the overall framework and logistics of the project. With experience, we also knew what specifics (all of them!) the IRB would want from us, and so we were sure to include everything in detail in order to avoid having to revise the initial submission. This worked out well, and within a few weeks we were approved to proceed with data collection.

Sampling

Since this study was part of a larger data collection effort, we did not face the task of creating a sampling frame. The sampling frame was the group of students who had been recruited for the observational and interview component of the larger study examining adolescents' digital media uses, skills, and participation. The overarching study was based on very rigorous sampling methodology, and so we knew that we were working with a random sample of students from a well-defined population. More specifically, the study was based on students enrolled in the one required course at the University of Illinois, Chicago. That study had achieved a high response rate of 82 percent, and the follow-up segment was similarly successful at 53 percent in recruiting students into the observational component of the project. Therefore, we knew that our participants would be a diverse group.

Working with the research assistants who were conducting the interviews with the participants in the observational study, we recruited students into the text-messaging project by using the end of the observational session as an opportunity to ask whether they would be willing to take part in this additional study. If they agreed, we asked them to sign a separate consent form for the texting project and gave them compensation for their anticipated messaging fees. Arranging these logistics at this stage of the process was important given that the whole point of this methodology was to avoid the need for physical copresence with participants for the actual data collection.

Compensation

Needless to say, paying people up front for their participation in a study is tricky since it raises concerns about respondents running off with the money without meeting their end of the agreement. We were nervous about this and addressed it by providing an incentive for participation that students would get after the data collection. We gave respondents $10 cash up front for subsidizing their text-messaging fees associated with the study. In addition, we committed to sending them a $15 gift certificate at the end of the data collection. We also conducted a drawing for an iPod where each text message sent to us in response to our requests added to the likelihood of a person being picked the winner. Our hope was that this would provide an added incentive for participation. Overall, most students readily participated, and only in a few cases did we need to send a few reminder messages (see below for more details on this point).

Integrating Participant Information

Since we wanted to study the participants throughout their waking hours, we needed to know when people would not be asleep so that we could tailor the schedule of messages accordingly. This is information one could collect about participants when they agree to be in the study, but we had neglected to do so. Contacting respondents for this information gave us the opportunity to remind people of the study. We had participants' e-mail addresses and cell phone numbers from our original recruiting, and so we were able to contact them using both voice and text messages, in addition to e-mail, if necessary.

We used a simple spreadsheet for keeping track of all relevant information about respondents, which concerned participants' e-mail addresses, mobile numbers, and availability during the day of the study.[4] The day before the study, we filled in any missing information about when respondents would be awake with our default values for availability (10:00 a.m.–10:00 p.m.), and we translated the information into a short Ruby script that scheduled the messages on the scheduler Web application. These scripts rarely exceeded 70 lines of code. The day before the study was also dedicated to setting up the system and conducting some preliminary tests to confirm that there were no problems with the configuration. The evening before the study, we scheduled a handful of messages to be sent to our own mobile phones. This allowed us to verify that we received the scheduled messages and that the software received and cataloged our responses. After we were confident that the system was sound, we ran the study script to schedule the messages for the upcoming data collection.

Reminders to Participants

Given the time that elapsed between recruitment of respondents into the study and the date of our data collection, it was important to remind participants of the project a few days before going live with data collection. We also wanted to verify that the cell phone numbers we had been given were in order and that we had people's awake hours to know when to send them our automated pings. Accordingly, we had to leave enough response time between the time of our notification and the study to hear back from students. After realizing from our first run that contacting students on Monday for a Wednesday study may be cutting it close, we started making e-mail contact on Friday for a Wednesday study.

While most of the e-mail confirmations we received verified the mobile numbers we had on hand, we did find a few errors where a mobile number had been miscommunicated, and so it was helpful to double-check these crucial details. In addition to the request for information about waking hours, these e-mail messages included reminders about the study as a whole, the goals of the project, and information about how to participate.

Even with the added lead time, not all participants responded to our requests in a timely manner, and in the days leading up to the study we resent the message to those who had not gotten back to us until we received a response. It was also useful for the lead investigator to e-mail the students to remind them that they had already been paid for their participation, and so while they were certainly free to decline participation—an important caveat in compliance with human subjects protection guidelines—they would have to return the money to us if they did not take part. (Of course, there was no way for us to pursue the money if students decided to back out and not send back the $10, but it was worth a mention.) Keeping a polite tone and explicitly acknowledging that the study was voluntary was important throughout this communication. If we did not obtain information about hours from a respondent then we scheduled the person's participation in the study using our default time window that stretched from ten o'clock in the morning until ten o'clock at night. This was extremely rare, however, and we only had to resort to calling people up to check on participation in a few cases.

Finally, to test the system and get the respondents into the mode of communicating with us through text messaging, we sent a reminder to respondents' phones the night before the study noting that the study would begin the next morning and suggesting that they add the message's sender to their address book. The challenge of writing this reminder message—and all other messages we sent—was that such messages had to comprise less than 140–160 characters in order to comply with restrictions that some phone companies put on the length of text messages. We ended up using the following 133-character text as the reminder message the evening before the study: "Tomorrow we will be conducting the SMS study you signed up for. Please respond to all messages you receive from this number tomorrow." We avoided using shorthand messages in case any of our participants were unfamiliar with them.

Going Live

Using the system that we built for text messaging, we collected diary data from 60 respondents in four stages over the course of three months. Because this project supplemented another one and relied on it for recruiting purposes, our time line was dependent on the logistics of the larger project. If we had not had this constraint, the entire study could have been run much more quickly. We conducted the study in several phases, because we wanted to make sure that data collection occurred close to the time when respondents were recruited into the study and thus less likely to forget about their participation.

While we managed to engage all of the people who had signed up for our first two groups, our third attempt proved less successful. Of the 26 people who signed up to participate, 5 did not respond to our text-messaging requests. We recontacted the absent participants and all of them enrolled in a fourth makeup study two weeks later. In the end, 4 of them responded to the messages in this last round of data collection.

Participants received messages from us during the course of the data collection day. A few minutes before our first request for information, we sent a message alerting the participant that the study was about to begin. The 136-character message read as follows: "Good morning. Thank you for agreeing to participate in our text messaging study today. You will receive our first request for info soon." After the morning reminder, we sent messages hourly requesting that the participants respond with their location, activity, social context, and any media in use. Again, we faced the challenge of fitting the instructions into a very short message, this one 147 characters long: "Please reply with your location, current activity, people you are with (number, your relationship to them, gender) and any media you are using now." We sent these messages fifteen minutes after the hour so that we avoided capturing any nontypical activities that may be associated with the top of the hour (start of a work shift, a class, or a meeting, to name a few).

After the last request for information had been transmitted, we sent a final 103-character message a few minutes later informing participants that the study was over, thanking them for their participation, and providing contact information in case they had any questions. ("The SMS study is finished for the day. Thank you for your participation. Questions? Call: xxx-xxx-xxxx.") We also included ourselves in the list of participants in order to ensure that we received all of the same messages as the participants. The goal was to identify any problems in the transmission process immediately. Fortunately, we encountered none.

While we encouraged participants to respond to the messages as soon as possible, we realized that immediate responses would often be infeasible. Students might be in class or a meeting and unable to respond. It was also possible that they would receive our messages while out of range. We instructed them to respond at the next nearest time they were able to do so with information on what they had been doing at the time they had received the message. To eliminate any confusion about the time a message was sent and because not all cell phones include an automatic time stamp on text messages, we included this information as the first few characters of each text message we sent out to respondents.

The process of running the study was largely automatic and only required one team member to contact the participants, collect their information, schedule the study, and monitor the study for any unforeseen problems. The bulk of the work was concentrated in the days before the study, with the majority of the effort focused on establishing contact with the participants. A moderate amount of effort was involved in writing the scheduling script, but this took less than an hour for the base script and less than twenty minutes for customization with any given case of data collection. It was important for one of us to be present with the system during the day of the study, but monitoring the progress was a background task that only required attention every hour or so. Shutting down the study the next morning required that we archive the collected data and shut down the software. This typically took less than half an hour. Overall, all four instances of our data collection went smoothly, something we attribute to our extensive testing and tweaking leading up to data collection.

Data Processing

After shutting down the study, we moved the collected data to a university-based shared network space for later use. In preparation for coding the collected data, we first combined the responses into a single file and cleaned the data set by getting rid of text messages that were not substantive in nature. (The participants often sent simple "ok" messages to our reminders about the study. We discarded these so as not to clutter our coding process later.) We used the resulting aggregated master file as the data set for coders.

LESSONS LEARNED

Since the actual data collection is in many ways the most essential component of such a research project, it is worth explaining why the section (see Going Live above) devoted to it in this chapter is one of the shortest. The lengthy description of doing the groundwork highlights the importance of careful preparation leading up to data collection. Respondents' time and attention is at a premium. Glitches occurring at that stage of the project can be fatal to a study. Therefore, it is imperative that researchers put much care into all phases of the undertaking leading up to the crucial moments where participants are directly involved and data collection begins.

We learned several important lessons during this project. Communication with respondents may be easier to achieve using a combination of media (e-mail, voice, text messaging), but one-on-one attention remains important regardless of the particular means of contact. That is, although we relied on automated template messages—with personalized greetings—to establish contact, it became clear that respondents often required additional information whose delivery would be hard to automate. This has implications for the scalability of the project. If one were to try such a study with thousands of respondents, it would be essential to devote resources to one-on-one contact with participants given the number of issues that tend to come up and that require resolution before data collection can proceed (e.g., clarification on both ends of logistical details about the study including means of subsidizing text-messaging costs, timing of message exchange, costs of messaging, and the time line for reimbursement).

In a technical sense, we confirmed the fact that open source and open standards are important tools for developing technical solutions to research problems quickly and cheaply. With the exception of the Flash coding interface, we built our entire system using free software available online. We resorted to Flash since it had better compatibility between browsers than the alternatives. If Flash were not available to us, we may have investigated more seriously the use of dynamic AJAX interfaces instead. We also confirmed that creating open and extensible architectures from the beginning of the project is very important. This allowed us to prototype and test the system with a readily available free network while we investigated more robust commercial alternatives for the actual study. We were able to adapt our system for the text-messaging services we found, but we were not locked in, and this allowed us the flexibility ultimately to create our own substitute service. An extensible architecture within the coding tool allowed us to extend our interface with a tree-view later in the process when we found that a simple list was not efficient from the coders' perspective.

Engineered extensibility is not only limited to the software and source code. By adopting a format that facilitated an easily modifiable coding scheme, we were more agile and responsive in the development of our scheme than would have been possible otherwise. This proved useful when we identified information that we were not previously capturing or options that we had initially overlooked. Our coding scheme benefited in the same way as software development when using a tight iterative cycle. Our scheme is more complete and was more responsive to the issues that our coders identified.

We also discovered that while the mobile text-messaging and instant messaging networks appear to be quite similar, that is not in fact the case. The text-messaging network is quite proprietary and requires more capital and work to establish a presence. If we wanted to create a presence on the network with a minimum number of middlemen and resellers, we would need to spend tens of thousands of dollars (and several months) to obtain a short code. Since this was beyond our means, we were forced to deal with resellers with their own short codes. These services are still expensive, and the resellers focus more on the lucrative marketing projects than the typical academic study. However, in the end, we discovered that we could still participate in this network through the creative use of a single mobile phone hacked together with some open-source tools.

We found that the Thumb Generation is comfortable with participating in this type of study and that our greatest difficulties were not caused by privacy concerns or text-messaging costs but the logistics of finding suitable software and the day-to-day logistics of setting up the project. Drawing on our lessons learned, however, we were able to run a second iteration of the project a year later much more efficiently. In this second study, we had 75 participants and collected data about each of them during three days (two weekdays and a Saturday). Overall, that study greatly benefited from the care we put into developing the details of the project in the first round.

A caveat must be made at this point about the generalizability of this study to other projects, particularly as it relates to the content of the information we collected. It is important to remember that we piggybacked on a larger project in which significant amounts of information had already been collected about our respondents. Therefore, we were not dependent on collecting baseline demographic data, to name one example, about participants using this method. Studies most likely to benefit from our experiences are ones that also use another methodology to collect some background information about respondents and then use text messaging for follow-up data collection.

Collaborative work can have both very rewarding and very frustrating components. We managed to avoid the latter thanks to a deep commitment to the project on behalf of team members, frequent and respectful communication, and explicit idea exchange. We considered each other's feedback seriously, and when not on the same page initially, we explained, patiently, the reasoning behind our positions in a detailed manner. Being comfortable with asking questions of others on the project was very important, especially given our different disciplinary backgrounds.

Pretesting various components of the study allowed us to address unanticipated challenges in a timely manner. Because various steps of the project are so dependent on each other (e.g., the coding interface is directly linked to the coding scheme), leaving the revision phase to the last minute would have left us with much to do and would have delayed the process as a whole. Not collecting initial data from our own trusted group of team members would have also jeopardized the quality of data we collected from study participants. Actively seeking input from our research group and research assistants was essential to being able to make the types of quick improvements to our coding scheme and interface that allowed continuous progress.

Finally, it is worth noting that being involved with every step of the process is important for having realistic expectations of what work is involved in a study, from building the technical aspects of the system to what data are realistic to collect and how they should be handled. We both took part in simulations of data collection, testing of the coding interface, compilation of the coding scheme, and communication with respondents. (Of course, we did the latter in a coordinated manner that presented a unified front to participants.) While we were certainly not equally involved with each aspect of the project (e.g., Karr gets credit for the programming work that went into building the technical systems), we both had a realistic idea of what we were asking of each other, what we were asking of our research assistants, and most important, what we were asking of our respondents. There is no substitute for such direct involvement, and it adds significantly not only to the final research product but also to the new skills and know-how the researcher is able to take away from such an experience.

NOTES

The authors thank Viktor Domazet, Alex Knell, and the members of the Web Use Project research team of 2006–7 for their helpful input. They also acknowledge the assistance of Elizabeth Anderson, Waleeta Canon, and Gina Walejko. The authors are grateful to the National Science Foundation (IIS0712874), the John D. and Catherine T. MacArthur Foundation, and the Northwestern University School of Communication for their support. Hargittai also thanks the Center for Advanced Study in the Behavioral Sciences and the Lenore Annenberg and Wallis Annenberg Fellowship in Communication for time to work on this project.

1. An application programming interface (API) defines the set of services that a software component provides to other applications and systems. Software developers create and document APIs so that others in the future may use the services with their own software projects. In this case, we defined an API so that others could write their own scripts for scheduling studies using their own preferred programming languages and environments.

2. Since this could end up being an imposition on the person whose phone is thereby taken up all day for the study, future studies may want to opt for purchasing a separate phone and data plan for the project.

3. Since we coded messages manually, it was relatively easy to identify such cases. In the future, if machine coding was implemented, messages of this sort may pose a special challenge.

4. For confidentiality purposes, any such information was always stripped of identifying information so we only had ID numbers and cell phone numbers without any names. These documents were kept in password-protected directories on university computers to which only research team members directly involved with this project had access.

REFERENCES

Carter, S., J. Mankoff, and J. Heer. 2007. *Momento: Support for Situated Ubicomp Experimentation.* SIGCHI Conference on Human Factors in Computing Systems, San Jose, CA.

Christensen, T. C., and L. Feldman Barrett. 2003. A Practical Guide to Experience-Sampling Procedures. *Journal of Happiness Studies* 4:53–78.

Feldman Barrett, L., and D. J. Barrett. 2001. An Introduction to Computerized Experience Sampling in Psychology. *Social Science Computer Review* 19:175–85.

Larson, R., and M. Csikszentmihalyi. 1983. "The Experience Sampling Method." *New Directions for Methodology of Social and Behavioral Science* 15:41–56.

Pentland, W. E., A. S. Harvey, M. P. Lawton, and M. A. McColl. 1999. *Time Use Research in the Social Sciences.* New York: Kluwer Academic/Plenum Publishers.

Robinson, J. P. 1977. *How Americans Use Time: A Social-Psychological Analysis of Everyday Behavior.* New York. Praeger Publishers.

GIVING MEGA ATTENTION
TO MACRO RESEARCH

The Rewards and Challenges of Quantitative
Cross-National Data Collection and Analysis

NINA BANDELJ

Comparison is central to any social scientific inquiry. As one scholar boldly stated, not only social science but *"thinking* without comparison is unthinkable" (Swanson 1971, 145, emphasis added). We usually understand things in reference to other things. As social scientists we want to know if patterns exist across the social groups or individuals that we study, and pattern finding of course necessarily involves comparing. In fact, one of the founding fathers of sociology, Emile Durkheim, claimed that "comparative sociology is not a particular branch in sociology; it is sociology itself" (1938, 139).

Where better then to highlight the salience of comparison than in a cross-national setting? The all-too-familiar notion of "culture shock" is based on the premise that countries differ from one another. In our own familiar environments we tend to take things for granted. We often conflate the way things are around us with the way the world *should* be in general. But almost as soon as we get off the plane in a foreign country, we are nudged into questioning this assumption. As many students who return from foreign exchange trips reveal, an extended period of time in a foreign country typically forces one to reexamine personal values and behaviors and the ways of one's home country. Such experiences quickly reveal that different societies are organized differently and that these different modes of social organization produce equally diverse social outcomes. A famous political scientist, Samuel Huntington (1993), has even argued that some national contexts are so starkly different from others that their interactions lead to a "clash of civilizations." At the same time, other researchers observing the increasing interdependencies in the world, which we often call globalization, have proposed that cross-national differences are diminishing and that the world is becoming more and more homogeneous (Meyer et al. 1997; Ritzer 2003). In fact, broad attention to globalization has put cross-national comparisons at the forefront of social science inquiry.

The goal of this chapter is to offer some concrete advice about quantitative cross-national research and its associated trials and tribulations. Like the other contributors to this volume, I use my own research experience to reflect on the logistics and challenges of doing work on a large-scale comparative project. My study examined foreign investment flows in eleven countries of Central and Eastern Europe in the first decade after the fall of communist regimes (Bandelj 2008). However, because the field of macrocomparative research is vast, this chapter also refers to a number of first-rate quantitative cross-national studies that provide insights into methodological issues related to the unit/level of analysis, case selection, and the assembling of a cross-national data set.

Before turning to the methodological issues, I want to give a sense of the diversity of topics that can be examined in cross-national research. What are some of the research questions that cross-national research has tackled? Or, perhaps better yet, what are the questions that it has *not* tackled? Indeed, any social scientific topic one can think of, including economic, political, social, cultural, and technological issues, has most likely been addressed in a cross-national comparative setting. One prominent set of cross-national questions that scholars in economics, political economy, and economic sociology continue to investigate concerns the determinants and consequences of national economic development (e.g., Smith 1900; Gerschenkron 1962; Evans and Rauch 1999; for reviews see Gereffi 1994; McMichael 2000). Using cross-national research, scholars have tried to specify the economic and noneconomic factors that contribute to broad disparities: that is, to the fact that some countries continue to enjoy great economic prosperity while others suffer persistent poverty and underdevelopment. But, of course, national development is not confined to economic dimensions. Hence, those interested in the political issues have compared and contrasted the political institutions and policy outcomes across different states, asking questions such as, Why is there so much diversity in national political organization and policy outcomes? What determines whether a country provides more or less social protections for its citizens? Moreover, how does the fact that countries have historically been characterized by distinct politicoeconomic institutions contribute to the different values that the nationals of particular countries are believed to share? What are the salient differences in cultures across national groups? Are these declining or persisting over time? To what extent do these differences impact issues such as inequality, prosperity, war, human rights? Needless to say, these are all extremely important questions that are of great interest not only to academics but also to citizens across the world.

I hope I have convinced you that engaging in cross-national research is not simply for those who enjoy the Travel Channel; it is a vital means of addressing pressing issues and social problems that are now, in our newly globalized era, closer to home than we often care to realize. The personal, scholarly, and policy rewards of cross-national research are truly great. However, as with any social scientific inquiry, these rewards can be realized only if we can trust that our research findings are based on sound and rigorous methodology. And, without a doubt, comparing and contrasting social processes and outcomes across countries can be a challenging enterprise.

In the next section, I place the quantitative cross-national method in the context of the broader cross-national research field. After that, I discuss issues related to the unit/level of analysis, case selection, and the assembling of a cross-national data set, with the goal of identifying common pitfalls and offering some concrete suggestions about how to handle the practical concerns associated with these aspects of the research process. Throughout, I refer to specific lessons learned from my own research experiences while also using illustrations from other successful cross-national studies. While these examples come mostly from sociology, the lessons are applicable to other social science disciplines as well.

CROSS-NATIONAL COMPARISON

In this chapter, I focus on *quantitative* cross-national comparisons, that is, research that uses quantitative analytic techniques to test the generalizability of hypothesized relationships about macroeconomic, political, social, and cultural issues in a number of country cases. But before we get to my recommendations about how to handle the practical issues associated with this type of research, I'd like to sketch, at least briefly, the cross-national approaches that have relied on *qualitative* data and analyses. This detour is useful because in-depth knowledge of cases, even if ultimately examined with quantitative techniques, is extremely helpful for understanding the cross-national findings that such analyses produce. In fact, I would argue that if a researcher can triangulate methods (i.e., use multiple methods and multiple sources of cross-national data) then the research, findings, and explanation provided are all likely to be more robust and more persuasive.

Those who pursue a cross-national comparison by relying on qualitative data usually select only a few country cases and employ a historical-comparative method to draw conclusions about social phenomena. Classic studies include Barrington Moore Jr.'s *Social Origins of Dictatorship and Democracy* (1966) or Theda Skocpol's *States and Social Revolutions* (1979). As Barrington Moore notes, by using a historical comparison macroanalysts try to specify "configurations favorable and unfavorable" (1966, xiv) to producing particular outcomes, such as modern Western democracy. The logic used in such analyses is similar to the logic used in a controlled experiment that tries to isolate cause and effect between two factors, by manipulating the influences on the key outcome of interest while keeping everything else constant. Such approximations of controlled comparison in qualitative cross-national analysis can be done in two ways. Cases can be selected that have in common many features that seem causally relevant with one exception that can be linked to the difference in the outcome of interest that is also observed. Alternatively, the selected cases may be very different but exhibit a common outcome of interest. Then, the task is to identify those features that these seemingly very different cases have in common and that can also be causally linked to the common outcome.

John Stuart Mill discussed these approaches, which are also known as Mill's Method of Difference (when the outcomes are different) and Mill's Method of Agreement (when the outcomes are similar). For instance, employing both the Method of Agreement and Method of Difference to support her theory on the social origins of revolutions, Skocpol first points out that despite the many different factors that theorists would consider decisive for revolutions, 1790s Bourbon France, late imperial China, and tsarist Russia experienced social revolutionary crises for similar reasons related to state structures and the activities of states (Method of Agreement). But Skocpol also presents evidence from select histories of England, Prussia/Germany, and Japan to show how the *absence* of successful social-revolutionary transformations in countries that had much in common with the analyzed cases of France, Russia, and China can be traced precisely to the absence of the identified causal conditions (Method of Difference). Skocpol and Somers (1980) provide further detail and additional examples about these two methods in their discussion of the comparative historical method. Other sources to consult on the topic of comparative-historical analysis include Clifford Geertz's *The Interpretation of Cultures* (1973); Charles Tilly's *Big Structures, Large Processes, Huge Comparisons* (1984); King, Keohane and Verba's *Designing Social Inquiry: Scientific Inference in Qualitative Research* (1994); Barbara Geddes's *Paradigms and Sand Castles: Theory Building and Research Design in Comparative Politics* (2003); and Mahoney and Rueschemeyer's *Comparative Historical Analysis in the Social Sciences* (2003).

One of the key challenges faced by those who use a small number of country cases to argue about the causes and consequences of macrolevel outcomes is generalizability. To what extent do the conclusions that we form based on an in-depth analysis of a few cases apply to a wider population of countries? In the attempt to move toward greater generalizability in cross-national research, sociologist Charles Ragin (1987, 2000) has pioneered a technique that uses in-depth knowledge of country cases but allows for the inclusion of more than a few in the analysis. Known as qualitative comparative analysis (QCA), it uses case-based Boolean algebra rather than the more commonly used variable-based regression analyses, as Ragin explains on the Web site that introduces this technique.

> Boolean methods of logical comparison represent each case as a combination of causal and outcome conditions. These combinations can be compared with each other and then logically simplified through a bottom-up process of paired comparison. Computer algorithms developed by electrical engineers in the 1950s provide techniques for simplifying this type of data. The data matrix is reformulated as a "truth table" and reduced in a way that parallels the minimization of switching circuits (see Charles Ragin, *The Comparative Method: Moving Beyond Qualitative and Quantitative Strategies*). These minimization procedures mimic case-oriented comparative methods but accomplish the most cognitively demanding task—making multiple comparisons of configurations—through computer algorithms. (2009)

By quantitatively manipulating the information gathered about many cases using Boolean algebra, Ragin's method can be likened, at least to a certain extent, and despite its self-identification as "qualitative," to the more commonly used quantitative approaches to cross-national comparison that rely on statistical regression techniques. However, Ragin's QCA approach is distinct because it is case oriented rather than variable oriented. It focuses on identifying configurations of conditions that lead to a particular outcome and allows for the possibility that *different* configurations can lead to the *same* outcome (equifinality). In contrast, regression analysis techniques assume only *one* causal path to any *one* particular outcome (unifinality). They produce coefficients, which indicate the level and significance of a relationship between an individual factor (variable) and the outcome of interest, assuming the "everything else being equal" conditions, as in a controlled experiment.

Because Ragin's QCA is not (yet) as mainstream as using regression techniques for quantitative cross-national comparisons (e.g., only one [Amenta, Caren, and Olasky 2005] of the articles published in 2005 and 2006 in the top two sociology journals, *American Sociological Review* and *American Journal of Sociology*, used this method), the rest of the chapter focuses on quantitative cross-national methods that use regression analyses to test relationships between hypothesized causal factors and particular outcomes of interest. However, much of the discussion on the unit of analysis, selection of cases, and assembling a data set is relevant also for those who wish to pursue QCA.

QUANTITATIVE CROSS-NATIONAL COMPARISONS

A review of articles published in the top sociology and political science journals, *American Sociological Review*, *American Journal of Sociology*, *American Political Science Review*, and *American Journal of Political Science*, shows that quantitative cross-national comparison is a frequently used method. Among the articles published in the 2005 and 2006 issues of these journals, about 20 percent used a cross-national quantitative comparison to present evidence on various economic, political, social, and cultural issues.

One of the most common cross-national strategies is to investigate country-level outcomes, using a large set of countries, often over a period of time, so that the units of analysis are country/year observations. For instance, in a recent article on women's political representation in a cross-national context, authors Pamela Paxton, Melanie Hughes, and Jennifer Green (2006) ask how the growth and discourse of the international women's movement has influenced when women in a country acquire suffrage, the timing of the first female parliamentarian installed in a particular country, and the achievement of 10, 20, and 30 percent of women in a country's national legislature. They use data on 151 of the world's countries over 110 years (1893–2003) and employ event history regression analyses. They consider both the domestic and international influences on nation-level outcomes as they pertain to women's acquisition of political power over time. They find that increasing pressures by international actors, in particular the international women's movement, have a substantial effect on women's national political representation, in addition to domestic factors such as colonial history, religion, industrialization, democracy, Marxist-Leninist ideology, and proportional representation political systems.

Similarly interested in how international influences affect domestic outcomes, but examining a different, economic topic, Henisz, Zelner, and Guillén (2005) studied the worldwide diffusion of market-oriented reforms, as part and parcel of the phenomenon often referred to as *neoliberalism*. Observing the telecommunications and electricity sectors in the 1980s, the researchers found that only 10 and 44 countries, respectively, had adopted market-oriented reforms. These figures were up to 124 and 94 countries by the end of 1999. What can account for this change? Examining 71 countries over a period between 1977 and 1999, the authors find robust evidence that countries implement neoliberal reforms not only because of domestic economic and political factors but also because of "international pressures of coercion, normative emulation, and competitive mimicry" (2005, 871). Specifically, whether a country decides to privatize its telecommunications or energy sectors significantly depends on the country's exposure to multilateral lenders like the World Bank and the International Monetary Fund (which espouse the neoliberal credo) and the competition with, and imitation of, peer countries.

While the studies by Paxton et al. and Henisz et al. are examples of research that is interested in state-level outcomes using country cases as units of analysis, another prominent body of cross-national comparative research is characterized by a multilevel design. This means that multiple levels of analysis are combined in a single study, usually at the individual and the country levels. An example of such a study is Jennifer Hook's (2006) research on men's housework. Instead of simply using survey data from the United States on men's housework and child-care behaviors, Hook situates men within the country and time period in which they live. She hypothesizes that not only attributes of individual men, such as their education, marriage, or work status, but also national contexts, characterized by broader women's employment practices and family policies, influence men's household and child-care work contributions. Hook uses 44 time-use surveys from 20 countries, conducted from 1965 to 2003, to test her hypotheses and finds that men's participation increases with national levels of women's employment. In addition, whether fathers contribute to households depends on women's national employment hours, the length of available parental leave granted by the national policies, and men's eligibility to take parental leave as stipulated in the policy.

Because they combine the individual- and national-level outcomes, the multilevel cross-national comparisons are particularly conducive to examining questions about individuals' attitudes and values, positing that these will vary across national contexts. One such study is Semyonov, Raijman, and Gorodzeisky's (2006) examination of the rise of antiforeigner sentiments in European societies, from 1988 to 2000. The authors use data from Eurobarometer surveys for 12 European countries. First, they document a substantial rise in antiforeigner sentiment over time in all 12 countries. In the next step, they try to identify the sources of this sentiment and trace it both to individual- and country-level factors. In this way, they find that antiforeigner sentiments tend to be greater in places with a large proportion of foreign populations, lower economic prosperity, and greater support for right-wing extreme parties. As other research has already shown, these attitudes also depend on individuals' socioeconomic characteristics, but while education has remained a stable influence over time, this study shows that the effect of one's political ideology has increased.

Semyonov and colleagues (2006) rely on Eurobarometer surveys, conducted under the auspices of the European Union. The other commonly used cross-national surveys are the International Social Survey Program (ISSP) and World Values Survey (WVS). An example of a study using ISSP is Osberg and Smeeding's (2006) analysis of the attitudes toward economic inequality, looking at beliefs about what individuals in specific occupations "do earn" and what they "should earn," with particular emphasis on how American attitudes differ from those held by individuals in other countries. An example of the use of the World Values Survey in a cross-national comparative framework is Schofer and Fourcade-Gourinchas's (2001) award-winning article on the determinants of voluntary association membership in 32 countries. While the number and type of voluntary associations people join seems to be a rather individual choice determined by individual-level attributes such as one's level of education, beliefs, age, gender, and employment status, Schofer and Fourcade-Gourinchas argue that these individual choices are shaped by "structural contexts of civic engagement" as the title of their article emphasizes. These structural contexts are apparent at the national level in the type of sociopolitical organization that states exhibit. Hence, states can be more statist versus liberal, or corporate versus noncorporate. These dimensions reflect historically developed differences in political and cultural institutions of nations that make certain types of individual action more or less appropriate or legitimate. The authors show that statism generally constrains individual associational activity and that corporateness encourages it. As with other cross-national studies that try to estimate effects of both individual-level and country-level variables, the authors use hierarchical-linear models (HLM).

All of the above listed studies have been published in top peer-reviewed journals. This means that they have been carefully scrutinized by other (peer) researchers and that the authors most likely had to revise their drafts substantially to address the reviewers' comments before the articles got published. Such scrutiny is necessary because researchers embarking on cross-national studies face multiple challenges before they can execute this method successfully. So what are some of the challenges associated with cross-national quantitative analyses? In what follows, I review issues related to the unit/level of analysis, case selection, and data set assembly.

THE UNITS AND LEVELS OF ANALYSIS IN CROSS-NATIONAL RESEARCH

Cross-national studies can be generally classified according to the units of analysis and levels of analysis that they employ. Unit of analysis refers to the entity about whom or which the researcher gathers information, be it individuals, dyads, groups, social artifacts (such as advertisements or texts), organizations, communities, or nations. The unit of analysis can also be thought of as the actor about whom the analysis tries to make certain claims. As should be apparent from cross-national design, not only individuals are considered actors, but so are states as well. It is important, however, that the researcher carefully considers who the actors are in order to specify the right unit of analysis and thus the origin of the causal forces shaping this actor's action.

Causal forces can originate from different levels of analysis. We can illustrate this by a series of concentric circles. If the individual is at the center of this circle because the actors about whom we want to make claims in our research are individuals, then the first belt surrounding the center is the individual level of analysis (e.g., individual-level attributes such as socioeconomic status, demographic characteristics, or values). Individuals can be seen as nested in a social group (such as households and their characteristics), which exerts influences on their beliefs and behaviors; groups can be seen as nested in organizations; organizations in communities; communities in municipalities/counties; and these in countries. Hence, one could potentially include many levels of analysis when investigating values/behaviors of individuals in a cross-national context. In practical terms, gathering data for causal forces operating at many different levels of analysis is not easy, but before one embarks on this process, it is important to stipulate theoretically what the potential influences would be. The determination of which (and how many) levels of analysis to use in a project should be based on theory and not solely on data availability.

For this reason, it may be perfectly appropriate to use only a single level of analysis in cross-national research, by focusing on countries. For example, if the researcher is interested in examining national state-level outcomes, such as the extent of women's representation in parliament, or likelihood of privatization of a country's telecommunication sector—both of which are country characteristics—then country cases are the most appropriate unit of analysis.[1]

Alternatively, researchers can be interested in individual-level outcomes, such as men's household work, people's sentiments toward foreigners, or their voluntary association membership. However, the researcher decides to use a cross-national comparison because she theoretically stipulates that individual-level outcomes are significantly shaped by country-level factors. Hence, the appropriate approach here is to combine individual- and country-level influences and use multilevel hierarchical model techniques, such as HLM. Certainly this multilevel modeling can be done also for organization-level outcomes, whereby one combines samples of firms from different countries in a single data set. In such a case, a third level of analysis could also be added, such as industry, since it is plausible that not only country-level but also industry-level factors will influence the behavior of firms.

CASE SELECTION

Whether the unit of analysis is the country (single level), or individuals/organizations nested within countries (multiple levels), the research will use a cross-national design and needs to deal with country-case selection issues.

A particular feature of cross-national research is that the country population is inherently limited to a little less than 200 cases. As of 2007, 192 countries are considered sovereign political units, and they are all members of the United Nations. Another sovereign political unit which is not a member of the United Nations is the Vatican City, which brings the number of countries to 193. Sometimes territories without complete political sovereignty are also considered as countries, such as Taiwan, Palestine, or Puerto Rico. There is no one right way of including or excluding certain countries from the analysis, but it is important that the researcher makes the choices theoretically grounded and transparent.

While we have seen the number of countries in the world increase in the past years, especially after the dissolution of the former Soviet Union and former Yugoslavia, the number of cases we work with in the cross-national research is nevertheless much smaller than for most other quantitative data sets, such as surveys of individuals. And unlike most survey studies of individuals where there are often more people that one could include in the project to increase the sample size, this is not easily done in cross-national research. Sample size is, of course, important in quantitative analyses because the greater degrees of freedom assured by a greater sample size allow us to test for more causal factors and combinations of these factors in the analysis.

In cases that involve sample limitations, the important issue becomes case selection. Which country cases should be included in our cross-national research? In answering this, the starting point should always be our research question and object of study. What do we want to know? Are we interested in knowing about women's political representation in all countries of the world, in particular geographical regions such as Europe or Latin America, or just particular types of countries, such as advanced democracies or lesser developed nations? Defining the population of interest is going to determine the extent to which we can generalize our conclusions.

It is important to note that even if our goal is to generalize to the whole population of the world's countries, because of data limitations, we often can include only some of these countries in the analysis. Thus, it is crucial that a researcher think carefully about which countries she did and did not include in the final sample. Are those countries that are excluded due to logistical data limitations somehow different on substantive grounds from those that are included? Maybe we only included countries with a long history and tended to exclude the more newly formed ones. Could this have consequences for the interpretation of our findings? If so, we need to remember this selection bias and limit the scope of our generalizations accordingly. For instance, Schofer and Fourcade-Gourinchas include 32 countries in their study of membership in volunteer associations, which they list in table 2 of their article (2001, 809). Perusing this list, one can notice that most of the included countries are European and North American. The list also includes four Latin American countries and two Asian countries but no African countries. This means that the list of included countries is biased toward the richer countries of the world. It is reasonable to assume, therefore, that the findings about the influence of statism and corporatism on associational membership may be relevant primarily for these developed countries and not for the world in general.

In order to increase the number of cases studied, researchers often extend the temporal dimensions in their cross-national projects. Considering longitudinal process is also theoretically valuable. While most studies ask about how one set of influences at a particular point in time relates to the outcomes at the same point in time, such cross-sectional design is not well suited for specifying the causal influences connecting the independent and dependent variables. Hence, a fruitful approach to addressing both sample size and causality issues in a cross-national data set is to include observations for each country at several points in time, if possible for every year over the period of interest. Hence, our units of analysis become country/years.

Such a research design relies on pooled cross-sectional time-series analysis because it combines (pools) multiple country cases across multiple temporal observations. All countries can be observed for the whole period under consideration (balanced panel of cases), or they can contribute only some observations during this period (unbalanced panel of cases). These characteristics of the data set will determine the specific analysis techniques that a researcher should employ. Most important, one should be mindful that several assumptions underlying the most commonly used ordinary least-squares (OLS) regression are violated in the pooled panel design, in particular those concerning independence between observations (as observations from the same countries will likely have much in common) and temporal correlations due to the time-series structure of the data. A great deal of methodological work is available to those who wish to ensure that the appropriate analytic techniques are used for the particular data structure. In political science, the scholar who has written most on these issues is Nathaniel Beck (Beck and Katz 1995; Beck 2001; and special issue of *Political Analysis* 2007 edited by Beck). A useful guide comparing strategies in sociology and political science is an *Annual Review of Sociology* piece on the topic by Charles Halaby (2004). For those who may be scared away by the apparently complicated equations and technical jargon often featured in methodology texts, consulting the applications of methods in actual studies may be a better way to go. The data and methods sections of empirical studies, including all the ones that I refer to in this chapter, are often more user-friendly than descriptions in methods volumes and provide many useful examples of how to handle methodological challenges.

Finally, in terms of case selection, I want to bring attention to the fact that sample size can also be significantly bigger if we use *pairs of countries* as units of analysis. These may be theoretically most appropriate if the outcome of interest is an inherently relational (international) phenomenon such as international trade (e.g., Hanson and Xiang 2004) or international conflict/war (e.g., Lemke and Reed 2001), not a mere country characteristic. I used this strategy in my research on foreign direct investment (Bandelj 2002) and benefited theoretically as well as methodologically. First, by definition, foreign direct investment (FDI) describes an economic relation between pairs of countries as investment flows from a source country to a host country. Second, I stipulated that the amount of FDI coming to a particular country will depend not only on that country's characteristics, such as economic prosperity, political stability, or policy environment, as most other research on the topic assumes. Rather, FDI will be crucially dependent on the characteristics of *relations between investor and host countries*, such as their migration ties, patterns of foreign aid disbursement, previous business connections, and historical/cultural ties. In fact, I would not be able to test these relational propositions if I used countries, and not pairs of countries, as units of analysis. And of course I would not be able to do much with a sample of only a dozen or so observation points (as my population was European postsocialist countries). So, for this study, I was fortunate that my theoretical concern also had methodological advantages; using pairs of countries as units of analysis allowed me to have a big enough sample to test several hypotheses about the relations between countries.

ASSEMBLING THE DATA SET

After we identify the units of analysis and select the country cases that we want to study, we need to find data sources for the factors that we want to examine in our cross-national research. Admittedly, as practitioners of empirical research we know that sometimes data sources find us, rather than the other way around. That is, we embark on a study because particular data are available instead of going to collect data after having identified a theoretically and empirically interesting research question. However, such data-driven research is bound to bring us trouble and ultimately be less convincing. It is like building a house without following a blueprint. Something will be constructed but would you want to live in it? It is also true that just having a blueprint is not going to get you far either. As with any other method, theory and data need to go hand in hand.

One of the major advantages of cross-national research is that there is a plethora of data sources that one could use for such research. Among the most popular cross-national surveys are the International Social Survey Program, the World Values Survey, Eurobarometer, and the European Values Survey. Sources of country-level data—most also available in a computerized data form—include World Development Indicators (World Bank's data on development, from 1960); CountryWatch (geopolitical information on all the world's countries, including news analysis, since 1993); Economist Intelligence Unit (EIU) Country Report and Country Profile (economic information, since 1996); Political Risk Yearbook (political and economic indicators, since 1990); SourceOECD (development indicators for advanced economies by the Organization for Economic Cooperation and Development); ProQuest Reference Asia (data on member countries of ASEAN—the Association of South-East Asian Nations); International Data Bank or IDB (including demographic data on all of the world's countries, published by the U.S. Census Bureau); the International Monetary Fund's International Financial Statistics Yearbook and the Government Finance Statistics Yearbook (economic and demographic data for most of the world's countries, over time); Foreign Labor Statistics (labor-related data on major industrial countries by the U.S. Department of Labor); Luxembourg Income Study (LIS) (income inequality data on major industrial countries); United Nation's University World Income Inequality Database (WIID) (income inequality data for many of the world's countries); and last but not least, UNCTAD's (United Nations Conference on Trade and Development) database on foreign direct investment and trade, which includes most of the world's countries, over time.

What I have found particularly useful in my research when ready-made cross-national data sets did not include information of interest to me is the fact that most of the world's countries have state offices that also publish yearly statistical accounts that contain a variety of kinds of useful research data. Collecting data from each country individually is often referred to as data from "national accounts." However, pursuing this strategy implies that data for a single variable are collected from different sources that likely use different modes of operationalization. This creates problems if we want to combine such information into a single variable to be used in the analysis, because we violate the assumption that any particular variable is measured in the same way for all the units in our sample. We run into similar problems when we use data for some countries from one data set and for others from another data set.

So what to do in such cases? I have a few recommendations along these lines. First, it is always important to find out how any particular piece of information was gathered or how a particular piece of data is measured, rather than blindly including the information in the data set. For instance, if data are collected on wages per household, this is not the same as total income per household, as wages are not the only possible source of income. Often, there will be discrepancies in operationalization, but should we immediately assume that such data are useless? We should not dismiss such sources outright, because that would prevent us from including many cross-national data in our analyses. What we should do, however, is check whether data from different sources for any single variable are substantially different from those from another source. A simple way to do this is to create a dichotomous variable that marks all the records coming from one source as 1 and the rest as 0. Then we include this variable in the analysis itself, and if the coefficient comes out as significant, then we know that that particular data source is significantly different from others. Hence, we should reconsider using it together with other data sources.

Finally, another challenge that cross-national researchers encounter is that some things they want to measure are not easily operationalized. For instance, concepts such as culture, history, institutions, and so forth all feature prominently in cross-national research, but how can one capture them in quantitative analyses? Again, there is no quick fix for this issue. Two golden rules of research need to be kept in mind: validity and reliability. The only way the readers are going to find the arguments convincing is if they believe that the measures are both valid and reliable.

Basically, the measures will have validity if they are closely coupled with the concepts that we are trying to capture. For instance, if the goal is to measure the level of a country's development, then just using a country's gross domestic product (GDP) is unsatisfactory, as obviously there are many different components of development in addition to economic production. Hence, if one cannot find a better indicator, one should at least concede that the measurement is not about development in general but economic development in particular. Following standard practice, that is, using measures that others have used for the same type of concept, is a safe way to go. However, if we are innovative in our analyses (which is a good thing!), we may not have such a standard to rely on and may need to construct proxy measures for our concepts.

Let me offer an example from my research on foreign direct investment between Western investors and Central and East European hosts (Bandelj 2002). My central theoretical claim in that article was that preexisting social relations between countries will influence subsequent FDI between them. Grounded in the extensive literature in economic sociology, this theoretical proposition seems sound, but how can we go about measuring social relations between countries? I suggested that we should distinguish between different kinds of relations, including institutional arrangements, political alliances, personal and business network ties, and cultural ties. Still, each of these could be measured in several different ways.

In particular, it seemed that the notion of cultural ties is particularly hard to quantify. Many researchers choose language similarity as a proxy for cultural ties, that is, they consider two countries to share a cultural tie if their official languages belong to the same language group, such as Roman, Germanic, Slavic, and so on. However, I did not think that language similarity captured well the causal mechanism linking the particular concept, in my case culture, to the ultimate outcome of interest, in my case foreign direct investment. And for a proxy to work well, it is supposed to do just that, that is, capture the stipulated causal logic. In my case, language was an inadequate proxy measure for cultural ties because I argued that it is not language *similarity* that is necessarily conducive to more foreign investment between two countries. Instead what matters is cultural *matching* or compatibility whereby both parties to an FDI exchange, based on the knowledge people in each country have of each other's culture, can envision each other as likely partners in a transaction. Therefore, the appropriate proxy would be something that captures the likelihood of members from two different national groups sharing a history of experiences and interactions. In fact, it would be something akin to colonial ties, which researchers have also used in similar studies.

The problem was that none of the countries in my study used to be colonies. So the question then was what kinds of factors could be compared to colonial ties in the Central and Eastern European context? Using analogy as an analytical device, I came up with the idea that historical divisions of territory and settlement in Europe could serve as a good proxy for cultural/historical processes for countries within Europe. That is, historically some nationals—so-called national minorities—were left in lands that are today subsumed under a different national boundary (e.g., ethnic Germans in Hungary or Romania). In the end, my measure of cultural/historical ties between investor and host countries was the presence of national minorities of investor country origin in the host country and vice versa. This measure is by no means perfect and would not likely work for studying different world regions that have experienced different sociohistorical processes. However, as I also explained in the appendix to data sources, the variable used "is the best available quantifiable measure that reflects a historical and cultural dimension of the relations between two countries [included in the data set]; this warrants its inclusion in the analysis, despite its possible shortcomings" (Bandelj 2002, 444).

The fact that I included detailed information about how I operationalized cultural ties in the appendix of the article, where anyone could read it, brings me to the issue of reliability. In addition to validity, the measures we come up with in cross-national research need to have reliability. This refers to the stability and consistency of operationalization so that any other researchers who wish to replicate the study will be able to collect information and measure a particular concept in a similar manner and, hence, reach similar conclusions. The only way to assure reliability when primary data collection is involved—that is, when novel measures are proposed—is to be as transparent as possible about the steps involved in constructing the measures.

Let us consider how this was done by Brooks and Manza (2006), who studied social policy responsiveness in developed democracies. The authors argued that policy preferences by popular masses in any particular country influence the size and scope of social welfare provided by the country. Mass policy preferences could be understood as opinions shared by the masses in a country. These preferences, the authors stipulated, have an effect on the welfare regimes. (Much research in sociology and political science shows that welfare regimes differ across countries.) The major contribution of Brooks and Manza was to link mass opinion and public policy and to find a convincing and reliable measure of mass opinion. To do so, Brooks and Manza used responses to two questions on the International Social Survey Program surveys about people's "preferred degree of government responsibility for providing employment opportunities and reducing income inequality" (2006, 482). In particular, they used questions that asked whether the respondent believed that it is the government's responsibility to provide a job for everyone who wants one, and whether it is the government's responsibility to reduce income differences between the rich and the poor. The responses to these questions included 1. definitely should not be; 2. probably should not be; 3. probably should be; and 4. definitely should be. The authors combined the responses to the two questions into a scale, which yielded a single score for each country in the sample. By providing concrete information on how they transformed survey data from a random sample of thousands of individuals from multiple countries into a country-level variable with one score for each country, Brooks and Manza ensure that any researcher who follows their steps will be able to reproduce the same indicator/measure of the "mass social policy preferences" construct.

CONCLUSION

The goal of this chapter was to describe some of the rewards and challenges associated with quantitative cross-national analysis. In today's global world, information about other countries is widely available, and "think globally, act locally" is not just a cute T-shirt slogan; it captures the fact that domestic outcomes in any one country are tightly intertwined with influences from others. In this context, cross-national research figures at the forefront of social science inquiry.

A researcher always confronts a wide choice of subjects to study and methods with which to study them. (This may actually be one of the most attractive features of social science!) The key challenge is to match a particular research question to the most appropriate method for answering it. Assuming this basic premise of research design, the first part of this chapter was devoted to spelling out the relevance of cross-national research for understanding domestic and international social, economic, political, technological, and cultural processes and outcomes. I have argued that the personal, scholarly, and policy rewards of cross-national research are truly great. However, as with any social scientific inquiry, these rewards can be realized only if the research is based on sound and rigorous methodology and a good and important research question. For this reason, the second part of the chapter identified the methodological challenges related to the unit/level of analysis, case selection, and assembly of a cross-national data set. Using illustrations and examples from some of the most recent and highly regarded studies involving cross-national comparisons, as well as personal research learning lessons, this chapter offered concrete advice on how to deal with the trials and tribulations of this kind of research enterprise. But reading about research is one thing and doing it, another. I hope that reading this essay has expanded your methodological tool kits, enabling you to sharpen and fine-tune these various tools in the course of your own cross-national research. Good luck!

NOTES

Thanks to Eszter Hargittai for inspiring this piece and providing helpful editorial advice. I am grateful to Bogdan Radu for research assistance, and to the Center for the Study of Democracy at the University of California, Irvine, for financial support.

1. However, it would not be appropriate to use the country-level findings to make inferences about organizational- or individual-level outcomes/behaviors. Such an attempt would result in an ecological fallacy. For instance, knowing what predicts the national levels of women's political representation in countries does not yet tell us about why any one particular woman is or is not partaking in the political process.

REFERENCES

Amenta, Edwin, Neal Caren, and Sheera Olasky. 2005. Age for Leisure? Political Mediation and the Impact of the Pension Movement on U.S. Old-Age Policy. *American Sociological Review* 70:516–38.

Bandelj, Nina. 2002. Embedded Economies: Social Relations as Determinants of Foreign Direct Investment in Central and Eastern Europe. *Social Forces* 81(2): 411–44.

Bandelj, Nina. 2008. *From Communists to Foreign Capitalists: The Social Foundations of Foreign Direct Investment in Postsocialist Europe.* Princeton: Princeton University Press.

Beck, Nathaniel. 2001. Time Series Cross Section Data: What Have We Learned in the Past Few Years? *Annual Review of Political Science* 4:271–93.

Beck, Nathaniel. 2007. From Statistical Nuisances to Serious Modeling: Changing How We Think About the Analysis of Time-Series-Cross-Section Data. *Political Analysis* 15:97–100.

Beck, Nathaniel, and Jonathan N. Katz. 1995. What to Do (and Not to Do) with Time-Series Cross-Section Data. *American Political Science Review* 89 (3): 634–47.

Brooks, Clem, and Jeff Manza. 2006. Social Policy Responsiveness in Developed Democracies. *American Sociological Review* 71:474–94.

Durkheim, Emile. 1938. *The Rules of the Sociological Method.* Chicago: University of Chicago Press.

Evans, Peter, and James Rauch. 1999. Bureaucracy and Growth: A Cross-National Analysis of the Effects of "Weberian" State Structures on Economic Growth. *American Sociological Review* 64:748–65.

Geddes, Barbara. 2003. *Paradigms and Sand Castles: Theory Building and Research Design in Comparative Politics.* Ann Arbor: University of Michigan Press.

Geertz, Clifford. 1973. *The Interpretation of Cultures.* New York: Basic Books.

Gereffi, Gary. 1994. The International Economy and Economic Development. In *The Handbook of Economic Sociology,* ed. Neil Smelser and Richard Swedberg, 206–33. Princeton: Princeton University Press.

Gerschenkron, Alexander. 1962. *Economic Backwardness in Historical Perspective: A Book of Essays.* Cambridge: Belknap Press of Harvard University Press.

Halaby, Charles. 2004. Panel Models in Sociological Research: Theory into Practice. *Annual Review of Sociology* 30:507–44.

Hanson, Gordon H., and Chong Xiang. 2004. The Home-Market Effect and Bilateral Trade Patterns. *American Economic Review* 94 (4): 1108–29.

Henisz, Witold J., Bennet A. Zelner, and Mauro F. Guillén. 2005. Market-Oriented Infrastructure Reforms, 1977–1999. *American Sociological Review* 70 (6): 871–97.

Hook, Jennifer. 2006. Care in Context: Men's Unpaid Work in 20 Countries, 1965–2003. *American Sociological Review* 71(4): 639–60.

Huntington, Samuel. 1993. The Clash of Civilizations. *Foreign Affairs* 72:22–49.

King, Gary, Robert O. Keohane, and Sidney Verba. 1994. *Designing Social Inquiry: Scientific Inference in Qualitative Research.* Princeton: Princeton University Press.

Lemke, Douglas, and William Reed. 2001. War and Rivalry among Great Powers. *American Journal of Political Science* 45 (2): 457–69.

Mahoney, James, and Dietrich Rueschemeyer, eds. 2003. *Comparative Historical Analysis in the Social Sciences.* Cambridge: Cambridge University Press.

McMichael, Philip. 2000. *Development and Social Change: A Global Perspective.* Thousand Oaks, CA: Pine Forge Press.

Meyer, John, John Boli, George M. Thomas, and Francisco Ramirez. 1997. World Society and the Nation-State. *American Journal of Sociology* 103:144–81.

Moore, Barrington. 1966. *Social Origins of Dictatorship and Democracy.* Boston: Beacon Press.

Osberg, Lars, and Timothy Smeeding. 2006. "Fair" Inequality? Attitudes toward Pay Differentials: The United States in Comparative Perspective. *American Sociological Review* 71 (3): 450–73.

Paxton, Pamela, Melanie Hughes, and Jennifer Green. 2006. The International Women's Movement and Women's Political Representation, 1893–2003. *American Sociological Review* 71:898–920.

Ragin, Charles C. 1987. *The Comparative Method. Moving Beyond Qualitative and Quantitative Strategies.* Berkeley: University of California Press.

Ragin, Charles C. 2000. *Fuzzy-Set Social Science.* Chicago: University of Chicago Press.

Ragin, Charles C. 2009. fuzzy-set/Qualitative Comparative Analysis. Retrieved April 16, 2009. http://www.u.arizona.edu/~cragin/fsQCA/index.shtml.

Ritzer, George. 2003. *The Globalization of Nothing*. Thousand Oaks, CA: Pine Forge Press.

Schofer, Evan, and Marion Fourcade-Gourinchas. 2001. The Structural Contexts of Civic Engagement: Voluntary Association Membership in Comparative Perspective. *American Sociological Review* 66 (6): 806–22.

Semyonov, Moshe, Rebeca Raijman, and Anastasia Gorodzeisky. 2006. The Rise of Anti-foreigner Sentiment in European Societies, 1988–2000. *American Sociological Review* 71(3): 426–49.

Skocpol, Theda. 1979. *States and Social Revolutions*. Cambridge, UK: Cambridge University Press.

Skocpol, Theda, and Margaret Somers. 1980. The Uses of Comparative History in Macrosocial Inquiry. *Comparative Studies in Society and History* 22:174–97.

Smith, Adam. [1776] 1900. *An Inquiry into the Nature and Causes of the Wealth of Nations*. London: G. Routledge and Son.

Swanson, Guy. 1971. Frameworks for Comparative Research: Structural Anthropology and the Theory of Action. In *Comparative Methods in Sociology: Essays on Trends and Applications*, ed. Ivan Vallier, 141–202. Berkeley: University of California Press.

Tilly, Charles. 1984. *Big Structures, Large Processes, Huge Comparisons*. New York: Russell Sage Foundation.

SECONDARY ANALYSIS OF LARGE SOCIAL SURVEYS

JEREMY FREESE

A prospective graduate student once explained his resolute lack of interest in quantitative social research to me by saying the work seemed to him akin to dying before one was dead. Although quantitative methodology encompasses a broad array of otherwise quite distinct types of research, those who view it as a soul-sucking craft seem often to be thinking primarily about the secondary analysis of large social surveys. Somehow, the prospect of a career spending much of one's time analyzing numeric data collected by other people does not capture the romantic imagination in quite the same way as doing fieldwork in some intriguing locale, having long face-to-face interactions with a small number of selected informants, or sitting in a coffeehouse debating the finer points of French social theory. Plus, as human lives and the processes by which human fates diverge are vastly more complicated than anything that can be represented by a few hundred variables, one might be leery of the whole premise that important insights into social life can be gained by gazing at numbers on one's monitor. In brief, a prospective quantitative social researcher might seem to be signing up for a career of boring, solitary labor contributing to a dreary mountain of incremental oversimplifications on whatever narrow topic they choose to specialize in. Talk about dying before being dead!

I have to confess that I started graduate school with similar preconceptions, and I planned to avoid quantification and questionnaires as much as possible. Now, however, much of my research involves working with large surveys, and, at this writing, I remain physically and otherwise alive. What I came to realize was that large-scale social surveys provide the best means for addressing a broad class of questions about social life that are theoretically interesting and important for broader social understanding and for social policy. The ability to work with large survey data knowledgeably allows one to engage such questions whenever they intersect with one's intellectual agenda. These surveys also offer important advantages when one wishes to do work on contentious topics, as I will discuss. The labor itself turns out to be intricate, challenging, and subtle, requiring both creativity and discipline to be done well. And even then it is vulnerable to the same kinds of setbacks and problem solving that characterize the research process more generally.

Doing quantitative research of course requires understanding matters covered in statistics or econometrics texts, but those are not the purview of this essay. Instead, my purpose is to introduce some of the practical issues that are part of the craft of analyzing large-scale surveys, and to provide my thoughts on navigating those issues. To keep matters concrete, I proceed using a single project as an extended illustration—a project I did as a graduate student (in essence, my own introduction to large-scale survey analysis) that was later published with my dissertation adviser and another collaborator in the *American Sociological Review* (Freese, Powell, and Steelman 1999). While I have mixed feelings about excavating a project I completed nearly a decade ago, the project illustrates the main points I wish to make, the methodology is fairly straightforward and transparent, and the benefit of hindsight makes it possible to reflect on ways the project could have been better. Even so, technological advances have meant that the practical work of quantitative analysis is much different now than it was then, and I make note of key differences along the way. At the end, I also discuss some possibilities for using survey data for reaching stronger and more satisfying conclusions than were possible in our study.

BACKGROUND

The story begins in 1996, with me reading a *New Yorker* article about a new book by a scholar named Frank Sulloway entitled *Born to Rebel* (hereafter *BTR*). The article intrigued me so much that I had a friend drive me to a bookstore so I could buy the book; then, I stayed up all night and read the entire thing. By the time I was done, I decided I wanted to try to test some of the book's claims for myself to see if they were true.

Sulloway has an impressive intellectual biography that includes being a member of the Harvard Society of Fellows and a recipient of a MacArthur "genius" grant. His theory in *BTR* is that sibling competition for parental resources causes children to develop ways of thinking and acting that maximize the resources they receive from their parents, and that these differences persist into adulthood. That is, children develop in ways that help them stake out a "family niche." Even though sibling rivalries play out uniquely within each family, firstborns have a consistent edge when competing with their younger siblings because, in the early years, firstborns tend to be larger, stronger, and more intellectually developed. As a result of all these advantages, Sulloway theorizes that firstborns tend to occupy the dominant position among their siblings, and they develop the attitudes and personalities that are optimally suited for protecting this position—namely, attitudes that are more conservative and tough-minded and personalities that are more jealous, conscientious, and dominant. Meanwhile, later-born children are chronic underdogs who have to work to differentiate themselves to increase their share of parental resources. Sulloway argues that later-borns tend to develop attitudes that are more liberal and compassionate and personalities that are more open and rebellious.

Granted, this brief description makes the theory sound a little hokey to me even as I type this. What makes *BTR* impressive is the voluminous evidence Sulloway presents in support of his theory, which he had spent over twenty years amassing. This included data on over 3,000 scientists from the eighteenth through twentieth centuries who participated in 28 different scientific controversies. He found that later-borns were twice as likely as firstborns to adopt scientific innovations early. For example, later-born scientists were disproportionately likely to adopt Darwin's theory of natural selection and Einstein's theory of relativity, while firstborns were overrepresented among doubters. He also gathered data on participants in numerous historical events, finding that those who were later-borns tend to drive liberal social movements while firstborns tend to be conservative and uncompassionate reactionaries. As examples, later-borns were overrepresented among the early leaders of the Protestant Reformation and French Revolution, and firstborns were overrepresented among their foes. In addition, Sulloway conducted an extensive review of the existing literature on birth order—notorious for its mixed results—and reported that when methodologically weak studies were excluded, the pattern of results was, in fact, quite consistent and supported the implications of his theory.

All this evidence certainly impressed others. Blurbs on the back of a book's jacket are invariably enthusiastic, and yet *BTR* featured what may be still the most impressive jacket blurbs I have ever seen. Edward O. Wilson, the eminent biologist and winner of two Pulitzer Prizes, is quoted as calling *BTR* "one of the most authoritative and important treatises in the history of the social sciences." Robert K. Merton, arguably the most important American sociologist of the twentieth century, adds, "A quarter century in the making, this brilliant, searching, provocative, and readable treatise promises to remain definitive for twice as long." And in case these glowing endorsements were somehow not emphatic enough, a renowned anthropologist predicts *BTR* would have "the same kind of long-term impact as Freud's and Darwin's." Elsewhere, the editor of *Skeptic* magazine— whom you might expect to be a tough sell—called *BTR* "the most rigorously scientific work of history ever written" (Shermer 1996, 63) and announced the possibility of the book being "comparable to the Kepler-Galileo-Newton impact in changing astrology into astronomy" (66). Freud, Darwin, Kepler, Galileo, Newton: rarely are authors of social science trade books included in such company!

All this, and yet the book did not contain any firsthand examination of contemporary population data, only Sulloway's own analyses of historical figures and his summary of studies of contemporary populations conducted by others. However, if Sulloway's theory was true, one should be able to observe implications of it readily in social survey data, provided one did not make any of the methodological errors or alternate decisions that Sulloway argued had obscured real birth order effects in earlier research. As I had bought and read Sulloway's book immediately upon its release, I thought that I could be the first one to address the theory using contemporary data if I worked quickly. I approached a faculty member in my PhD program, Brian Powell, and we agreed to work on the project with a longtime collaborator of his, Lala Carr Steelman.

FINDING DATA

The plan was always to test the theory using some existing set of data, rather than attempting to collect new data on birth order and personality or social attitudes ourselves. The obvious advantage of using secondary data is that one's project benefits from all the hours and expertise other people have invested in putting the original data together. After all, major survey projects convene experts in sampling, questionnaire, and survey fielding operations, and then spend millions of dollars and employ dozens of interviewers to implement their design. The obvious disadvantage of using secondary data is that one has to take the data on their terms, which may be more or less well suited to one's animating question.[1] In our case, we believed we could find secondary data that would allow us to contribute to the evaluation of Sulloway's theory far more efficiently and effectively than anything we could do by collecting our own data. Internet surveys today do make it more plausible for graduate students to conduct surveys cheaply on geographically distributed samples, but at least for now, this works much better for projects with well-defined samples of individuals expected to be online (e.g., surveys of academics; see the chapter by Walejko in this volume for more on this), not when one is looking to do research on the general population.

Originally, we set to work looking at the National Educational Longitudinal Study of 1988 (NELS:88), which is based on a representative sample of American students who were eighth-graders in 1988. In retrospect, I have no idea why we decided this was a good data set for studying Sulloway's theory, other than that Powell was already using it in other projects and we knew that it had birth order information. The NELS data set includes various indicators of student performance and achievement, and while Sulloway's book makes some claims about achievement, it was a stretch to think any of the measures there could really make a direct contribution to testing the parts of his theory I thought were most interesting, namely, those related to political and personality differences by birth order. Even so, I tried mightily to convince myself that I could make it work, as if I could somehow will new and more suitable questions to appear magically on a survey that had been administered years before. I spent so much time considering the data set and how I might make it work for the project that I had an entirely separate idea for an article that Powell and I wrote and published in the *American Journal of Sociology* while the project on *BTR* floundered (Freese and Powell 1999).

Then one day I was sitting in the sociology department's computer lab and started idly flipping through a General Social Survey (GSS) codebook that was sitting on a table. GSS has many measures of social attitudes and so would have been a more obvious fit for our study than NELS, but it did not collect information on respondent's birth order. I discovered from the codebook, however, that in 1994 GSS had asked respondents to list all their brothers and sisters, dead and alive, and the years they had been born. (I presume this is obvious, but if you know when a person was born and when their siblings were born, you can infer their birth order.) I told Powell about this and immediately we dropped the idea of using NELS and instead focused on testing Sulloway's theory using GSS.

In this respect, I was lucky, and I suppose could opine here about the role of serendipity in social research. But the more appropriate lesson, I think, is that it would have been well worth my time to have made a more systematic and thorough search of available data resources rather than focusing immediately on NELS even when it seemed unpromising. The paper I did get using NELS was developed "inductively," by looking at the data and realizing the NELS would be appropriate for testing a different theory, while my efforts to use it more "deductively," for a question for which it was ill suited, went nowhere. As one becomes more familiar with a data resource that contains all kinds of information, ideas emerge on how the unique strengths of those data can be used to answer other questions. When one begins with a question one wants to answer, meanwhile, time searching for and confirming that one is using the right and best data is time well-spent. Expanding online resources are making it ever easier to plumb the contents of different data sets quickly, and technological advances and institutional imperatives are also increasing the availability of data to researchers outside the immediate circle involved in the original data collection.

To draw an even more general lesson, a common tendency in social research is to carry over a belief that is useful and true in many life contexts, which is that the ultimate quality of a finished product with our name on it is basically up to us. That is, if we work hard enough, are clever enough, write lucidly and insightfully enough, or whatever, the paper we are working on can attain a level of quality suitable for any goal we might have, such as publication in the top journal of one's field. Journal editors, however, are not judges in some abstract intellectual virtue pageant but are instead looking for convincing work that contributes to the field. The quality and suitability of one's data set a ceiling on how convincing an argument a researcher can ultimately make, just as a chef in charge of salad can only do so much with wilted lettuce and stringy carrots. Investing time in finding the best data, and working to secure access to the best data if such work must be done, is not only typically rewarded with better publication prospects but can also save time, as it reduces the number of iterations a paper goes through as the author tries to figure out how to make the best of a bad situation. (When the limits of data are plain, the better route may be to finish a modest paper intended for a modest venue and seek either to find a more tractable question for the same data, or better data to answer the same question. The modest paper you finish can provide a call for better data, and, at least later in one's career, one might use this call for better data to attempt to convince a granting agency to give one the resources to collect it.)

As it was, GSS still only allowed me to address one of the parts of Sulloway's theory that I found interesting—the relationship between birth order and social attitudes. (By social attitudes, I mean political and moral opinions, such as attitudes about abortion, animal rights, giving benefits to immigrants, the importance of teaching children obedience, or the trustworthiness of government.) I was as interested in the parts of Sulloway's project that concerned personality as social attitudes, but trying to tendentiously interpret various GSS items to press them into service as personality items would not have been especially convincing. Instead, we narrowed the question to what the GSS could answer well and went ahead as though social attitudes were our primary interest all along. Ultimately, because one is working with data that have already been collected and is thus stuck with what one has, I think secondary data analysis often proceeds best when one begins with a broad research question that has room for shaping and narrowing when applied to real data. The ideal is to be able to present a focused and interesting question for which the data allow the possibility of compelling evidence.

MAKING ANALYTICAL DECISIONS

The analysis strategy for the project was relatively straightforward: take some social attitude items in the GSS, and see if they were associated with respondents' birth order. Simple as this sounds in the abstract, trying to enact it invoked numerous complicated concrete details. What I quickly learned is that trying to test theories using social surveys involves a large number of small decisions. One obvious issue for the study of birth order is what to do about respondents who had reported stepsiblings—does having an older stepsibling make one a later-born? What to do about only children? Twins? What measures of social attitudes should be used? What variables should be used as covariates ("controls") in the models? How should these covariates be measured? What should be done with cases that did not answer one of the items used to construct one of the covariates?

Usually minor decisions do not make major differences for one's results, but sometimes they do. If a particular study involves 25 decisions between two alternative ways of doing the analysis versus another—25 being, at least in my experience, a low-end estimate of the number of such decisions in an actual study—this implies there are over 30 million (2^{25}) different configurations of decisions one could make.

Many questions involve statistical points that have been subject to much exposition and debate, and my purpose here is not to get into the specifics of those. Instead, I wish only to reflect upon the general strategy for dealing with the rapidly multiplying decision forks in quantitative studies. My basic counsel is that, with each decision, one should figure out first what one thinks is the right way of proceeding given the purpose of the study. At the same time, however, one should consider the consequences of different ways of doing the analysis, especially for decisions that seem major or especially debatable.

Most emphatically, the point of doing the analysis alternative ways is not that one should reconsider decisions when they turn out to make a difference. It is intellectually dishonest to use one's decision latitude in quantitative research to simply hunt for the results that one wants. Plus, post hoc decisions are all too easy to rationalize after the fact. One gets a result one doesn't like, then runs it another way and gets something more desirable and then—not necessarily disingenuously—"realizes" there is some reason why the first analysis was a mistake and the second way is right. This is dangerous reasoning, and certainly makes the *p*-values and significance tests reported in one's analysis misleading.[2] Instead, the point of doing the analysis multiple ways is that readers will often wonder whether particular decisions are consequential or not, and one can pre-empt their questions by telling them. Still, the infeasibility of looking at all configurations of possible decisions means that the usual strategy is to look at the consequences of different ways of making any one decision when all the other decisions are made according to what one has decided is best.[3]

What is the right decision? When a study is testing a theory, decisions should, to the maximum extent possible, follow from the substantive implications of the theory. In our study, we were testing Sulloway's theory, and we sought to think through the implications of his theory as he articulated it in *BTR*. Because the GSS did not provide sufficient information to be able to determine whether stepsiblings were part of the child's early childhood environment, we decided simply to exclude them from our analysis, although we also looked at the implications of this decision. (If models are correctly specified, excluding cases based on explanatory variables does not bias estimates for the more restricted sample that remains; by contrast, excluding cases based on values of the outcome—aka "sampling on the dependent variable" [see King, Keohane, and Verba 1994, 129–35]—does bias results.)

In general, my experience is that when people are trying to answer abstract research questions rather than speak to specific theories or at least ideas about processes, decisions about how to do the analysis become much harder. If we had been trying to answer "What is the effect of birth order on attitudes?" then questions of, for example, what to do about only children or children with much older siblings cannot be answered straightforwardly, as different answers follow from different ideas about *why* birth order might affect attitudes. For example, there exist biological theories of birth order effects that attribute effects to differences in the mother's reproductive system with successive births; these imply that older siblings who died in infancy should still be counted and thus make the second child a later-born. By contrast, an environmental theory like Sulloway that attributes birth order to interactions among siblings and their parents would suggest that children who die in infancy should not count. Indeed, if there was evidence of birth order effects generally, these would be competing theories, and the case of children whose only other sibling died in infancy would be one way of testing between them.

In practice, the vague character of much theory in social science—even for theories that are "formalized"—only goes so far toward providing direction for the many decisions made during a survey analysis project (e.g., Raftery 1995). Having some principled grounds based on substantive or statistical reasoning is better than just acting arbitrarily. Following conventional practice in an area can serve as grounds and is especially helpful in contexts in which one frames work as following an established literature except for some key innovation that is the intended contribution of the paper. (The political scientist Gary King [2006] has said this is one of the best strategies for graduate students to get an early publication that makes a genuine contribution.) I worry about research that is slavish to conventional practice in ways that can seem intellectually lazy, but unexplained deviations from conventional practice are easy targets for reviewers. Researchers often refer to including "the usual suspects" covariates (a set that includes at least age, sex, race, educational attainment, and some income measure), often without any additional explicit rationale for doing so, and omitting one of these variables as a covariate may prompt a reviewer to wonder why. Reviewers find enough unpredictable things to object to, and too many reviewers let one or two readily addressed problems color their entire reaction to a paper, so one wants to be cautious to close down as many obvious lines of objection as one can. More broadly, writing successful research articles requires being able to take the perspective of a reviewer when reading the article yourself. You do not get the opportunity to answer questions for the reviewer, or elaborate points to clear up misunderstandings, and so the text needs to read well to a reader who may not be giving it complete attention and may not understand the methodological and substantive issues as well as you do.[4]

Our article estimated the effect of birth order on different social attitudes using several different model specifications. This allowed readers to see how estimates were affected by the addition of different covariates. In our case, as I will discuss more shortly, results did not change as new variables were added. When results are substantively affected by the addition of covariates, one wants to be sure to know what covariates yield the change and consider why they do (in the abstract, covariates change the coefficient of a key explanatory variable when they are associated with *both* the explanatory variable and the outcome, and the exact change depends on the product of the direction and magnitude of both associations).[5]

Just so we are clear, when we are using regression analysis as a tool for testing theories, the reason one includes covariates is usually to attempt to adjust for sources of spuriousness (or "confounding") that would otherwise bias our interpretation of the influence of the theorized explanatory variable on the theorized outcome (much can be said about the limitations of this approach; see Berk 2004). For example, in the case of birth order, an obvious confound is family size. Sulloway's theory concerns differences between firstborns and later-borns. A family with two children has one firstborn and one later-born. A family with six children has one firstborn and five later-borns. Consequently, the average later-born has more siblings than the average firstborn. If family size is itself causally related to an outcome and one's study is based on a sample of unrelated individuals—about which I will say more later—this will make birth order correlated with that outcome even if birth order per se has no influence. As a result, we need to adjust for family size, so we are effectively comparing firstborns and later-borns with the same number of siblings. Using regression methods and including family size as a covariate (or "control") is a strategy for adjusting for the potential spuriousness of family size. Note that a very closely related strategy would be to restrict analyses to only respondents with only one sibling, or run separate analyses for respondents with one sibling, two siblings, three siblings, and so on. (We did this as well, and found the same results as in our combined analyses.)

To take a somewhat different example, it is commonly argued in the birth order literature that one also needs to adjust for the socioeconomic status of the respondents' families. Sulloway's and other attempts to quantitatively summarize ("meta-analyze") the birth order literature have typically excluded studies that do not adjust for both family size and socioeconomic status. The argument goes that lower socioeconomic status is associated with family size, which means that later-borns are more likely to come from lower socioeconomic status families than firstborns. But this argument does not actually follow: if one already adjusts for family size, then this solves the problem without also needing to adjust for parents' socioeconomic status. Issues like this arise regularly in quantitative research, where conventional ways of conducting research are either not optimal or not correctly justified. Practically speaking, one is put in a position of having to choose one's battles. In this case, there is no reason to expect that controlling for socioeconomic status of one's family would bias results, and it turns out that one gets similar results whether or not it is controlled. In our study, we included socioeconomic status in the models we presented, rather than risk failing to persuade reviewers that controlling for socioeconomic status was unnecessary.[6] However, if an alternative way of doing the analysis both seems more justified and does produce different substantive conclusions, then obviously the alternative analysis is what one must present, even if relying on convention would be easier.

Importantly different is the idea of adjusting for respondents' *current* (i.e., adult) socioeconomic status. In social science, one will commonly see researchers "control" for variables determined after the key causal variable has been established. We did exactly this in our study, by including respondents' education and income in what we present as our "final model." If birth order affects respondents' socioeconomic status, and that status, in turn, affects social attitudes, then socioeconomic status is a mediating variable—part of one of the *mechanisms* by which birth order affects attitudes—rather than a source of spuriousness. What we say in our article is, "To account for the possibility that observed birth-order effects may be caused by birth-order differences in achievement, our final model adds controls for the respondent's education and occupational prestige" (215). Sulloway's theory is quite clear that the birth order effects shape attitudes by shaping psychology, not by shaping social attainment outcomes that later shape attitudes, so this wording is correct. Still, I wish that we had been clearer that, when including these measures, we had moved from estimating the total causal effect of birth order to including covariates that were actually potential mediators of the effect of birth order on attitudes. Sometimes people approach regression analysis as though the appropriate strategy is to include everything at one's disposal as a covariate; variables that are consequences of the key explanatory variable are not "controls" and should only be included in an analysis when the researchers intend to isolate the effects of mediators of the relationship.[7]

Covariates in regression analysis are commonly used as a strategy for "ruling out" other explanations; for example, that an observed bivariate association between birth order and an outcome is really the result of a spurious relationship with family size. One aspect of this strategy that needs emphasizing is that it only works to whatever extent the proposed source of spuriousness is accurately and fully measured. There are many social science research questions, for instance, for which researchers believe that socioeconomic status poses a very plausible confound that absolutely must be taken into account. This is commonly done by including a measure of the respondent's educational attainment and family income (or, the respondent's parents' educational attainment and income). To whatever extent what is relevant about "education" is not totally captured by response to survey reports of highest degrees attained, and what is relevant about "financial resources" is not totally captured by response to survey reports of annual family income, and what is relevant about "socioeconomic status" is not exhausted by "education" and "financial resources," this strategy will not fully control for the spurious influence of socioeconomic status. If the coefficient of one's key causal variable is partly diminished by the inclusion of a faulty control, one would expect it to be further diminished had the control been more completely measured. Ways of correcting for measurement error in control variables exist (although they still involve some technical debate when the outcome variable is not continuous). My hope is that social research that relies on the strategy of providing statistical controls for sources of spuriousness will make greater use of these techniques in the future.

ESTABLISHING FINDINGS

What quickly became clear when I started looking at the relationship between birth order and social attitudes using GSS was that there did not appear to be *any* relationship. Powell had expected this; I was enchanted enough by Sulloway's book that I had thought there was a good chance our study would support his theory. In any case, what we had were "null findings," the general term for results in which a theoretically predicted relationship between an explanatory variable and an outcome variable is not observed. Null findings are said to be much harder to publish, especially in prominent venues, than are studies that find positive support for a theory. I have no doubt this is true, and yet our study with null findings was successfully published in the *American Sociological Review*. How?

In order to publish null findings, you need to do two things. First, you need to establish that there are people who believe the theory that your null findings call into dispute. We were able to argue that Sulloway's book had made the long-studied topic of birth order timely again, and to use selections from the extremely positive press the book received as grounds that the theory was one some people believed. Second, you need to establish that your study really does provide a good test of the theory. Null findings are exactly what one expects if measures are so weak or biased that they are effectively meaningless, or if the sample is small and the effects observed are of a magnitude that would be statistically significant in a reasonably sized sample. Another way of putting the point is that you need to establish that your findings really are null rather than just equivocal.[8] Here, I do not think null findings are especially different from positive findings: the researcher needs to establish that one's findings are *news to someone* and that they are *credible*. The greater the combined success on these two fronts, the greater the ultimate prospects of the paper.

Because we wanted our own results to be as credible as possible, we never considered looking at only one or two measures of social attitudes. If we had, then no matter what we found, readers would be apt to wonder why we didn't take a broader view that would take fuller advantage of all the measures of social attitudes available in the GSS. They might worry that we were only showing them results for the measures that happened to fit our conclusions. Instead, we considered 24 measures that we had decided beforehand most closely reflected the dimensions of attitudes on which Sulloway focused in *BTR*. We selected these 24 measures by first identifying what we regarded as the six broad areas of attitudes that were emphasized by Sulloway and covered in the GSS: conservative political identification, opposition to liberal social movements, resistance to racial reforms by Whites, belief in traditional gender roles, support for authorities, and "tough-mindedness." We then chose what seemed to be the most apt measures available in the GSS for each area. Thus, we were able to provide a justification for why each measure we used followed from some part of Sulloway's argument.

In our models that included all controls, birth order was significantly associated with only 3 of these 24 measures (Freese, Powell, and Steelman 1999, 216). Moreover, for all of these three measures, the association between birth order and the attitude was actually *opposite* the direction predicted by Sulloway's theory. For instance, in direct conflict with Sulloway's chapter on how firstborns are more tough-minded—reflected, as one example, in the disproportionate number of firstborns who voted for the execution of King Louis XVI—firstborns in GSS were actually less likely to support the death penalty than were later-borns.[9]

Even here, we were worried that we could be open to the charge that we simply picked measures of social attitudes that happened to support a particular conclusion. So, in addition to looking at these 24 measures, we looked at all 202 measures in GSS that could be interpreted as tapping into liberal-conservative differences. We found again that there was no pattern of significant results supporting Sulloway's theory, and in fact the number of significant results and number of results in the predicted direction were roughly in line with what one would expect by chance alone (Freese, Powell, and Steelman 1999, 221).

All that said, I was bothered that our study (as well as most of Sulloway's) was ultimately deficient because it compared firstborns with later-borns from other families. It would certainly be more revealing to compare firstborns and later-borns from the *same* family, as that strategy, known more generally as a fixed-effects design (see Halaby 2004), would solve problems caused by differences between respondent families of origin by only comparing individuals with their own siblings. As I learned by following up on an obscure footnote in the GSS codebook, the 1994 GSS included a companion study, the Survey of American Families (SAF), of telephone interviews with randomly selected siblings of GSS respondents. This allowed us to compare siblings from the same family for those cases where one of the selected respondents was a firstborn and another was a later-born. This comparison was not without problems of its own: the SAF did not have as good a response rate as the GSS, and the survey included fewer measures, but that analyses of SAF also yielded null results increased my confidence that our findings were correct and strengthened the presentation in our paper. An advantage of drawing on multiple data sources in the same paper is that concerns about the imperfection of each may be mitigated if they yield similar or complementary results.

It is worth noting here that many questions that social researchers study are fraught with moral and political implications and the people who choose to study a particular topic are often among those who have the strongest opinions about it. I did not have any psychological investment in Sulloway's theory being true or false, but that isn't to say a reader could not wonder if our findings partly reflected some secret determination we had to contradict his work. Here is where the secondary analysis of publicly available data shows one of its greatest strengths. Recall that *BTR* was based on remarkable data that Sulloway himself compiled over many years. I have talked to some people who have cited all his labor as *grounds for skepticism:* since Sulloway was himself responsible for so much of the data collection, perhaps some of the decisions resulted in data that were biased in favor of his theory (see Harris 1998). One does not have to suspect *conscious* bias to raise this possibility: to be absolutely clear, I regard Sulloway as a remarkably conscientious and committed scholar. Sulloway indeed did various checks against undue subjective influence, but some of these were not fully convincing. As one example, a key strategy that Sulloway uses to show that his study was insulated against the possible influence of his own biases was that many ratings were obtained by independent experts. Many of these ratings, however, were obtained in interviews conducted by Sulloway himself, and his participation could easily have affected the resulting ratings in various ways.

Contrast this with our study. We did *far less* work than Sulloway but had an important advantage precisely *because* of that. We had nothing to do with the collection of the 1994 General Social Survey—all we did was download it. Someone disinclined to believe our results would not be able to argue that the data on the GSS Web site have been contaminated by any biases of ours against Sulloway's theory. The data are publicly available if anyone wonders whether we reported our results accurately. Although the steps used to generate results are straightforward and described in the article, I also have the computer code that I used to generate the results and can share it with anyone who asks. From this, a person can reproduce the numbers in the article, meaning that one does not have to take our word that these numbers really did come from an analysis of the General Social Survey.[10]

People are skittish around words like *objective* for good reason, but it is hard to imagine how results can be more "objective" than when someone hands over the data that were used—data that the person had no hand in collecting—and says: *here, I beseech you to look at these data yourself and tell me how one might reasonably arrive at any other conclusion than mine.*[11] In sum, a major advantage of quantitative research on large surveys that enables it to speak effectively to policy questions is that researchers can show precisely and compellingly how their conclusions follow from available data and thereby limit the degree to which others can dismiss their work as just one person's (misleading, wishful, ideologically biased, etc.) interpretation.

Importantly then, when conducting quantitative analysis of secondary data, one should conduct analyses in such a way as to have computer code that reproduces all the steps necessary to go from an original data set (e.g., the GSS file I downloaded) to all the numbers presented in the article.[12] Statistical software packages that allow one to conduct analysis using point-and-click menus still typically generate code that allow one to automatically reproduce the commands being executed by the menus. Any software that does not allow one to do this should be avoided. Major economic journals presently require authors to deposit this code (and also the data if they have the rights to do so) at the time their article is accepted for publication, and the code is then posted on the Internet. My hope is that other social sciences will adopt some version of this practice (Freese 2007). If a key strength of secondary quantitative analysis is that findings are less open to subjective biases—or, at least, that the influence of subjective biases is easier to establish because of the potential for other researchers to scrutinize the same data—then such analyses are especially convincing when work maximizes this advantage by making the relevant procedures as transparent as possible.

CONCLUSION

We live in an age of rapid technological change, and large-scale survey analyses may stand to benefit more than any other common social research methodology in how ongoing changes will expand and strengthen our ability to learn new things. Repeated investments in major survey instruments—both those based on asking similar questions to new cross-sections of the population in different years (like the GSS) and those based on tracking the same individuals over time (longitudinal studies like the National Longitudinal Studies of Youth or the Health and Retirement Study)—allow these studies to afford stronger and more comprehensive research each time they are fielded. Ubiquitous digital record keeping has created all kinds of novel possibilities for matching survey and administrative records to these data. For example, the Health and Retirement Study allows researchers to use data from the Social Security Administration on earnings and from Medicare claims data regarding health care utilization.

Advances in Internet surveying will allow for the possibility of more frequent and much cheaper collection of repeated measures, affording possibilities for a much more fine-grained understanding of the unfolding of biography than even those studies that talk to the same respondents every year or two (although this volume's chapters by Walejko and by Williams and Xiong note some challenges to these approaches). Advances in biomarker collection portends possibilities for integrating studies of biological, psychological, and sociological processes (see, e.g., the Adam, Doane, and Mendelsohn chapter in this volume). Advances in the collection and manipulation of spatial data will allow better work on the effect of environments on individuals' lives. Sure, there will always be buzzkills who regard disciplined research with numbers as anathema to their personal aesthetic, but exciting possibilities lay ahead in quantitative research involving large-scale survey resources.

This is not to say all is bright. Surveys have suffered from declining response rates in recent years, for a variety of reasons (one of which is that the amount of surveying in society has increased so much that, even if individuals spent the same amount of overall time participating in surveys, the response rate of individual surveys would still be lower). Surveys are improving in their understanding of how to collect data to allow for the best possible inferences in the face of nonresponse (Groves et al. 2002), and estimation techniques for working with nonresponse are becoming increasingly well incorporated into regular data analysis practice (King et al. 2001). Especially as their work has been more infused with cognitive psychology, survey methodologists have discovered all kinds of ways in which survey responses are sensitive to the wording of questions and responses, their placement in the larger survey, and the mode and context in which the interviews are done (Tourangeau, Rips, and Rasinski 2000; Stone et al. 2000). This work will ultimately make surveys stronger, although part of their immediate impact has been to provoke anxiety about whether we really know all we thought we did—but, of course, this is itself an opportunity for new research. Some work I have collaborated in, for example, suggests that many of the subscales of a leading measure of psychological well-being seem actually, once proper statistical adjustments are made, to be largely indistinguishable from one another, raising the possibility that a whole preceding literature of studies finding distinctions among these subscales has been mostly just chasing chance variation (Springer, Hauser, and Freese 2006).

In addition to technological advances, social science is also making methodological strides that are improving the craft. What may be ultimately of most lasting importance here, perhaps, is not what is now happening on some statistical or computational frontier but rather the steady elaboration and diffusion of a clearer understanding of how quantitative research interested in identifying causes or predicting the consequences of policy manipulations should think about research questions. Here, social scientists are becoming increasingly adept at thinking about research questions in *counterfactual* terms: that is, thinking about quantitative research on causes as asking whether and how our expectations about an outcome would be different if the key explanatory variable had been different (Morgan and Winship 2007). So, a study of the effect of attending an elite college on later earnings, for instance, is asking how a given person's earnings would be different if they had gone to a nonelite college rather than an elite one (see Brand and Halaby 2006). This, in turn, allows clearer thinking about the appropriate comparison to substantiate any attempted answer to this question, which helps move well beyond simply taking some large data set, putting a bunch of variables into a regression routine, and looking at the coefficient of the ELITECOL variable. For example, it leads one to question how much value there is to including in one's analysis people whose background and academic record together give them practically no chance of attending an elite college, as these people are so different from those who actually attend elite colleges that the idea that one is estimating a causal effect by comparing the two seems implausible.[13] Some try to expand the heuristic value of thinking about counterfactuals and "potential outcomes" into a full-fledged philosophy of causality (Holland 1986), which runs aground quickly in various ways (e.g., Glymour 1986). Practically, though, counterfactual thinking seems an extremely useful cognitive tonic for clarifying various kinds of muddled thinking that have chronically beset many areas of quantitative social research.

As researchers have become more sophisticated in their thinking about causality, this has increased awareness of just how hard it is to draw strong causal inferences from ordinary single surveys, such as in our study utilizing just one year of GSS. Moreover, developments in this regard have underscored the limited gains from fancier statistical techniques in comparison to improvements in the quality of data. A recent movement in economics and in policy evaluation research has sought increasingly to isolate instances in which data would afford a relatively clear inference about causes in that situation, even at the expense of broader generalizability.

Two strategies, pervasive in economics but only intermittently considered in the quantitative methods curricula of other social sciences, deserve special mention. One, which I call *inference from discontinuity*, involves identifying the point in a series of data at which we would expect, if a given cause is operating, a relatively discrete change in the observed data. The most obvious application of this is time: if the cause is an event, then we would predict a discrete change just after compared to just before the event occurs. We can use familiar techniques to model any larger background trend over time and then specifically estimate the change associated with the event. In the case of estimating effects of widowhood on health, for instance, we can estimate the overall trend of aging and then look at whether there is a discrete difference before and after the spouse's death. Inferences from discontinuity are not limited to time, though, as different policies may lead us to predict discontinuous changes immediately above and below specific levels of income (Berk and Rauma 1983), different school district boundaries (Black 1999), or different test scores (Van der Klauuw 2002). When evidence over multiple cases reveals a sharp discontinuity at a point for which it is hard to imagine some explanation other than the postulated cause, this can serve as quite compelling causal evidence.

The other strategy, which I call *inference from exogenous variation* (or inference using "instrumental variables"), involves trying to isolate a "natural experiment" within some larger set of data and using it to estimate the effect of a cause. Consider trying to estimate the effect of family size on educational attainment. This is a notoriously difficult problem because parents who choose to have more or fewer children differ from one another in ways that are also likely related to how much education their children receive. The strategy of simply controlling for confounding variables is only satisfactory if one really believes all the pertinent differences are accurately and fully captured by the variables included as controls. An entirely different strategy may be derived from the finding in other research that there are some parents who prefer having a child of each sex enough that they will have a third child if they do not get one of each with their first two births. This creates a natural experiment: if having a son or daughter is basically random, some of these parents will have a son and daughter and then stop, whereas some will have two sons or two daughters and then have a third child. If we could somehow isolate these parents, we could estimate the effect of two-child versus three-child families on educational attainment in a way that would not be confounded by background differences across families (since, at least as posited here, it is random—*exogenous* to any parental characteristics—whether the first two children are opposite or same sex, and so random whether these parents on the margin stop or try to have a third child). If we are willing to defend certain assumptions, however, we do not actually have to isolate these families. Instead, putting things simply, we set aside the information on how many total children there are in the family, and we just compare the first two children in cases in which they are both boys or both girls to cases in which they are one boy and one girl. If we believe the only reason the educational attainment of the former would be different than the latter is that the former are more likely to have additional younger siblings that causally affect educational attainment, then we can rescale this difference to produce an estimate of the effect being in a three-child versus two-child family (see Angrist and Evans 1998 and Conley and Glauber 2006 for examples; see Imbens and Angrist 1994 and Morgan and Winship 2007 for a discussion of these issues in a counterfactual framework).[14]

Perhaps we can imagine other plausible explanations why the educational attainment of same-sex sibling pairs would be different from opposite-sex pairs. Perhaps there is greater competition for parental resources in same-sex pairs in ways that affect achievement.[15] If so, then this would bias our estimates and so not provide an effective strategy. Other instances make it harder to devise alternative explanations. In trying to estimate the effect of military service in Vietnam on earnings, we know there are some men who only served in Vietnam because their birthday was selected high in the draft lottery and other men who did not serve but would have if their birthdays had been selected high instead (Angrist 1990). If we observe that men in those cohorts whose birthdays were on March 15, June 9, August 25, September 24, and December 11 have higher average earnings than those born on March 14/16, June 8/10, August 24/26, September 23/25, and December 10/12, and if the former dates were selected high in the draft lottery and the latter were not, then what other explanation would there be except that the earnings of the former group are higher because of their higher probability of being drafted? The inference is compelling to whatever extent we imagine that the two groups (same vs. opposite-sex sibling pairs; individuals with one set of birthdays vs. another) otherwise would be the same, and so the only reason we would observe a difference is because of the effect of the "natural experiment." Other examples include using election years as a source of exogenous variation in the size of city's police force (Levitt 1997), exogenous variation in number of rivers and streams for the number of school districts in an area (Hoxby 2000), and exogenous variation in how judges are assigned for the length of prison sentences (Kling 2006) (see Angrist and Krueger 2001 for a list of examples). Inference from exogenous variation is tricky, and its virtues can be oversold, but it is attractive because it offers the possibility of compelling inferences in cases that would otherwise seem hopelessly ambiguous.

In closing, I will admit I am ambivalent about how much of my work has relied on large-scale survey data. I find surveys often frustrating to work with given how little we can know about the contours of an individual case, and even extensive longitudinal surveys provide only very indirect insights into processes of individual development or social life. Still, they are indispensible tools for characterizing populations, and clear-eyed and conscientious survey research has afforded all kinds of subtle insights into the workings of social life not otherwise available. Plus, survey technology continues to improve, as do techniques for analyzing survey data. Even so, I and many other social scientists find that a comprehensive research agenda involves seeing surveys as a complement to other kinds of research. For carrying forward such an agenda, the three most invaluable resources seem to be an open and enthusiastic mind, broad training, and collaborators.

NOTES

1. One might presume this changes radically when one gets to be involved in constructing items for a survey, but the economy of large-scale surveys is so tight that one has to choose only a subset of the items one would ideally ask, and my experience has been that what one learns from the items one does ask leads to remorse about the items that were cut.

2. Significance tests using p-values can be misleading for various other reasons I cannot get into here, but the heuristic value of p-values is especially undermined by making post hoc decisions and then reporting p-value and significance tests as though those decisions were a priori.

3. This point does not deny the use of model fit (e.g., R^2 values) as a criterion for some matters, perhaps such as how a control variable should be measured. One can decide that the right decision before running the models is to make it on the basis of model fit. Again, what is wrong is to run the models, look at the results, and then choose the results one prefers and rationalize this result on the basis of model fit.

4. Helpful for this, of course, is having other people read one's paper. The

most useful readers in this respect are those who are as much as possible like those who would be candidates to review the paper. Worth emphasizing again about the feedback one receives from readers is that any elaborations or clarifications you have to make for them afterward is exactly the kind of interaction you will not get to have with a reviewer—one needs to *preempt* concerns, not have ready answers to them.

5. Sometimes researchers will show that the bivariate relationship between two variables is dramatically reduced when several covariates are added to the model, but then not give any indication which covariates were actually responsible for the change. I always find this unsatisfying.

6. For that matter, one can make a reasonable argument why controlling for socioeconomic status is still a good idea, e.g., if one is worried about either measurement or specification error in the family size measure. Also, if it is unnecessary, the expectation is that it will have no effect on the estimated effect of birth order (which is mainly what we observed), not that estimates will be biased.

7. A separate consequence of this is that regression analyses are much more readily interpreted when considered in terms of attempting to estimate the effect of a single explanatory variable rather than imagining that one is estimating the causal effect of all the explanatory variables in the regression at once.

8. In this last respect, null findings are probably easier to publish than findings that are highly ambiguous as to whether they do or do not support a theory.

9. Not that our conclusion is that firstborns and later-borns really differ in their attitudes about capital punishment: given that one expects roughly 1 result out of 20 to be significant by chance alone if one is using a significance level of $p <$ .05, 3 out of 24 measures being significant seems like it may also just reflect chance.

10. Besides, as already noted, I looked at GSS as comprehensively as I was able, which strengthens my own confidence that there is not some defensible alternative way of doing the analysis that would have yielded different conclusions from those we drew.

11. Or, alternatively, why the data are inappropriate for the conclusion drawn from them.

12. The code needs to be carefully documented, so one can figure out what one is doing. I have gotten much better at this with time, less because of increasing skill but because of greater appreciation of the importance of replicability and greater humility about the fallibility of my memory.

13. To elaborate, one is on much stronger grounds for estimating the effect of attending an elite college if one compares those who attend elite colleges to those who are like them but do not (ideally, for completely random reasons—that this ideal is implausible is the great challenge for research using nonexperimental data). In this case, one is estimating the average effect of attending an elite college for those who did attend an elite college, which may be very different from the average effect of attending an elite college for students as a whole. Only by (often implausible) extrapolation can we claim to estimate the causal effect of an event on a group of people if that event has happened to practically no one in that group.

14. Of course, what one is really estimating is the effect of being in a three-

child versus two-child family for those families where the sex composition of the first two children determines whether or not the family has a third. Whether the effect can be generalized to three-child versus two-child families more broadly is a question of external validity that is hard for these designs to address and is often underappreciated in evaluating studies using instrumental variables designs.

15. As a different possible concern, Currie and Yelowitz (2000) use sibling sex composition as an instrument for public housing because public housing supplements in some areas favor families with two opposite-sex children over two same-sex children (giving the former an extra bedroom).

REFERENCES

Angrist, Joshua D. 1990. Lifetime Earnings and the Vietnam Era Draft Lottery: Evidence from Social Security Administrative Records. *American Economic Review* 80:313–36.

Angrist, Joshua D., and William N. Evans. 1998. Children and Their Parents' Labor Supply: Evidence from Exogenous Variation in Family Size. *American Economic Review* 88:450–77.

Angrist, Joshua D., and Alan B. Krueger. 2001. Instrumental Variables and the Search for Identification: From Supply and Demand to Natural Experiments. *Journal of Economic Perspectives* 15:69–85.

Berk, Richard A. 2004. *Regression Analysis: A Constructive Critique*. Thousand Oaks, CA: Sage.

Berk, Richard, and David Rauma. 1983. Capitalizing on Nonrandom Assignment to Treatments: A Regression-Discontinuity Evaluation of a Crime-Control Program. *Journal of the American Statistical Association* 78:21–27.

Black, Sandra E. 1999. Do "Better" Schools Matter? Parental Valuation of Elementary Education. *Quarterly Journal of Economics* 114:577–59.

Brand, Jennie E., and Charles N. Halaby. 2006. Regression and Matching Estimates of the Effects of Elite College Attendance on Education and Career Achievement. *Social Science Research* 35:749–70.

Conley, Dalton, and Rebecca Glauber. 2006. Parental Educational Investment and Children's Academic Risk: Estimates of the Impact of Sibship Size and Birth Order from Exogenous Variation in Fertility. *Journal of Human Resources* 41:722–37.

Currie, Janet, and Aaron Yelowitz. 2000. Are Public Housing Projects Good for Kids? *Journal of Public Economics* 75:89–124.

Freese, Jeremy. 2007. Replication Standards in Quantitative Social Science: Why Not Sociology? *Sociological Methods and Research* 36: 153–72.

Freese, Jeremy, and Brian Powell. 1999. Sociobiology, Status, and Parental Investment in Sons and Daughters: Testing the Trivers-Willard Hypothesis. *American Journal of Sociology* 106:1704–43.

Freese, Jeremy, Brian Powell, and Lala Carr Steelman. 1999. Rebel Without a Cause or Effect: Sociobiology, Birth Order, and Social Attitudes. *American Sociological Review* 64:207–31.

Glymour, Clark. 1986. Comment: Statistics and Metaphysics. *Journal of the American Statistical Association* 81:964–66.

Groves, Robert M., Don A. Dillman, John L. Eltinge, and Roderick J. A. Little. 2002. *Survey Nonresponse*. New York: Wiley.

Halaby, Charles N. 2004. Panel Models in Sociological Research: Theory into Practice. *Annual Review of Sociology* 30:507–44.

Harris, Judith Rich. 1998. *The Nurture Assumption*. New York: Free Press.

Holland, Paul. 1986. Statistics and Causal Inference. *Journal of the American Statistical Association* 81:945–60.

Hoxby, Caroline M. 2000. Does Competition among Public Schools Benefit Students and Taxpayers? *American Economic Review* 90:1209–38.

Imbens, Guido W., and Joshua D. Angrist. 1994. Identification and Estimation of Local Average Treatment Effects. *Econometrica* 62:467–75.

King, Gary. 2006. Publication, Publication. *PS: Political Science and Politics* 39:119–25.

King, Gary, James Honaker, Anne Joseph, and Kenneth Scheve. 2001. Analyzing Incomplete Political Science Data: An Alternative Algorithm for Multiple Imputation. *American Political Science Review* 95:49–69.

King, Gary, Robert O. Keohane, and Sidney Verba. 1994. *Designing Social Inquiry: Scientific Inference in Qualitative Research*. Princeton: Princeton University Press.

Kling, Jeffrey R. 2006. Incarceration Length, Employment, and Earnings. *American Economic Review* 96:863–76.

Levitt, Steven D. 1997. Using Electoral Cycles in Police Hiring to Estimate the Effect of Police on Crime. *American Economic Review* 87:270–90.

Morgan, Stephen L., and Christopher Winship. 2007. *Counterfactuals and Causal Inference: Methods and Principles for Social Research*. Cambridge, UK: Cambridge University Press.

Raftery, Adrian E. 1995. Bayesian Model Selection in Social Research. *Sociological Methodology* 25:111–63.

Shermer, Michael. 1996. History at the Crossroads: Can History Be a Science? Can It Afford Not to Be? *Skeptic* 4:56–67.

Springer, Kristen W., Robert M. Hauser, and Jeremy Freese. 2006. Bad News Indeed for Ryff's Six-Factor Model of Well-Being. *Social Science Research* 35:1119–30.

Stone, Arthur A., Jaylan S. Turkan, Christine A. Bachrach, Jared B. Jobe, Howard S. Kurtzman, and Virginia S. Cain. 2000. *The Science of Self-Report: Implications for Research and Practice*. Mahwah, NJ: Lawrence Erlbaum.

Sulloway, Frank J. 1996. *Born to Rebel: Birth Order, Family Dynamics, and Creative Lives*. New York: Pantheon.

Tourangeau, Roger, Lance J. Rips, and Kenneth A. Rasinski. 2000. *The Psychology of Survey Response*. Cambridge, UK: Cambridge University Press.

Van der Klauuw, Wilbert. 2002. Estimating the Effect of Financial Aid Offers on College Enrollment: A Regression-Discontinuity Approach. *International Economic Review* 43 (4): 1249–87.

DOING ARCHIVAL RESEARCH

How to Find a Needle in a Haystack

JASON GALLO

The National Archives is a public trust on which our democracy depends. We enable people to inspect for themselves the record of what government has done. We enable officials and agencies to review their actions and help citizens hold them accountable. We ensure continuing access to essential evidence that documents the rights of American citizens, the actions of Federal (and other) officials, and the national experience.

—Allen Weinstein,
Archivist of the United States, March 7, 2005

Archival research can often feel like a test of endurance and patience. Multiple storage sites, elaborate naming conventions, and a matrix of rules and regulations that govern access to and use of primary source material make doing archival research a challenging enterprise. Nevertheless, the payoffs can be extraordinary. Finding a key memo or report buried in thousands of cubic feet of archived files can make all of the difference to the successful completion of a truly original research project. By following a strategy based upon three principles, it is possible to locate valuable historical documents in an efficient and cost-effective manner.

The first principle is to prepare assiduously in advance of an archival site visit. It is important to determine the location and availability of the most relevant documents and make all preparations for the visit before leaving home. A good rule of thumb is to start preparations at least six weeks before you plan to visit your intended research destination. This will provide you with the requisite time to locate an appropriate collection and inquire about its availability, contact administrators and archivists at the site, prepare your equipment, and make appropriate travel arrangements without having to scramble for last-minute tickets or accommodations. Second, it is essential to plan the logistical details of the site visit in advance by developing a working knowledge of the archive's operations and regulations. This will maximize primary source research precisely by minimizing the amount of time and energy spent dealing with the bureaucratic regulations and idiosyncrasies of the particular archive. Finally, one must be willing to seek advice and learn from the expertise of on-site professionals. They will be familiar with the scope and content of their collection and in most cases be ready to provide researchers with time-saving suggestions. This chapter gives a detailed account of the various steps that can be taken to navigate the maze of federal archives.

The chapter is divided into the following major sections: thoughts about archival research as a scholarly practice, pretrip preparation, general guidelines for doing on-site archival research, a concrete example of conducting research using the federal resources of the National Archives collection, what to do once you return home, and finally major takeaway lessons. The advice in each section is generally applicable to research in any archive, regardless of its size or the scope of its collections. I will discuss common bureaucratic regulations, security measures, the appropriate use of equipment, and effective techniques for organizing findings for later use. While the chapter focuses primarily on finding and duplicating textual files, the use and duplication of audio, film, and photographic records is also discussed briefly.

WHY ARCHIVAL RESEARCH?

At its core, archival research involves the search for and use of existing information to provide answers to scholarly research questions. Before embarking on a costly and time-intensive archival research trip it is vital to assess whether conducting archival research is right for you. This entails determining what your research questions are and whether primary source data will help you to answer them. Broadly stated, archived information constitutes a data set that is generated, collected, and organized by third parties, and available for analysis by scholars. According to Hill (1993, 2), "The institutional fabric of modern societies captures traces of individuals, organizations, and social movements in a variety of complex ways, including physical traces collected in cultural monuments such as libraries, museums, and formal archives." These "physical traces" of individuals, organizations, and social movements constitute a set of archived information that can include, but is not limited to, government documents, personal correspondence, memos, voting records, photographs, audio and visual recordings, databases, and quantitative public records.

There are two common misconceptions about archival research that should be addressed. The first is that archival research constitutes a *method* for data analysis. Instead, as Harris (2001, 330) notes, archival research cannot be contained by a single methodology, as most decent-sized archives represent "an enormous body of relevant information contained in quite different types of documents, each presenting distinctive challenges and subtleties." One of the advantages of conducting archival research is that it often provides scholars with a diverse array of sources and thus lends itself to mixed-methodological research. It can supplement ethnographic, interview, and oral history research by providing scholars with independently created data to corroborate findings derived from these other methods. Archival research also lends itself to scholarly work that employs both qualitative and quantitative methods, even though it has been commonly associated almost exclusively with the former. But it is in fact an effective research practice for uncovering third-party quantitative data upon which statistical analyses can subsequently be run. It is therefore necessary to draw a clear line between archival research as the practice of locating primary source evidence and the variety of scholarly methods that can be used to analyze the data once gathered.

The second common misconception is that archival research is the exclusive domain of historians. While it is particularly useful for uncovering historical documents, it also has become an important tool for scholars in a wide variety of other disciplines, including geography (Harris 2001), international relations (Thies 2002), media and communications (Berger 2000), mediation (Bercovitch 2004), psychology (Simonton 2000), race relations (Stanfield 1987), and the general social sciences (Hill 1993). Archival research is broadly applicable to almost any discipline that does not rely strictly on empirical experimentation, and it complements research methods in most social science and humanities fields, as well as some scientific disciplines.

To assess the value of archival research for your research agenda it is important to ask *what data do I need to answer my research questions, how do I locate the data,* and *are the data reliable?* If your research depends in any capacity on the location of third-party data housed in a unique repository by third-party actors, you will need to engage in archival research to some degree. In addition, if your research questions are primarily answered using data gathered through alternative methods, archival research still might represent a useful secondary method for collecting information that complements or corroborates your primary research thrust. Whether archival research is a primary or secondary data-gathering method, it is absolutely essential to plan your research trip in advance in order to maximize the efficiency of the data-gathering process. However, it is equally important to recognize that archival research is an ongoing process and that one needs to be open to following the evidence on hand to sometimes unexpected destinations. This flexibility is critical, as a "previously unknown collection, stumbled upon, may suggest a different, more rewarding line of inquiry" (Harris 2001, 331).

To be adequately prepared to conduct archival research you should consult the academic literature that engages research questions similar to your own in order to hone your research questions and acquaint yourself with the scholars with whom you are in conversation. The literature review will point toward the types of data commonly used by scholars in your field, the primary sources associated with your research questions, and the repositories where they can be found. Since unique archival data tend to be located in only one place (Fisher 2004) and many rare or fragile resources have not been digitized, the cost in time and financial resources required to conduct research at a remote repository will help determine if archival research is a practical option.

Finally, it is important to consider the reliability of the data that you plan to collect. Primary sources that are housed in archives reflect the context in which they were created and collected, and their selection for inclusion in an archive itself represents a series of editorial and curatorial decisions. Each actor in the chain of custody of a particular archival source, from the author of a particular letter or sponsor of a statistical report through the archivist in charge of its storage and categorization, exerts influence on the materials that are available. It is imperative to support your findings with multiple data points. By making the discovery of corroborating evidence a priority of your archival research strategy you ensure both that claims supported by weak evidence are eliminated and that your reported findings are as strong as possible.

BEFORE LEAVING HOME: GATHERING INFORMATION AND PLANNING THE TRIP

Once you have determined that archival research is necessary and valuable, the next step is to figure out which archives house the collections you wish to use. While your review of relevant secondary literature should provide a good starting point, it is advisable to conduct an online search to determine if other repositories house collections pertinent to your work. Be sure to use a variety of search terms derived from your research questions and secondary literature, and devote several hours to doing online keyword searches. Even if it feels redundant, search for as many keyword strings related to your topic as possible, and thoroughly examine all promising results. Keep in mind that each search will return a wide array of answers, some useful, others not, and continue searching until you are satisfied that you have located a collection of documents that you wish to use. If a specific person, group, company, or university is associated with your topic, conduct a series of online searches using associated proper nouns as well. Papers related to particular individuals are often housed at the institution where they worked, institutions and scholarly associations with which they were affiliated, or a historical society or research center dedicated to the person's field of study.

Once you have determined your target archive, conduct preliminary research on the Web about the collection or collections that you plan to use. From this point on in your preparation process you will encounter various bits of information that will be useful for your site visit. Create a list that includes each important detail and be sure to consult it before you embark on your journey. Each regulation that you will need to follow and each piece of identification or equipment that you will need to bring should be listed in an inventory as well.

Examine the archive's Web site or browse the archive's online collections to determine what is available and what format it is available in. The level of detail available online varies depending on the archive; however, almost all include an online search function and an overview of the collection divided into categories, subcategories, and series. Most archive Web sites will provide users with online finding guides and the ability to search the collection for specific thematic areas. As a general rule, archives will provide enough information online for you to determine whether they hold files that are pertinent to your research interests, how those files are organized (whether chronologically or thematically), in what format they are available, and where they are located. The actual work of sifting through the individual files is left up to the researcher. Some archives may provide detailed data on a limited number of individual files, and in rare cases a digital duplication of the document may even be available to download.

Do as much online research about the collection as possible. If you come across files or a series of files that you wish to view in person, note any identifying numbers provided. Using a laptop to store your information is strongly recommended as most archives allow laptops but have stringent rules about bringing outside paper products and writing utensils into their collections. Often, one can bring outside notes on loose-leaf paper into an archive only after inspection and approval, but notebooks, bound paper products, and ink writing utensils are often banned. The rules governing laptop use or bringing outside paper products into the archives are generally posted on the Web or can be obtained by calling the archive directly. If you do not own or have access to a laptop, see if it is possible to borrow a laptop from work, school, a university IT department, a university library or multimedia lab, or a friend or associate.

Use the Web site or call ahead to determine the location of the archive, its opening hours, the credentials that one needs to bring, when and how often it allows documents to be pulled from the stacks, equipment regulations, paper restrictions, if duplication is allowed, and if lockers or storage areas are provided to researchers. Larger archives often provide a dedicated customer service line to deal with your questions. Smaller archives may only provide a local telephone number that is answered by a receptionist, who will be able to answer general questions and route you to the appropriate person for specific inquiries. Remember to call during archive business hours to ensure that someone is available. Once you have an appropriate authority on the phone, politely ask precise and appropriate questions. General questions about opening and closing times should be addressed to the receptionist for the general helpline, while questions regarding the availability and use of a specific file should be addressed to the archivist or collection specialist responsible for that document. Asking the right person the right question will save you time and energy.

Prepare for your site visit by making sure that you possess all of the relevant identification documents required to gain access to the archive. This information can either be found online or by calling the archive directly. Most archives only require a valid government-issued identification card, like a driver's license or passport; however, some collections may require you to obtain additional documentation. These additional documents may include a researcher pass, library card, or visitor pass—all of which are usually available to visiting scholars on-site. If you plan to use documents that require a security clearance, be sure to call in advance to ascertain what forms of identification one will need to present in order to gain access to classified material. In some limited circumstances researchers may also be required to either arrange for accreditation in advance or set up a research appointment with an archivist. Information about these extra requirements can either be found online or by calling the archive. Nothing can be more frustrating than arriving at an archive ready to do research and being turned away because you forgot to bring the appropriate forms of identification, you failed to schedule an appointment, or you neglected to obtain extra accreditation in advance. The rules and procedures employed at an archive may seem bureaucratic and arbitrary, but they have been deemed essential for the protection of the collection by those who work there. Understanding and respecting these rules is essential for efficient research.

A Concrete Example: Planning a Trip to the National Archives

If you have determined that the documents that you would like to locate reside at the National Archives Annex in College Park, Maryland, the repository for the majority of U.S. government records, for example, you should begin preparing for your research trip to this location just outside of Washington, DC. The National Archives Web site provides a page dedicated to trip preparation. One of the first things to do is to call the Archives' toll-free number to inquire about the availability of the records that you wish to view. Records are rarely removed from circulation; however, rare, delicate, sensitive, or classified documents may be unavailable for a variety of reasons. Calling ahead will alert you to any possible problems that may arise regarding access to the relevant files and to any other restrictions. Prepare for the call by having the information that you gathered online at hand. You will need to tell an Archives staff member what types of records you are seeking, and the person will help route you to the appropriate contact.

While e-mailing the Archives is also a possibility, do not take this route no matter how appealing it may seem. You will get faster and better answers if you speak to a live person. While you may not need to speak with an Archives staff member if you are interested in general records and your online research has shown that they exist in bulk at a particular facility, it is a good idea to call ahead anyway just to reassure yourself before making concrete plans. Ask the staff member to help you approximate the amount of time you will need to use the materials without being rushed. It is often cheaper to make one visit and stay for an extra couple of days than it is to have to make a second trip. In addition, if you are researching an area that contains classified material, restricted access material, or very fragile material, a staff member will be able to advise you on best practices for proceeding efficiently with your research.

Once you have confirmed that the records you wish to use are available, it is time to plan the practical aspects of your trip. Using the Archives' trip planning Web page you can locate the dedicated Web site of the facility that you wish to visit, complete with information about opening times, pull times, transportation, and on-site regulations. The Web site for the Archives Annex lists all of the above information and even includes information about the on-site bookstore, cafeteria, and snack bar. Note that the Archives Annex has extended hours one week per month. This is listed on the Web site and is something to consider when planning your trip. The site has a link to a list of local hotels, motels, amenities, and restaurants.

Regardless of the destination, it is generally helpful to familiarize oneself with local transportation options as that may enable you to extend your hotel search to a wider area. It will be important to find a mixture of convenience, access, and price that works best for you. But, above all, make sure that wherever you stay you have access to public or private transportation to and from the Archives location. Do not lose sight of the fact that doing archival research is your primary concern, and make your lodging decisions with that in mind.

Equipment

The final step of your pretrip planning involves determining what type of equipment you can and should bring. By this point, you should have a good idea of the types of primary source material with which you will be working: paper-based documents, photographic documents, audio recordings, video recordings, or film recordings. The use of a laptop is strongly recommended for working with each medium. A laptop will help in taking notes, organizing the research, and storing digital captures of primary source documents if necessary. If you plan to use visual records, audio recordings, video recordings, or film recordings, search the archive's Web site to determine any special regulations governing the use and duplication of these materials. Archives that house these types of records will be equipped to view or listen to audio and visual materials, provide listening and viewing carrels, and offer access to duplication equipment.

You are strongly advised when dealing with audio and visual recordings to call the archive in order to talk with a specialist who handles these materials. Ask the specialist how you can view or listen to these records, what duplication equipment is available, whether you will be provided duplication media (video/audiotape, CD, DVD), or if you should bring your own, and if there are any duplication fees that you will be required to pay. Archives generally do not allow backpacks, bags, or equipment cases to be carried into the document viewing area. Be sure to inquire about the availability of lockers or another secure area in which you can store your belongings, and if a deposit or charge is required.

Paper-based records are the most common type of material housed in non-media-specific archives. In addition to laptops, most archives will allow you to use digital cameras, and in some cases flatbed scanners, to replicate textual records in their facilities. Archives also generally provide photocopying services. Again, look online for specific regulations governing the use of these tools or call the archive directly. Each of these methods will allow you to capture an image of a historical document for later use at your home or office. However, using a digital camera with a tripod is recommended both for ease of use and because digital images can be stored, indexed, and easily recalled from either your home computer or laptop. If you do not own or have access to a camera, and you feel that purchasing a camera is outside of your budget, inquire whether you can borrow one from your institution, a university-based digital resource center, university library, a university film or fine arts department, or from a friend or associate. If this is impossible, photocopying documents is an alternative. If you intend to photocopy documents at an archive bear in mind that you will need to bring cash (or in some cases a credit card) to purchase a copy card. For duplicating a limited number of documents, using the on-site copiers can be preferable to lugging equipment with you. However, if you plan to duplicate large amounts of material or odd-sized documents, a digital camera will save you tremendous amounts of time and effort. For large copying jobs consider that at 5 to 10 cents per page your costs can add up quickly.

If you already own a digital camera or decide to purchase one, check to see if the camera has a grooved recess on its base to accept a tripod. The odds are that it will. An inexpensive camera tripod with the ability to pivot the camera to face downward will suffice for the purposes of indoor photography. A tripod is not strictly necessary, but it will lend stability to your photographs and speed up the process of duplicating longer documents, as you only need to flip between pages and shoot. Once you have set up your tripod and focused on a standard-sized document you will rarely need to adjust your setup. Remember, even if you are alternating between taking photographs of documents in varying layouts (upright, landscape, two-sided) you can always resize and rotate on your machine.

Using a camera's flash mechanism is generally forbidden, and so you will need to rely on either a desk lamp or the archive's overhead lamps for proper lighting. One concern that does arise when using a tripod is the possibility that the tripod may cast a shadow across the document being photographed. Repositioning the tripod or swiveling the desk lamp easily eliminates this problem. However, in a room where you are dependent on a fixed, overhead light installation, or where outside light streams in and shifts throughout the course of the day, there may be nothing to do except move the equipment to a desk or carrel not affected by this problem.

There are several other considerations to bear in mind when using a digital camera. Be sure to bring a fully loaded second battery with you in case your first battery runs out. Always have the battery charger on you as well. If you anticipate a multiday trip to an archive, make sure to charge each battery fully overnight. If you bring a laptop with you to the archive you can dump the images stored in your camera's memory directly to your computer when you have exhausted the memory card's capacity. Alternately, it is best to bring an additional memory card to save time on processing the images locally. If you have access to an external hard drive that you can bring with you on your trip, it is a good idea to save your freshly captured files to it each night to ensure against potential data loss.

A final alternative for capturing images is to use a flatbed scanner attached to a laptop. This is a cumbersome option that will take up a good deal of work space, but fine nonetheless. Using a scanner will produce digital images with roughly the same fidelity as a photocopy but provide the convenience of capturing digital images that one can later manipulate, resize, and index. Not every archive allows the use of a scanner, so like all other logistical information, this should be verified ahead of time as well.

THE SITE VISIT

Once all of the preliminary preparations are complete, select a date to visit the destination archive. Consult the list of regulations and inventory of equipment and identification documents before you leave, and be sure to bring each item that you will need. Get to the archive early. Be prepared to spend up to an hour going through security, getting credentialed, having your equipment inspected, finding a locker, and locating a desk or carrel at which to work. Each collection has a different protocol for admitting and credentialing researchers. Some require you to pass through airportlike security (certainly true of federal archives), while others simply require that you present an identification card. Your bag may be x-rayed, and you will need to present a valid form of identification each time that you enter the facility. Most archives, including the National Archives system, are open to researchers of all nationalities. If you are not a U.S. citizen and do not possess a valid U.S. government-issued identity document, bring your passport. For those with special needs, it is worth noting that public archive facilities must comply with the Americans with Disabilities Act, and so the premises will be accessible. If you are concerned about accessibility at a private collection, however, you should call in advance and inquire what arrangements can be made for the visit.

Once you have passed security you may be required to obtain a guest pass, library card, or researcher identification badge before using the collections. Your pretrip research about the archive's regulations should prepare you for this step. Present the required identification documents to the appropriate staff member, fill out the necessary forms, and wait for your temporary pass to be issued. In the National Archives, for example, you will have to view a short computerized presentation on the rules and proper handling techniques for archived documents before being issued a researcher card. Your equipment will likely be inspected, and you may be issued a property pass that will allow you to bring your equipment into the collection. This is both for the protection of the archived material and your equipment. Researchers cannot take equipment in or out of the research area without a property pass and personal identification that match. Finally, if you are required to leave your bags and carrying cases outside of the collection, inquire about the location of lockers or a secured area. The lockers often require a deposit that will be refunded when you collect your things at the end of the day. Wheeling carts are generally available for use if you have more equipment than you can handle unassisted.

Having gained access to the collection, locate a suitable desk, table, or carrel to set up your equipment, and then head straight to a reference librarian or archival specialist. This is perhaps the most important task on your first day. The archive's staff deals with new researchers all day, every day. These people will be happy to assist you personally or find someone who can help you. On your first visit you will make dozens of mistakes; however, the biggest mistake that you can make is not to ask a trained professional to help you with your research.

Consulting professionals is useful for a variety of reasons: they can point you toward the appropriate finding guide for the collection, they can show you how to request documents, and they can provide hints about how to handle the documents once you have them. Be polite and courteous; the time that you spend with the archivist may be some of the most important of your entire trip. An inability to be patient or friendly could be detrimental to the successful completion of the project. Misunderstandings may arise out of the imprecise phrasing of a question or the failure to use the appropriate technical language when making a query. If a misunderstanding does occur, politely ask follow-up questions until you are satisfied that the archivist understands exactly what is of interest to you. The tips and advice that you receive could save you hours of research time.

In the Nation Archives Annex, for example, staff members in the main reading room will happily arrange a meeting with an archivist who specializes in your subject area and the record group(s) of interest. When you meet with an archival specialist, clearly describe your project and the types of records for which you are looking. Be polite, patient, and pay close attention to what the archivist has to say. You have the attention of an expert who knows more about these files than almost anyone else. The archivist will describe what is available and help you locate the files that best suit your needs.

At the National Archives Annex, meetings usually take place in the reference room that houses the most detailed and annotated finding guides in the building. Most stacks are not publicly accessible; therefore you will need to consult the finding guide to find the exact location of the files that you wish to view. These guides are housed in a series of binders that are arranged by record group and contain information on every box, folder, or file available in that group. The guides constitute the holy grail of federal archival research. Have the archivist walk you through how to use the guide (it is confusing), and also have the archivist help you fill out your first pull slip to request documents. The naming protocols in archives can be puzzling, and you will need to fill out the pull slips correctly in order to en-sure that you receive the files that you want.

All archives provide finding guides or catalogs that help describe the scope of their collections and the division of content into subject areas, boxes, and individual files. Finding guides are either physically stored in binders in the archive or are available digitally on dedicated computers lo-cated in the archive. An archival professional can be of great assistance in helping to locate records in a particular subject area across several related series. For example, records relating to the urban housing policy of a par-ticular state in the 1960s may be found in the records of the state's housing agency, but also in the individual files of state politicians and administra-tors of the era. Once you have located the files that you wish to view, the next step is to request that the files be pulled from the stacks. Be sure to keep an eye on the clock so that you do not miss the next pull.

If you run into trouble with the pull slips, ask someone at the archive for help. It is their job, and you are not the first researcher to be baffled try-ing to fill out a pull slip. You must list a series of alphanumerical identifiers in proper order on a pull slip, along with the name of the requested files, your name, institutional affiliation, and researcher number. Using the housing policy example, a pull slip for the files of a state's housing author-ity for the construction of a housing project in 1955 may look something like this: 201/13/04/17/06 referring to Record Group 201 (State Housing Authority), shelf 13, row 04, series 17 (Housing Authority 1955 Chrono-logical Files), and box 06. There are various permutations of this, and it is important to get these protocols right to ensure the delivery of the proper files.

Since many archives only pull files at specific times of day, usually in two- to three-hour intervals, you will want to have as many boxes as possi-ble on hand to maximize your research time. A pull can often take an hour, so failure to fill out your request form accurately can lead to disappoint-ment and a loss of valuable time. Archives often set limits on the number of boxes that an individual researcher may have out at any one time. Fill your quota, and do not be hesitant about going over this limit; the archive staff will only provide you with what you are allowed to have. One of the most time-consuming mistakes one can make is to neglect to have docu-ments pulled. Even if you have a full load of boxes at your desk, be sure to take the time to submit new requests if you think that you may need more documents. If you miss a pull it will be several hours before you can make a new request and even longer before you have a chance to examine the documents.

Once you submit your pull slips, note when the files will be delivered, and begin setting up your equipment. Most carrels and desks will come equipped with a reading lamp and an electrical socket, or be within close vicinity of one. Plug in your gear. Set up your tripod if you are using one, attach your camera, turn off your flash, and take a practice shot of something to make sure everything is functioning properly. Many archives do not allow flash photography, and frankly, if you are capturing textual documents for research purposes a desk lamp should provide ample lighting. If you plan to photocopy documents locate the copy machine. If it requires a copy card find out where you can purchase one. There are often machines nearby that sell cards, or they can be purchased from archive staff.

After the designated amount of time has passed, you can collect your pulled files from the archive staff, usually at the same desk where your request was submitted. Often your boxes will be arrayed on a pushcart for easy transport back to your work area. Archives usually request that you view only one file or folder at a time, and this is a good strategy to use no matter what the regulations are. Always work in the order that files are presented in each box and each folder. This allows you to work systematically through the files and prevents the files from being returned out of order. Boxes generally contain a series of folders arranged chronologically or thematically. Locate the folder that corresponds with the time period or subject matter of interest.

The standard unit of measure for archival research should always be the folder. Review the entire folder, take note of each document that you wish to duplicate, receive approval from the staff, and then copy, photograph, or scan all of the documents. After you are done with this part of the work, return each document to its proper place in the folder, and then put back the entire folder to its location in the box before moving on to another folder. View each document in the order that it is presented in the folder and do not skip a single page. Even though the file should be organized chronologically, previous researchers may not have returned the documents in the proper order. You do not want to miss an important document by assuming mistakenly that a previous user of the material had returned everything in order. Archives usually provide paper slips (akin to bookmarks) for you to use to mark files of interest. Place a slip in front of each file in a folder that you wish to duplicate, and completely review the entire folder before presenting the folder to a staff member for review. Take the files over to a staff member and let them know of your intention to either photograph or copy the files. This is not an arbitrary step as there are very delicate or photosensitive documents that can only be photographed or copied with staff assistance.

Always duplicate the documents in the order in which they are presented in the folder. This not only prevents you from returning files out of order but will also help you store and sort your copies for later use. Note any identifying numbers associated with each document and make a record for your later use. If you find a letter from the mayor of a large city to the State Housing Authority, for example, you could record the file as "Housing Authority, Chronological Files, Box 06, Folder 2, Letter from Mayor John Doe of Large City to State Housing Authority, 01/01/1955." This will allow you to organize your duplications efficiently and properly cite the documents in your research. The use of a laptop is, again, strongly recommended. Each of the identifying characteristics for your documents can be entered into a spreadsheet using the naming convention mentioned here. Maintaining your notes in the order in which you duplicate documents will help you organize your research once you leave the archive. This is especially useful for labeling digital photographs once you have completed your trip. The entry on line 1 of your spreadsheet will correspond to the first photograph in your digital inventory, and so on.

Keep an eye on the clock and remember to leave yourself enough time to submit more pull requests if necessary. If you have submitted new requests you can proceed in peace knowing that new boxes of documents will be waiting for you when you are ready for the next batch. Once you are finished with all of the boxes from your first pull, return them in exchange for the new files that you have requested, and continue the process of examining documents. Be aware of the next pull time if necessary, and also be aware of the closing time of the archive. You should allow at least half an hour to wrap up everything in time, return all of your boxes, shut down your equipment, exit through any archive security measures, get everything out of your locker, and vacate the premises before the staff locks up. Archives will generally hold the files that you pull overnight for use the next day if you ask them. You will be able to retrieve the files without having to wait for the regularly scheduled pull times the next morning. Conversely, if you are finished with the materials that you have out you should make the staff aware of this fact. This will allow them to return the files to their proper place and will make them available for the next researcher who wants to use them. As you depart the archive, you may be asked to submit any photocopies that you have made and your equipment to scrutiny to make sure that you are not walking out with original documents.

The Case of Doing Research at the National Archives

The principles touched on in the previous sections can be applied to doing research in most archives including federal archives. In this section, I will use the National Archives Annex in College Park, Maryland as an example, as well as the regional and presidential libraries of the National Archives system. I will also discuss the unique online search functions for federal records as well as including information on using classified records.

I have chosen the National Archives Annex for two reasons. First, it is the archive with which I have the most experience, and second, it is the repository for the majority of U.S. federal records and is therefore the likely first destination for anyone making use of public records or doing research on any aspect of the U.S. government. The National Archives Annex is located just outside of Washington, DC, near the University of Maryland, and within easy reach of the National Archives main building and the Library of Congress in central Washington, as well as the headquarters of most federal agencies scattered across the Washington metropolitan area. The headquarters of federal agencies sometimes house recent records that have yet to be transferred to the National Archives or else have their own libraries where additional material can be found.

If you are doing research on a specific agency or a project that is primarily associated with a particular organization, inquire in advance of your trip to DC whether any additional material may be available at the institution's headquarters, and plan to stay an extra day or two if possible. For example, a quick review of the Housing and Urban Development (HUD) Web site indicates that HUD maintains its own library and lists its location and a telephone number. You should call and talk to a librarian on staff about your research. Some of the information that can be found at the institutional level cannot be found elsewhere in the federal system. If an agency has an official library or historian's office, the staff in either of these can be of invaluable service to you since the agency is intimately involved in the preservation of historically significant documents. If you are unable to find contact information for either of these, get in touch with the public affairs office and ask about on-site research opportunities at the organization's headquarters. A public affairs officer may not be able to assist you with your research but should be able to tell you about the availability of records or put you in touch with someone who is better qualified to assist you.

Once you have gathered information and gained access to a federal archive, the procedures for conducting research are the same as mentioned in the previous section. The only thing to bear in mind is that security measures at federal archives may be more stringent than private or state collections. Plan to spend some extra time passing through security and having your equipment inspected.

National Archives Research Online

The recurring theme of this chapter is to do as much online research as possible before investing time and money in a research trip. As more scholarship has shifted online, academic publications are increasingly available digitally, and centers of digital history create tools and services to enhance the online research process. The best place to start planning a research trip to a federal repository is the Web site of the National Archives and Records Administration (NARA), the umbrella agency that oversees the diverse federal repositories located across the United States including the National Archives Annex and the presidential libraries. There is a preponderance of information and a multitude of links that will tell you everything about the National Archives systems, its constituent parts, the millions of documents in its various collections, hours of operation, and directions to its facilities by car, bus, and train. You will be able to find record group, and possibly series-, subcategory-, and box-level information about federal archival holdings, but you may not be able to get a file-by-file view of what is available. The Archives' Web site will be crucial in helping you figure out if your area of interest has a collection, what is in that collection, and where that collection exists.

The NARA Web site presents several online finding guides, catalogs, and digital collections that aid the research process. The fact that there are multiple online guides may appear daunting at first; nevertheless spending an hour or so viewing and searching each is a valuable process as these resources range from general databases about NARA holdings to specialized collections of digitized material. Be sure to note the specific details of each online guide, paying close attention to exactly what files and file types you are able to review and possibly retrieve. Taking the time to become acquainted with the online finding guides will minimize the time spent searching the wrong database for information that does not reside there. Critical hours may be lost searching for paper records, for example, in a database that only returns results on digital holdings.

Once you are comfortable using NARA's online resources, it is a good idea to begin your research with a search for the record group number that covers your research area. The record group number is the top-level identifier for an entire thematic collection of documents. For example, all documents pertaining to the Department of Housing and Urban Development are in Record Group 207. Note the number of the record group, as you will continually use this number both online and on-site during your research process. The contents of Record Group 207 are listed in the fashion in which they are organized, often moving from a set of general records to more specific divisional and then program records (207.1, 207.2, 207.3, 207.3.1, etc.). Once you have found information on your specific area of interest on the NARA Web site, carefully note the identifying details of the collection that you wish to view. The online finding guides will provide details about the type (textual, microfilm, photographic, motion picture, machine-readable) and scope of records available and may even link to related record groups in which material pertinent to your subject areas also appears.

Other Search Mechanisms

The Archival Research Catalog, ARC for short, is a good place to start digging a little deeper. If your subject cannot be found in ARC or only returns a limited number of resources, bear in mind that according to the ARC Web site, only a portion (50 percent at the time of this writing) of the Archives holdings are listed in ARC. This is not ideal for a comprehensive search but will help locate specific documents and provide you with a better feel for what is available. As mentioned earlier, it is best to search for several keyword strings of varying specificity to ensure that you do not miss important documents by simply conducting a single search that is either too broad or too specific. The results will be limited only to files in the ARC system. When these are specified properly, they can be highly informative and provide the most detailed description of federal records that you will find online.

ARC describes the type of files available (textual, maps, photographic, motion picture) and the historical function and use of the files, and it includes a note about the scope and content of the files. Often issues of practical interest will be listed, such as the removal of all oversized items from the general file or any restrictions on viewing or reproducing the files. A series of tracking numbers, transfer numbers, and disposition authority numbers may be listed. Ignore them. You will not be provided with the numbers that you will need to use when having these documents pulled. The importance of an ARC search is that it allows you to familiarize yourself with the types of files that may be available and how the National Archives describes them.

Finally, review the National Archives list of finding aids listed on the NARA Web site that have been compiled by Archives staff, employees of federal agencies, or independent scholars. These aids are listed in six overlapping sets, each of which is short and easily browsed in a few minutes. Scan each set for reference to your record group, bearing in mind that not all record groups have prepared inventories, preliminary inventories, or special lists. Ordering information can be found on the Archives' ordering Web site. Although you may have found an inventory for your record group in one set of finding aids, take some time to browse the others. Much of the information is redundant, but there are other compilations that may be of use. Spending a few minutes locating and ordering a finding aid may save hours of on-site research time.

Regional Archives and Presidential Libraries

There are a number of other locations outside of the Washington, DC, area that house federal archival collections. These include the presidential libraries, the regional National Archives centers (Atlanta, Chicago, Kansas City, Seattle, etc.) that contain the regional records of federal agencies and courts, and subregional centers (e.g., Albuquerque, Anchorage). Check the Web site of the National Archives and Records Administration for links to each of these centers. Each U.S. president, from Herbert Hoover to William Jefferson Clinton has his own library where documents related to the operation of the executive branch during the president's tenure are housed. The documents generated by the president, his staff, and administration officials, in addition to audio and visual records of the administration, are stored in the presidential libraries for use by researchers.

As a general rule, when using the presidential libraries, do as much online research as possible at the Archives' presidential libraries Web site to determine what records are housed in Independence, Missouri (Truman),

Abilene, Kansas (Eisenhower), or Simi Valley, California (Reagan) before spending money on a plane ticket and hotel only to find out that the records that you are looking for are located in the National Archives Annex in College Park, Maryland. Each Web site will provide information about doing research on-site as well as provide an overview of the collection. Any additional regulations regarding identification documents or equipment of the library or collection will also be listed.

The presidential libraries are organized differently than the other repositories in the Archives system. Since presidential papers were considered the personal property of the president until the passage of the Presidential Records Act (PRA) of 1978, papers had to be donated to the federal government by former presidents or by representatives of his estate. The PRA transferred the ownership rights of the documents and materials belonging to the president and vice president from the holders of those offices to the United States. The PRA took effect in 1981 and has applied to every administration from Reagan onward. The PRA makes it possible for researchers to make Freedom of Information Act (FOIA) requests for presidential materials five years after an administration leaves office. An outgoing president can protect certain documents for up to twelve years, after which they are subject to FOIA requests by researchers. However, the Nixon Presidential Historical Materials fall under the Presidential Recordings and Materials Preservation Act of 1974, which transferred control of Nixon's presidential material to the Nixon staff at Archives II. There is also a Nixon presidential library in Yorba Linda, California, that stores Nixon historical material. If you are conducting research that involves the Nixon administration visit the Archive's Nixon Web site and call ahead.

Classified Records and the Freedom of Information Act

If your online research indicates that your project requires access to classified records, your first action should be to call the Archives' toll-free number and talk to an archivist who specializes in classification/declassification issues in general, or an archivist familiar with the classified portion of the record group that is of specific interest to you. This person will be able to address any questions that you have about classified material. It may be impossible for you to gain access to these records if you do not already possess an active security clearance. There is very little that you can do in this instance, save filing a request to have the documents released to you under the provisions of the Freedom of Information Act (FOIA). Visit the

FOIA section of the Archives' site and call an archivist to determine whether the files that you wish to view can be made available, and whether you have a strong chance of having the documents released. Bear in mind that FOIA requests can take months or years to be approved or denied. Do not waste your time filing FOIA requests if the documents that you wish to view are not essential to the completion of your project or you are working under a tight deadline.

ONCE YOU GET HOME: BACKING UP AND ORGANIZING YOUR FILES

Now that you have completed the work of finding and duplicating primary sources and have returned home, it is of paramount importance that you back up all of your electronic primary source files if you have not already done so. The loss of your electronic files could render your recently completed research trip worthless and set your research project back months. An external hard drive, or any other method of remotely storing a large volume of digital data that you have at your disposal, is highly recommended. You should back up your data every time you make changes to the organization of your files so that the most current and up-to-date version of your primary source documents is available should you experience catastrophic data loss. In addition, a very low-tech but effective backup system is to print and store each of your documents in binders or in a physical filing system. If possible, err on the side of caution and keep your original data physically separated from your digital backup system. This precludes both sets of data being compromised by a single catastrophic event such as a fire or flood at your home or office.

The second thing that you should do upon your return home is devote at least one to two days, depending on the number of documents that you have collected, to the continued organization of these files. As mentioned earlier in the chapter, you should have detailed notes, preferably stored in an electronic spreadsheet, chronicling the identifying characteristics of the documents that you have duplicated. If you have photocopied primary source material, you should have noted these characteristics on each reproduction and kept your copies in the order in which you created them. In fact, you should always keep paper or digital copies in the order in which you found them until you are ready to establish a filing system. This ensures that your files remain grouped by folder and box, and it simplifies the process of sorting your material. One of the most important decisions that you face is determining how to create and order a physical or digital filing system for storing your primary-source files. A filing system using your computer's native folder function is recommended if you have made digital duplications of primary-source documents. Not only does it make sense to organize digital photos using a digital system, this method will also allow you to search your computer quickly for specific files once you have named them.

You should allow the demands of your project and the scope of your findings to determine how you organize your materials for storage and retrieval. You will need to create a system of physical or digital folders, apply the naming conventions from the archive to your files, name your folders, and sort the individual files into their appropriate place in your system. There are several organizing principles that have proven effective when dealing with large numbers of documents: keeping the files in the folder, box, and series order used at the archive; organizing the files chronologically or thematically; and, finally, storing the files in a hybrid thematic/chronological system. There are advantages to each method. The first is ideal if you are primarily concerned with maintaining files in the order in which an archivist or curator has arranged them. This method is extremely simple since you should already have the documents stored in this order. Chronological organization is well suited to a research project on a single, unambiguous theme, with a good number of dated files like memoranda and personal letters. Thematic organization is useful for broader topics that have a number of distinct aspects, which must be dealt with individually. Finally, the hybrid thematic/chronological system will allow you to organize your files to deal with the demands of a research project that is broad, has a number of discrete subtopics, and relies upon a majority of dated files. Each topic and subtopic of your project can be organized in a thematic hierarchy that makes sense to you, while the dated material can be arranged chronologically in each subtopic folder.

CONCLUSION: LESSONS LEARNED

In this chapter, I have introduced the basic principles of archival research, focusing on practical measures that will make this process more efficient and rewarding. The ultimate goal of an archival research trip is to return home with the physical and/or digital copies of everything that you set out to find—and, perhaps, additional finds as well. The practical advice presented in this chapter should familiarize you with the general procedures for planning and organizing a research trip, the equipment that you will need, the regulatory maze that you will have to navigate, the process of conducting on-site research, and the file-storage and organization principles that will allow you to access the fruits of your labor easily. All of the general recommendations made in this chapter are applicable to doing research in any archive that you choose to visit: large or small, public or private. Bear in mind, however, that each archive is as unique as its holdings, and that each site that you visit will have rules, regulations, and procedures unlike any other repository.

This chapter has dealt exclusively with archival collections in the United States, but many of the general principles apply to international archives as well. However, if you plan to do archival research abroad, be prepared to deal with the additional complications that may arise. The best way to plan for unforeseen contingencies is to be both proactive and flexible. If you are going to work in a collection in a country where your native language is not widely spoken and you do not speak the native language, arrange in advance for interpreting or contact an individual at the archive that handles foreign visitors. When preparing your equipment for an international research trip find out if you will need electrical adaptors and if your equipment is interoperable with the equipment at your destination. For example, the United States operates on a different electrical current than many other countries in the world, and U.S. videocassette standards are drastically different than those of most other nations as well. Finally, it is extremely important to be sensitive to cultural and workplace differences and to respect the customs of the nation in which you plan to do research. It is advisable to acquaint oneself with local customs prior to departure and to learn several key phrases, especially how to say "please" and "thank you" in the local language. This brings us back to the recurring themes of this chapter: planning ahead, calling in advance, asking for help, and always being polite.

When conducting archival research you should never assume that you have the entire process completely figured out. Archival research is similar to hunting, fishing, or scavenging. Positive results are not guaranteed, but the chances of success increase dramatically with comprehensive preparation and perseverance. Seeking the assistance and guidance of an archivist, a librarian, or a collection specialist is perhaps the single most important thing that you can do. Many errors can be corrected through extra effort, but failure to consult a professional can mean the difference between a successful research trip and a failed one. No one has as much experience with, and understanding of, an archival collection as the individuals who work with it every day. A professional can point you toward the record group, box, series, or folder of documents that contains the missing piece—the needle in the haystack—of your research puzzle. Finding that one golden document that ties everything together is what this process is all about, and doing everything in your power to maximize the chances of doing so is well worth the effort.

NOTE

The author would like to thank Eszter Hargittai for the opportunity to publish this chapter and the reviewers that provided critical suggestions.

REFERENCES

Bercovitch, Jacob. 2004. Social Research and the Study of Mediation: Designing and Implementing Systematic Archival Research. *International Negotiation* 9:451–28.

Berger, Arthur Asa. 2000. *Media and Communication Research Methods.* Thousand Oaks, CA: Sage.

Fisher, Steven, ed. 2004. *Archival Information: How to Find It, How to Use It.* Westport, CT: Greenwood Press.

Harris, Cole. 2001. Archival Fieldwork. *Geographical Review* 91 (1–2): 328–34.

Hill, Michael R. 1993. *Archival Strategies and Techniques.* Qualitative Research Methods Series no. 31. Newbury Park, CA: Sage.

Simonton, Dean Keith. 2000. Archival Data. In *Encyclopedia of Psychology,* ed. A. E. Kazdin, vol. 1, 234–35. New York: Oxford University Press.

Stanfield, John H. 1987. Archival Methods in Race Relations Research. *American Behavioral Scientist* 30 (4): 366–80.

Thies, Cameron G. 2002. A Pragmatic Guide to Qualitative Historical Analysis in the Study of International Relations. *International Studies Perspectives* 3:351–72.

CONTRIBUTORS

EMMA K. ADAM is Associate Professor in the School of Education and Social Policy and Faculty Fellow at the Institute for Policy Research at Northwestern University. She received her Ph.D. from the University of Minnesota. A developmental psychologist, she is interested in how social relationships and everyday life experiences influence levels of psychological stress, health, and well-being in parents, children, adolescents, and young adults. In addition to being an investigator on several National Institute of Mental Health–funded research projects, Adam is the recipient of a National Academy of Education/Spencer Foundation Postdoctoral Fellowship (2003–4) and received a five-year William T. Grant Scholars Award.

KAREN ALBRIGHT is a National Institute of Mental Health Fellow at the Center for Culture and Health in the Semel Institute for Neuroscience and Human Behavior at the University of California, Los Angeles, and an Instructor in the Department of Community and Behavioral Health at the University of Colorado, Anschutz Medical Campus. She received her Ph.D. in sociology from New York University and was previously a Robert Wood Johnson Foundation Scholar in Health Policy Research at the University of California, Berkeley. Her research interests lie in three main areas: the experience and treatment of poor mental health in socioeconomically disadvantaged communities, the structure and consequences of inequality within the family, and the social-psychological effects of trauma. Her work has been funded by the National Science Foundation, the National Institutes of Health, and the Radcliffe Institute for Advanced Study at Harvard University, among others.

NINA BANDELJ is Associate Professor of Sociology and Faculty Associate at the Center for the Study of Democracy, University of California, Irvine. She received a Ph.D. from Princeton University and was awarded the Seymour Martin Lipset Dissertation Award from the Society for Comparative Research. In 2005–6 she held fellowships at the European University Institute, Florence, Italy, and the Max Planck Institute for the Study of Societies, Cologne, Germany. Her research examines social and cultural bases of economic phenomena, determinants and consequences of globalization, and social change in postsocialist Europe.

LAURA CLAWSON is a senior writer at Working America, community affiliate of the AFL-CIO. She received her Ph.D. in sociology from Princeton University and has taught at Dartmouth College and the Princeton Theological Seminary.

LEAH D. DOANE is a postdoctoral scholar in the Department of Psychiatry and Behavioral Neuroscience at the University of Chicago. She received her Ph.D. in Human Development and Social Policy from the School of Education and Social Policy at Northwestern University where she was the project director of the Northwestern Sleep and Stress Study. Her research focuses on chronic and short term interpersonal and psychological stressors. Specifically, she examines how these stressors influence physiology and health in adolescents and young adults.

JEREMY FREESE is Professor of Sociology and Fellow of the Institute for Policy Research at Northwestern University. His primary research interests are in social psychology, technology, and the relationship between biological and social processes. He is also the coauthor of a book on the analysis of categorical data.

JASON GALLO is a Research Staff Member at the Science and Technology Policy Institute, a federally funded research and development center in Washington, DC. His doctoral research in the Media, Technology, and Society program in the School of Communication at Northwestern University focused on the role of the National Science Foundation in the development of the U.S. information infrastructure.

ESZTER HARGITTAI is Associate Professor of Communication Studies and Faculty Associate of the Institute for Policy Research at Northwestern University, where she heads the Web Use Project. She received her Ph.D. in sociology from Princeton University, where she was a Wilson Scholar. Her work focuses on the social and policy implications of information and communication technologies and the methodological challenges of studying related questions. In 2006–7 she was a Fellow at the Center for Advanced Study in the Behavioral Sciences at Stanford. In 2008–9 she was a Fellow at the Berkman Center for Internet and Society at Harvard University. Her work has been funded by the John D. and Catherine T. MacArthur Foundation, the National Science Foundation, and the Markle Foundation, among others.

CHRIS KARR is the founder of and chief software developer at Audacious Software, a Chicago technology firm. In 2009 he received his master's degree from the Media, Technology, and Society Program at Northwestern University, where he worked on creating in situ systems and methods for conducting time-based surveys and diary studies. In the summer of 2009, he founded the Pennyworth Project, a nonprofit company dedicated to providing and promoting context-aware technology in mainstream computing environments.

KATHRYN MENDELSOHN is a clinical psychology doctoral student at Northwestern University, Feinberg School of Medicine. She is particularly interested in child and adolescent internalizing disorders and works with Dr. Mark Reinecke on the Treatment for Adolescent Depression Study. Prior to graduate school, Kathryn was the Project Coordinator for the Northwestern Sleep and Stress Study for Dr. Emma Adam from 2005 until 2007.

DEVAH PAGER is Associate Professor of Sociology and Faculty Associate of the Office of Population Research at Princeton University. Her research focuses on institutions affecting racial stratification, including education, labor markets, and the criminal justice system. Pager's current research has involved a series of field experiments studying discrimination against minorities and ex-offenders in the low-wage labor market. Her book, *Marked: Race, Crime, and Finding Work in an Era of Mass Incarceration* (University of Chicago Press, 2007), investigates the racial and economic consequences of large-scale imprisonment for contemporary U.S. labor markets. Pager holds master's degrees from Stanford University and the University of Cape Town and a Ph.D. from the University of Wisconsin-Madison.

CHRISTIAN SANDVIG is Associate Professor of Communication and Media Studies and a Research Associate Professor at the Coordinated Science Laboratory of the University of Illinois at Urbana-Champaign. He studies communication technology and public policy. In 2002 Sandvig was named a "next-generation leader in science and technology policy" in a junior faculty competition organized by Columbia, Rutgers, and the American Association for the Advancement of Science. In 2006 he received the Faculty Early Career Development Award from the U.S. National Science Foundation (NSF CAREER).

GINA WALEJKO is a Ph.D. candidate in the Media, Technology, and Society program at Northwestern University. Her research focuses on the use of computers and the Web in survey research as well as on methods to increase the data quality of digital media use survey measures. Walejko has also been a research assistant at Professor Eszter Hargittai's Web Use Project. There she studied how college students use the Web, focusing on content creation and sharing.

JOAN WALLING is an independent scholar and research consultant. She received her Ph.D. in sociology from Princeton University and has been Assistant Professor at Azusa Pacific University, Adjunct Professor at the Lutheran Theological Seminary in Philadelphia, and Researcher at Insight Research Group in New York City. She has enjoyed advising students on qualitative research methods at all of these institutions. Her research interests include the cultural meanings of gifts, giving, and altruism; the sociology of religion; and working class culture.

DMITRI WILLIAMS is Assistant Professor at the Annenberg School for Communication at the University of Southern California, where he helps direct the Annenberg Program in Online Communities. He received his Ph.D. in communication from the University of Michigan. His research interests are in online community, online games, and the social impacts of new technologies more generally.

LI XIONG is a Ph.D. student in the Annenberg School for Communication at the University of Southern California. His research focuses on the sociotechnical interactions in the design, engineering, and use of new communication technologies.

INDEX

Abrams, Courtney, 169, 170, 171, 172, 175, 184, 185, 186, 188
Academic Blogger Survey. *See* online survey
Adobe Flash, 205
Alabama, 61, 64, 65, 66, 69, 70, 72
Alaska, 132
Allentown, PA, 83
American Journal of Political Science, 222
American Journal of Sociology, 222, 242
American Political Science Review, 222
American Sociological Association, 188
American Sociological Review, 222, 239, 250
Anniston, AL, 72
AOL, 200, 201, 202
Asheron's Call 2, 123, 126, 133, 137, 138
Asia, 228. *See also* Association of South-East Asian Nations; ProQuest Reference Asia
Association of South-East Asian Nations (ASEAN), 230

Beagan, Brenda, 88
Beck, Nathaniel, 228–29
Bernstein, Basil, 146
Bertrand, Marianne, 40, 41, 57
Bethlehem, PA, 83, 89
Bethlehem Steel, 83, 89

Binney & Smith, 83
biological processes, 9, 10, 15
biomarkers, 17, 28
   collection, 4, 6, 18, 254
   incorporation, 14, 15
   salivary, 9
Birmingham, AL, 69
bloggers, 3, 6, 102, 145, 152, 155, 180
   graduate student, 103, 105
   political, 101, 160
   university, 105
   See also online survey
blogrolls, 106–7, 108, 115
Boolean algebra, 221
Brooks, Clem, 233, 234
Burawoy, Michael, 68, 71, 75–76, 77
Bush, George W., 164

Carnegie Commission for the Advancement of Teaching National Faculty Survey, 109
Castellas, Gilbert, 53
causality, 38, 39, 220, 221, 222, 224, 225, 226, 227, 229, 232, 248, 249, 255, 256
cell phone(s), 91, 141, 145, 192, 193, 194, 211
   number, 208, 209
   owner, 194
   plan, 17, 199